# Genocide and International Relations

*Genocide and International Relations* lays the foundations for a new perspective on genocide in the modern world. Genocide studies have been influenced, negatively as well as positively, by the political and cultural context in which the field has developed. In particular, a narrow vision of comparative studies has been influential in which genocide is viewed mainly as a 'domestic' phenomenon of states. This book emphasizes the international context of genocide, seeking to specify more precisely the relationships between genocide and the international system. Shaw aims to re-interpret the classical European context of genocide in this frame, to provide a comprehensive international perspective on Cold War and post-Cold War genocide, and to re-evaluate the key transitions of the end of the Second World War and the end of the Cold War.

MARTIN SHAW is a historical sociologist specializing in global politics, war and genocide. He is Research Professor of International Relations at the Institut Barcelona d'Estudis Internacionals; Professorial Fellow in International Relations and Human Rights at Roehampton University, London; and Emeritus Professor of Sussex University.

Shaw's books *What Is Genocide?* (2007) and *War and Genocide: Organized Killing in Modern Society* (2003) have established him as a major authority in the genocide field. He is the author of several books on war, most recently *The New Western Way of War: Risk-Transfer War and Its Crisis in Iraq* (2005) and *Civil Society and Media in Global Crises: Representing Distant Violence* (1996), and on global change, notably *Theory of the Global State: Globality as Unfinished Revolution* (Cambridge University Press, 2000). His website is martinshaw.org.

# Genocide and International Relations

## Changing Patterns in the Transitions of the Late Modern World

MARTIN SHAW

CAMBRIDGE
UNIVERSITY PRESS

# CAMBRIDGE
## UNIVERSITY PRESS

University Printing House, Cambridge CB2 8BS, United Kingdom

Published in the United States of America by Cambridge University Press, New York

Cambridge University Press is part of the University of Cambridge.

It furthers the University's mission by disseminating knowledge in the pursuit of education, learning and research at the highest international levels of excellence.

www.cambridge.org
Information on this title: www.cambridge.org/9780521125178

© Martin Shaw 2013

First published 2013

Printed in the United Kingdom by CPI Group Ltd, Croydon CR0 4YY

*A catalogue record for this publication is available from the British Library*

*Library of Congress Cataloguing-in-Publication data*
Shaw, Martin, 1947–
Genocide and international relations : changing patterns in the transitions of the late modern world / Martin Shaw.
     pages   cm
Includes bibliographical references.
ISBN 978-0-521-11013-6 (Hardback) – ISBN 978-0-521-12517-8 (Paperback)
1. Genocide–Research.   2. Genocide–History.   3. Genocide–Political aspects.
4. International relations.   I. Title.
HV6322.7.S529 2013
364.15′1–dc23   2013013916

ISBN 978-0-521-11013-6 Hardback
ISBN 978-0-521-12517-8 Paperback

*To the memory of my father,*
*Roy Shaw*
*1918–2012*

# Contents

# Acknowledgements

This book has been in the making since I completed *What Is Genocide?* in 2006. The intervening years have been a period of career change. I began them as Professor of International Relations and Politics at the University of Sussex, where I first formulated the project which is brought to completion in this book. By the time I began serious research and writing, I had given up my full-time teaching role at Sussex and become a Research Professor; I am now Emeritus Professor of the University. I subsequently took on roles at two other institutions: as Professorial Fellow in International Relations and Human Rights at the University of Roehampton, London, and as Research Professor of International Relations at the Institut Barcelona d'Estudis Internacionals (IBEI). All three institutions have provided research support and library facilities which have aided me in this project. The research was also financed by a visiting professorship at IBEI in 2010, supported by a grant from the Spanish Ministry of Education.

I have greatly benefited from presentations of parts of this work to seminars at Sussex, Roehampton and IBEI. The (mainly Master's) teaching on war and genocide which I have undertaken at all three institutions has been equally important. My students may not always have realized it, but their courses were for me an opportunity to test the ideas and different ways of presenting them that were maturing in the writing of this book. Students often highlighted problems in the argument and exposition, and sometimes made connections which I had not made. For example, a member of my last group of Sussex undergraduates pointed out that Carl von Clausewitz's famous trinity of government, generals and people as actors of modern war is mirrored in Michael Mann's recent trinity of radical party elites, paramilitaries and core social constituencies as the makers of genocide. I had presented both, but missed the overlap.

I have also gained much from the new global framework for the field which the International Network of Genocide Scholars (INOGS) has provided since 2005, and from feedback at its conferences at Sheffield in 2009, where a version of Chapter 2 was presented, and Sussex in 2010. The latter I co-organized with my Sussex colleague Nigel Eltringham, with whom I earlier organized the conference 'Genocide 60 Years After the Convention' in Brighton in 2008, where a first version of Chapter 5 was presented. The *Journal of Genocide Research* (*JGR*) has been a crucial reference point, and I have benefited greatly from discussions with its current editor, A. Dirk Moses, and his predecessor, Jürgen Zimmerer. I have also enjoyed the many opportunities that its reviews editor, Adam Jones, has provided for me to comment on new publications in the field: several reviews have been drawn on for the argument of this book. I have presented parts of the present work, too, at the Sheffield University Centre for Genocide Research, the Universities of Sydney, Melbourne and Queensland, and at conferences on 'Partitions in 20th Century Global History', at the University of Sydney Institute of Social Sciences; 'Contested Boundaries: Contested Rights', at Roehampton University; 'The Holocaust and Other Genocides', at the Wiener Library, London; 'New Directions in Genocide Research', at the European University Institute, Florence; 'Preventing Genocide', at the University of Antwerp; 'The Wannsee Conference – 70 Years After', at the University of Sussex Centre for German-Jewish Studies; and 'Armed Conflicts in Comparative Perspective', at the National University of Ireland, Galway.

An early version of the argument of Chapter 9 was published as 'Genocide in the Global Age', in Bryan S. Wilson, ed., *The Routledge Handbook of Globalisation Studies*, London: Routledge, 2009, pp. 312–27. Part of the argument of Chapter 4 was published in 'From Comparative to International Genocide Studies: The International Production of Genocide in Twentieth-Century Europe', *European Journal of International Relations*, 18(4), 2012, 645–88. A more general statement of the case appeared as 'Shifting the Foundations of Genocide Research' in a review forum on Donald Bloxham's *The Holocaust: A Genocide*, in the *Journal of Genocide Research*, 13(2), 2011, 111–16. The project has also had two major spin-offs: the annual War Studies Lecture at King's College, London, in 2010, published as 'Britain and Genocide: Historical and Contemporary Parameters of National Responsibility', *Review of International Studies*, 37(5), 2011, 2,417–38; and 'Palestine in an International Historical Perspective on Genocide', *Holy Land Studies*, 9(1), 2010, 1–24, which led to

'The Question of Genocide in Palestine, 1948: A Debate between Martin Shaw and Omer Bartov', *Journal of Genocide Research*, 12 (3–4), 2010, 243–59.

Many specific intellectual debts will be apparent in the text. However I must specially thank Andrei Gómez Suárez, whose thesis I supervised during the writing of this book, whose argument stimulated mine, and who commented on the entire manuscript, providing valuable suggestions and corrections. I am also very grateful to Dirk Moses for helpful comments on two chapters.

I could never have written this book without Annabel's constant support, encouragement and love.

# Introduction

Genocide has never been talked about more than it is today. Representatives of every group whose members have been victims of atrocities are quick to claim the genocide label. In Western countries a new kind of anti-genocide activism has come into its own, urging politicians to act. Although leaders remain reluctant to acknowledge the occurrence of genocide, genocide prevention is now an institutionalized policy objective of the United Nations and the United States. At the same time, genocide has been established as an academic field, many historical episodes have been uncovered, major works have appeared, conferences have been held, and student interest continues to expand.

What, if anything, does this level of interest tell us about the extent, character and causes of genocide in the twenty-first-century world? Does growing genocide consciousness reflect a still-high or even heightened danger of genocide, or merely greater awareness of dangers that may actually be less than in the past? Do episodes such as those in Rwanda and Darfur – the focal points of recent debate – tell us that genocide today is the same kind of problem that it was in the eras of the Armenian genocide and the Holocaust? Or do they indicate a new pattern? How do growing genocide awareness and policy affect the actual incidence of genocide?

All these questions are different angles on the issue of whether, in the twenty-first century, we are in a new historical period of genocide on a world scale. They thus raise the question of historical change, of how the phenomenon changes from one historical period to another, which is the fundamental question of this book. The historical contextualization of genocide has been an emerging interest in genocide research, and I build on some significant work that has been done in the last few years. However comparative genocide studies, as the field is generally known, is mostly interested in continuity rather than change in the forms and causes of genocide. At the same time, the field mostly looks at genocide in domestic or national, rather than world or international,

1

political contexts. Investigating the significance of *world-historical change* for genocide, as I propose to do, goes against the grain of much of the genocide literature, and necessarily involves a critical standpoint towards it.

In the first two chapters, therefore, I criticize the set of assumptions that mostly frames the field today, and ask why the themes of change and world-historical perspective have been difficult to address. In Chapter 1, I link these problems to the political and cultural contexts which have powerfully shaped intellectual agendas around genocide. I argue that without emancipating the genocide field from simplistic moral-political interests, it will not be possible to move on. In Chapter 2, I directly criticize the limited, indeed sometimes naive, conceptions of comparative studies that are linked to these interests and significantly shape the field as it exists. These critiques are, of course, preliminaries to the main tasks of the book. I aim to make two specific contributions to the emergent world-historical genocide literature that I discuss in Chapter 3. The first is simply to extend systematically the temporal frame of this strand, which has so far been concerned mainly with colonial and early twentieth-century European genocide, into the Cold War and post-Cold War eras. The second, however, is more theoretically ambitious. I argue that we cannot explain genocide in terms of the most general properties of the 'international system'. Rather, we must recognize that the 'systemic' characteristics of international relations are historically variable. So my key argument is that major changes in international relations have had fundamental implications for patterns of genocide.

In order to explore this case, I examine genocide across the major late-modern historical changes, paying particular attention to periods of transition. In Chapter 4, I revisit the classical locus of genocide, Europe in the early and mid twentieth century. I argue that the reasons for genocide's extreme prevalence and particular forms in this period lay in how nationalist conflicts and political polarization were entwined with the conflicts of the core powers of the international system, in the largest military struggles, and in key regions. These conditions were historically specific: they did not prevail either before the late nineteenth or after the mid twentieth century. Rather, different international contexts produced patterns of genocide in earlier and later periods of modern history which were different from this 'classical' pattern.

Here I take a distinctive position on international relations as well as on genocide. I explain in Chapter 5 that I see the outcome of the Second World War as a fundamental change, in which the multi-imperial international system that had produced both the colonial and European contexts of genocide was fundamentally undermined. The beginning of the end of this system had a double significance for genocide, which we can see in the transition of the late 1940s. On one hand, the newly named phenomenon was internationally criminalized and disappeared from Europe for several decades. On the other, genocide began to appear widely in processes of decolonization and in conflicts in post-colonial states, in what would come to be called the Third World. I argue, therefore, that this was a transition in the history of genocide, not a transition from a genocidal to a post-genocidal world.

In Chapter 6, I argue that between the late 1940s and the late 1980s, the Cold War (after which this period has generally been named) was a crucial international context of much genocide. However genocide was at least as much a manifestation of more fundamental changes in states, societies and international relations in the global South (another new naming of this time), which are the second major focus of this chapter. In Chapter 7, I consider the significance of the end of the Cold War for genocide. I see this as a further important turning point in worldwide international relations with major implications for my subject, but as a less fundamental change than that of the 1940s. The changes of the late 1980s involved the collapse of the quasi-imperial Soviet bloc, leading to patterns similar to the earlier unwindings of empires, but with some important new features. I discuss these, focusing on how the end-of-Cold War transition was associated with new genocidal violence in former Soviet republics and in Yugoslavia. I argue too that the wars resulting from the new US supremacy also produced genocide, in Iraq after 2003.

However Southern regions remain the main arenas of violent political and armed conflict, and hence also of genocide, as they were during the Cold War. Yet this is not simple continuity: I argue that the 'global' context of the new era has considerably changed both the locations and the forms of these conflicts. This is partly because of the dynamics of regional international relations, but also through the unintended as well as intended consequences of 'global' norms and interventions. Conflict resolution, 'humanitarian' intervention, and democracy promotion have all sometimes accentuated, as well as relieved, genocidal conflict. In Chapter 8, I evaluate some of the conceptualizations of and generalizations about anti-population violence that social scientists have produced in recent years. In Chapter 9, I move into a discussion of the regional and global international contexts of genocide in the current period.

In proposing a historical interpretation in which changes in modern genocide are linked to changes in international relations, I inevitably confront the continuities in both. Clearly it would be foolish to deny their significance. The simple fact that some regions have been sites of genocide in different historical periods indicates that historical change does not create blank slates for new conflict. The Balkans were a genocidal region before and during the First and Second World Wars as well as in the 1990s, as were the African Great Lakes in the aftermath of decolonization as well as in the post-Cold War years. More generally, structural forces that shape the international system in one period continue to mark it, albeit in different contexts, in subsequent eras. If 1945 saw the collapse of the classical inter-imperial system, empire remained a key feature of Cold War international relations, due to the superpowers' imperial ambitions, the protracted fallout from European imperial decline, and the quasi-imperial make-up of many new post-colonial states as well as of the Soviet Union. Similar issues remain in the twenty-first century. I discuss these implications of my argument more fully in Chapter 10.

## The scope of genocide

A key question for any historical evaluation of trends is how to understand the scope of genocide. One of the reasons why much research fails to historicize genocide is because it has reified a particular historical pattern as a timeless norm. Genocide has been increasingly defined narrowly in terms of large-scale intentional mass murder, with the Holocaust as the standard. Defined in these terms, it is easily concluded that genocide is rare, and that the task is to compare its relatively few cases *across* the different historical periods in which they happened, rather than to link them to other violence *within* those periods. If the few cases are seen to differ, this will appear an outcome of specific national conditions, rather than of the changing general patterns of international relations over historical time.

Clearly genocide is not a 'thing' which exists outside human discourse, so there is no absolutely right or wrong definition of the phenomenon. It is an idea, of relatively recent origin, and it is right that it should be developed in response to new challenges. Nevertheless we must be able to provide clear and coherent rationales for the definitions we adopt. The core rationale for the 'mass murder' criterion can only be that killing is the most fundamental type of violence against fellow humans, more heinous than others, making this alone the 'ultimate crime'. But this rationale should be questioned: first, because people often suffer more in torture, rape, separation and dispossession than they do in being killed; and, second, because these different forms of violence are usually combined in any given situation, so that what links them is more important than their distinguishing features. Genocide is generally violent, but it cannot be defined by a particular violent method.

For these reasons, most scholars have actually defined genocide as the 'destructive' targeting of a population on the basis of its presumed 'group' characteristics, rather than as mass murder. Historically the 'mass murder' definition is a departure from the mainstream of thinking about the problem. The original concept of Raphael Lemkin (1944) described multi-method group 'destruction', with physical violence as only one of a number of methods. The adaptation of this concept in the United Nations' Genocide Convention (1948), while steering closer to an emphasis on 'physical' destruction, maintained the multi-method idea. I have discussed these ideas and the subsequent debates in my last book (Shaw 2007: 17–36), leading me to a concept of genocidal action as 'action in which armed power organizations treat civilian social groups as enemies and aim to destroy their real or putative social power, by means of killing, violence and coercion against individuals whom they regard as members of the groups'. I also argue that in a broader sense, genocide can be seen as 'a form of violent social conflict or war, between armed power organizations that aim to destroy civilian social groups and those groups and other actors who resist this destruction' (Shaw 2007: 154).

A common objection to this and other definitions that see genocide as more than mass murder is that they are 'too loose', so that 'everything' counts as genocide. This misunderstands Lemkin's original rationale for 'genocide', which was precisely to have an *overarching* concept for targeted, socially destructive anti-group violence. I find this idea useful in the same way that 'war' makes sense as a general term for violent action and conflict between organized armed actors. Indeed the two concepts go together in specifying two fundamental types of violence and conflict that are often combined, their fundamental difference being the types of enemy. In war, armed power targets other armed actors; in genocide, it targets largely unarmed civilians. I have remarked that those who confine genocide to the narrow meaning of mass murder are obliged to reinvent general, overarching concepts for anti-population violence, such as Rummel's (1997) 'democide' and Mann's (2005) 'ethnic cleansing'. In my view, neither of these concepts has the power of 'genocide' (Shaw 2007: 64).

Genocide is a general type of violent action and conflict, and should not to be equated with a particular type of historical event, called 'a genocide'. Genocide can occur on a wide range of scales from huge episodes involving millions of victims, to small episodes involving hundreds or even tens. The term 'genocidal massacre' has long been used to refer to localized genocidal killing. However we need equally to recognize limited-scale genocidal expulsions, genocidal mass rapes, genocidal starvation policies, etc. Thus I propose 'genocidal violence' as a general term for targeted, destructive violence against population groups which is perpetrated episodically, locally or on a small scale, in situations where it does not seem appropriate to talk of 'a genocide'. One way to think about this is to compare it to the way we think about war: this too is a type of violence and conflict that can occur on a wide range of scales. 'Wars' are events of a certain size and duration – conventionally, involving 1,000 battle deaths per year – and thinking about war has long recognized the importance of localized clashes, skirmishes, etc., which involve military violence but are not sufficiently sustained or of a sufficient scale to be called 'wars'.

Of course, the idea of genocide as a general concept of destructive anti-population violence, like any useful concept, still has limits. Two are essential: the boundaries between genocide and war, on the one hand, and non-genocidal coercion against civilian populations, on the other. Neither of these distinctions is easy. Genocide frequently, indeed most commonly, occurs in the context of war, so that we often need to determine whether a civilian population is targeted as a means of fighting a conventional armed enemy or because it is regarded as an enemy in itself. This determination is manifestly difficult in many cases, because of imperfect knowledge of armed actors' aims, and because of their combined and/or changing aims. Nevertheless it is essential to make the best possible estimate of the relationships of war and genocide, in what can often be called 'genocidal war'. I return to these issues in discussing the contemporary political science literature on armed conflict, in Chapter 8.

Likewise, genocide often develops in the context of non-destructive political conflict, in which armed political actors engage in coercion against population groups. Imperial and authoritarian rulers (that means virtually all governments until recent times) have long practised targeted coercion against specific sections of their populations, defined culturally, linguistically, religiously and economically. Yet we can talk of genocide only when they aim to *destroy* those groups' social networks, institutions, way of life, and territorial or physical existence. Again, the determination of when the violence that is generally part of coercive rule becomes destructive is not always easy. Rulers and other armed political actors may move from non-destructive coercive rule to destruction and back again. Non-destructive rule may involve violence, and coercion always remains part of destruction. But this too is an essential distinction.

While both these distinctions are often difficult, they are vital to pinpoint genocidal dynamics in conflict. It is possible to have war and other forms of conflict without genocide, but it is not possible to have genocide without prior social, political or armed conflict. Genocide usually follows from more conventional conflicts, but it may also be followed by them. The relationships are in principle as complex as social, political and armed conflicts themselves. Genocide may be a matter of a general destructive campaign by a central political authority, or a regional strategy by military or paramilitary commanders, or a localized action by informal local social, political and armed networks, or any combination of these.

I have referred more or less interchangeably to 'civilian social groups', 'population groups' and 'populations' as targets of genocide. This is because, while the concept of 'group' that has been used since Lemkin in defining genocide expresses the idea of targeting particular populations, it is sociologically weak (as I explained in Shaw 2007: 97–105). Perpetrators ascribe group characteristics to populations which their members, or others, may not necessarily accept or see in the same way. Moreover, while violence may be thought of by perpetrators (and academic observers) as targeted, it may be experienced as arbitary and indiscriminate by victims. Mark Levene (2005a: 56) abandons the group concept altogether and talks of 'aggregate populations'; I believe the understanding of genocide needs to capture both sides of this process, hence my somewhat looser, more variable language.

The relevance of this understanding of genocide to my project is this. I stated above that genocide has too often been identified with only one of its methods, mass killing, although even in cases (like the Holocaust and Rwanda) in which mass killing became the dominant method, other forms of coercion and violence such as expulsions, dispossession and rape were also involved. I could have added that it has also been too identified with one type of perpetrator (centralized, particularly totalitarian, regimes), although even where this kind of actor organized genocide, others such as local paramilitaries and supportive social groups were often involved.

The crucial issue for my study is that a complex understanding of the methods and actors of genocide action and genocidal conflict points us towards looking for *shifts* in the structures of genocide over time. It is not just that different world-historical contexts produce different patterns or extents of genocide. They may also manifest different forms of genocidal organization, action and conflict, and different combinations of the principal methods of genocide. War, Carl von Clausewitz (1976: 80) famously stated, is more than a chameleon: it constantly changes its forms as well as its appearances. The same is true of genocide.

## On theory and method

Most conceptual work on genocide has been produced by sociologists and social theorists. The most substantial body of empirical work, in contrast, has been produced by historians, although anthropologists, political scientists, legal scholars and others have also contributed. The disciplinary gulf between sociology and history is probably the deepest in the world of genocide research. This situation has arisen although Max Weber long ago made a cogent case that the difference between the two fields should be understood as a division of labour between general concept-producing and individual event-explaining disciplines (I have discussed this in relation to genocide in Shaw 2007: 86–90).

The distinctive sub-field of historical sociology offers to combine the contributions of both. However it is modestly sized; while it has produced intellectual giants such as Barrington Moore, Charles Tilly and Theda Skocpol, of its major figures only Michael Mann (2005) has dealt with genocide (I continue to engage with his work in this book). Historical sociology has also begun to influence International Relations (Hobden 1994, Hobden and Hobson 2002), within which I partially frame the present project, but there is no large body of historical-sociological IR. Most work follows the major thinkers I have just mentioned in dealing primarily with earlier phases of modernity and the modern state; very little of it deals with the later twentieth and twenty-first centuries, the main empirical focus of this book. I complained some time ago (Shaw 1998) that we lacked a 'historical sociology of the future' able to deal with the 'global', 'transnational' and 'regional' as well as the 'national' and 'international'. Indeed I proposed my own historical-theoretical account of 'globality' (Shaw 2000), on which I draw in modified form in the present volume. But in applying historical sociology to late-modern and global-era genocide, there are few guides.

Historical sociology implies methodological commitments: abhorring alike 'abstracted' empiricism and ahistorical 'grand theory', it tends, as C. Wright Mills (1959) classically proposed good sociology should, towards middle-range, historically grounded generalization. But what this means methodologically remains underdeveloped. An impressive model is Mann's (1986, 1993) deployment of a theoretical framework to develop concrete historical analyses, using the work of historians as raw material for macro-historical interpretation. This approach has been hailed too in IR (Hobden and Hobson 2002), because he goes beyond comparative history to international analysis, replacing national societies by transnational networks as the units.

A similar approach inspires the present study, but I neither propose a new general social theory nor methodically apply an existing one to the history of genocide. Rather, I move to and fro between critical theoretical engagement and substantive historical-sociological analysis. Partisans of strict theoretical models and rigorous empirical analysis may be equally dissatisfied, but my discursive method reflects my sense of where we are at, not only in the general development of historical sociology, but in the historical understanding of the international system and above all of genocide. There is no tight theoretical model that can be simply applied; indeed there is no agreed universe of cases of genocide that any such model could be applied to.

In this book, I have therefore opted for a narrative approach, part critical-theoretical and part historical-theoretical. I simultaneously discuss ideas about international relations and genocide, on the one hand, and the changing historical realities, on the other. If I don't engage in quantitative analysis, this is not because I think the numbers of people murdered, starved, raped, expelled or dispossessed in different situations unimportant; indeed I often quote estimated numbers as indicators of the scale of events. It is rather because numbers are often hugely difficult to establish with certainty – all the more so once we move (as we must) beyond simple body counts to more complex measures of victimization – so that once debates about numbers were made a major focus of the analysis, they would have tended to dominate it. I felt that, before such analysis could usefully be done on a macro-historical scale, it was necessary to develop a narrative frame within which to identify the different kinds of genocidal situation that we find in modern world history.

This book mainly spans 'late' modern history, effectively the twentieth century and the first decade of the twenty-first, with nods to the earlier modern history of genocide. It might be thought that this reduces genocide to a manageable number of cases (from the Armenians to Rwanda) in each of which the writer might be expected to have a fair level of expertise. However my approach to the scope of genocide, and especially my argument that more limited genocidal violence should also be recognized, means that I actually have a shockingly wide range of cases to cover. Thus I am exclusively dependent on secondary sources and the empirical judgements of others, although the uses to which I have put their work are my own. It also means that I may have missed some relevant cases and sources, and have got others wrong at least in part. I ask readers' patience with such issues, and I shall be happy to receive corrections and suggestions for improvement. I ask that they consider the overall aims of the book and its chapters, in which world and regional international patterns are the objects of analysis and specific local and national cases constitute supporting evidence.

A further qualification is necessary. I have stated that it is analytically crucial to distinguish genocide from both war and non-destructive coercion, while showing relationships between them. This kind of analysis has been attempted in some empirical work, and where possible I quote scholars who have done it (although they too often emphasize its difficulties in practice). In the broad survey attempted here, however, it has often not been possible to *complete* either the demarcation of or the demonstrations of relationships between different types of violence. On the contrary, I have had to limit myself to indicating genocidal elements and their relationships to wider patterns of conflict. Once again, the reader should bear in mind the aim of the volume, to understand general patterns rather than to achieve definitive analyses of all the elements within them.

This book aims, therefore, to establish the variety in the patterns of modern genocide, primarily between historical periods but also within them, and to show how changing patterns of international relations have been causally implicated in changing genocide. I argue that genocide has been much more widely prevalent than many existing analyses suggest, and that international relations have been more changeable than suggested by notions of a more or less fixed international system. As I have said, the book moves back and forth between critical social and international theory and more concrete historical-sociological analysis. The reader will decide whether this combined method, which one might call critical-theoretical historical sociology, has served its purpose.

# PART I

# Perspectives

# 1 | *Emancipating genocide research*

I begin this study with the political, cultural and legal contexts of genocide research, rather than directly with issues arising from the understanding of genocide. This might seem a surprising choice, but it reflects my belief that the academic field has been imbued with similar assumptions to those which have shaped popular consciousness of genocide. Scholars in this field have strong moral and political commitments, and these inevitably affect their research activities. Since genocide is always a matter of great political, cultural and legal import, dialogue between academic research and wider debates is necessary and often fruitful. However we need to be critically aware of these contexts and how they affect scholarship. The argument of this chapter is that genocide research has been heavily skewed, and even distorted, by issues arising from its origins in mid-twentieth-century Europe and how these continue to ramify in twenty-first-century world politics. This skewing is a matter not just of scholars' personal outlooks but of how powerful political, cultural and legal paradigms have affected the conceptual, methodological and theoretical frameworks within which academic research has developed.

## Political and legal origins of 'genocide'

The idea of 'genocide', first proposed in Lemkin's (1944) study of Nazi rule, was from the start both a sociological concept, used for analysing historical developments, and a political-legal one, designed to show how genocide might be outlawed and its perpetrators punished. It came to prominence at the end of the Second World War as the victor states and their new United Nations Organization sought ways of, on the one hand, stigmatizing Nazism's policies towards civilians, and, on the other, criminalizing similar policies by others in the future. The UN adopted, in the Convention on the Prevention and Punishment of the Crime of Genocide (1948), a relatively broad definition of genocide – not limited to mass killing like some later definitions – influenced by the approach of Lemkin who lobbied for it.

Thus the idea of genocide was never neutral between perpetrators and victims, but assumed the criminality of the acts and agents of genocide. It is impossible, therefore, to imagine perpetrators describing themselves as genocidists, although nowadays many show awareness of the idea by projecting accusations of genocide on to others. So while most formulations define the act by the subjective orientation of the perpetrators (their 'intent'), the concept has always presupposed more than *their* meanings. It has always taken into account the destructive consequences for victims and condemnation by international authority. The concept of genocide originated in a politically as well as legally charged context, and this necessarily affected its later academic study.

This context was manifestly complicated. The UN powers were themselves directly (in the case of the USSR) and indirectly (in the cases of the USA and Great Britain) responsible for genocide during the war (as I argue in Chapter 4), and they and the UN itself were implicated in new genocidal processes (see Chapter 5). Although the UN definition was capable in principle of encompassing the crimes committed by the USSR and other member states of the UN, it was understood in practice in ways that excluded them. It has been widely noted that the Convention, under Soviet influence, excluded violence against political groups and social classes from the scope of genocide. It is even more pertinent, however, that it *deliberately* excluded specific mention of what is now called 'ethnic cleansing' (see discussion in Chapter 5). However the forced removal of populations was the most common form of group destruction, perpetrated on many sides and even authorized by the UN powers. So genocide was implicitly, and conveniently, narrowed to the kinds of acts and ideology involved in the Nazis' mass murder of the Jews, although Lemkin's original understanding and the Convention definition were much broader.

Yet as the Convention was adopted in late 1948, the Second World War and Nazism were beginning to recede into history. The Cold War was beginning and would shortly change the international context in ways which would have profound implications for the history of genocide. The Genocide Convention became a dead letter – it was not enforced internationally in the Cold War period – and hardly any academic study was forthcoming in the first three decades after the idea emerged. In the near-absence of legal and academic elaboration, the field was therefore clear for political and cultural development of the idea. And it was catching on: genocide became, Dirk Moses (2010) points out, 'a rhetorical weapon wielded during decolonization and the Cold War', while the term was also increasingly used to describe historical episodes. Some terrible new events came to be understood as genocide, notably the Khmer Rouge's violence in Cambodia in the late 1970s despite its partial lack of fit with the UN definition (it was directed against educated elites and city dwellers as well as ethnic, national and religious groups). Cambodia underlined how the idea had gained cultural and political reach beyond the legal framework.

## The Holocaust as a 'sacred evil'

However interest in genocide, especially in the West and above all the USA, was primarily driven by renewed interest in the Nazi genocide. When the UN Convention was adopted, 'there was no "Holocaust" in the English language in the sense that word is used today. Scholars and writers used "permanent pogrom" ... or "recent catastrophe," or "disaster," or "the disaster." Sometimes writers spoke about annihilation and destruction without use of any of these terms.' (Korman 1972: 259) Moreover, as Peter Novick points out (1999: 160):

For most Gentiles, and a great many Jews as well, [the Holocaust] was seen as simply one among many dimensions of the horrors of Nazism. Looking at World War II retrospectively, we are inclined to stress what was distinctive in the murderous zeal with which European Jewry was destroyed. Things often appeared differently to contemporaries ... Jews did not stand out as the Nazis' prime victims until near the end of the Third Reich ... Even when news of mass killings of Jews during the war reached the West, their murder was framed as one atrocity, albeit the largest, in a long list of crimes.

In the late 1950s, however, '"Holocaust" took on a specific meaning, stimulated by Yad Vashem (established by the state of Israel in 1953 as a "Martyrs' and Heroes' Remembrance Authority") which from the late 1950s switched from "Disaster" to "Holocaust" ... Within the Jewish world the word became commonplace, in part because Elie Wiesel and other gifted writers and speakers, in public meetings or in articles ... made it coin of the realm.' (Korman 1972: 261).

If the word 'Holocaust' initially gained its new meaning from Israeli and Jewish usage, it was much wider cultural and political currents that determined, in Jeffrey Alexander's words (2002: 5), that it 'gradually became the dominant symbolic representation of evil in the late twentieth century'. It came to be widely perceived that 'this mass murder was fundamentally different from the other traumatic and bloody events in a modern history already dripping in blood, that it represented not simply evil but "radical evil", in Kant's remarkable phrase, that it was unique' (Alexander 2002: 10; see also Moses 2008: 152–3). Indeed these killings

> became what we might identify, in Durkheimian terms, as a sacred-evil, an evil that recalled a trauma of such enormity and horror that it had to be radically set apart from the world and all of its other traumatizing events, and which became inexplicable in ordinary, rational terms. As part of the Nazi scheme of world domination, the Jewish mass killing was heinous but at least it had been understandable. As a sacred evil, set apart from ordinary evil things, it had become mysterious and inexplicable.
>
> (Alexander 2002: 27)

Thus the episode was framed as the prime tragedy of modern history, and 'this perception of its moral status [was] not a natural reflection of the event itself. The Jewish mass killings first had to be dramatized – as a tragedy' (Alexander 2002: 33). Alexander traces this process through key cultural moments such as the publication of the diary of Anne Frank, the Amsterdam Jewish schoolgirl murdered by the Nazis; the televised 1961 trial of Adolf Eichmann in Jerusalem; the 1978 TV series *The Holocaust*; and the 1993 film *Schindler's List*. Of course, 'millions of persons were victims of Nazi mass murder in addition to the Jews – Poles, gypsies, homosexuals, handicapped persons, and political opponents of all types'. But in the process of sacralizing the Holocaust evil, 'virtually all of these non-Jewish victims were filtered out of the emerging collective representation'. This, Alexander argues, 'underlines the "arbitrary" quality of the way the trauma is conceived' (2002: 65, n.28). Indeed the sociological idea of a 'sacred evil', Alexander (2002: 44) points out,

> suggests that defining radical evil, and applying it, involves motives and relationships, and institutions, that work more like those associated with religious institutions than with ethical doctrine. In order for a prohibited social action to be powerfully moralized, the symbol of this evil must become engorged. An engorged evil overflows with badness. Evil becomes labile and liquid; it drips and seeps, ruining everything it touches. Under the sign of the

tragic narrative, the Holocaust became engorged, and its seepage polluted everything with which it came into contact.

## Analogical bridging and political campaigning

The growing academic status of the Holocaust also did not primarily reflect scholarly distinctions between different cases of mass violence. Rather scholarship reflected the wider cultural definition of the Holocaust as a 'sacred evil'. The historian Omer Bartov (2010: 2) underlines the extent to which this was a quasi-religious influence:

like any other historical event, the Holocaust had both unique features (such as the extermination camps) and features common to many other genocides (such as communal massacres). It is also obvious that like any traumatic national event, the Holocaust is unique within its national context: to the Jews and to some extent to the Germans. Related to this, certain theological and philosophical interpretations also view it as a unique event. But for historians, the notion of the Holocaust as entirely unique extracts it from the historical context, and converts it into a metaphysical and metahistorical event, a myth and a focus of religious or national identification, thereby sacrificing its status as a concrete episode in the annals of human history.

And yet this was the context in which not only Holocaust, but also genocide, studies have developed. Holocaust 'seepage', Alexander argues, occurred through what he calls 'analogical bridging', in which other atrocities were reinterpreted through its prism. Bridging, too, has not been primarily an academic process: in the 1960s and 1970s, it 'powerfully contributed to a fundamental revision in moral understandings of the historical treatment of minorities inside the United States. Critics of earlier American policy, and representatives of minority groups themselves, began to suggest analogies between various minority "victims" of white American expansion and the Jewish victims of the Holocaust.' (Alexander 2002: 46) Later, Alexander claims, 'the engorged Holocaust symbol ... propelled first American diplomatic and then American-European military intervention against Serbian ethnic violence' (Alexander 2002: 47). Alexander (2002: 53) sees in this an overwhelmingly positive process, broadening the understanding of evil:

Evoking the Holocaust to measure the evil of a non-Holocaust event is nothing more, and nothing less, than to employ a powerful bridging metaphor to make sense of social life ... Metaphorical bridging shifts symbolic significance and audience attention from the originating trauma to the traumas that follow in a sequence of analogical associations. But it does not, for that, inevitably erase or invert the meanings associated with the trauma that was first in the associational line.

Thus for Alexander, the 'sacred' character of Holocaust evil does not preclude the event's generalization and universalization: 'For those committed to human betterment, a touchstone of evil does not preclude but rather invites comparisons' (Alexander 2002: 80, n.90). 'The contemporary "omnipresence" of the Holocaust symbol has more to do with "enlarging the circle of victims" than with focusing exclusively on Jewish suffering' (Alexander 2002: 72, n.57). Bartov (2010: 6) agrees: 'other genocides came into public and scholarly view thanks to the emergence of the Holocaust as a major historical event and not despite it'. Certainly this is how it has seemed to Armenian advocates, who have used the 1915 Armenian genocide's similarities to the Holocaust as a means of gaining recognition in the face of Turkish denial. And of course bridging is infinitely extendible: just as Armenian campaigners have bridged from the Holocaust, so Greek campaigners have bridged from the Armenian genocide to gain recognition of the genocide of the Pontian Greeks at the hands of the same Ottoman regime. Indeed it is argued that Ottoman genocide was directed too against Assyrians and Yezidis (Genocide Prevention Now 2011). The Armenian genocide becomes the centre of a larger genocide of Christians (Hofmann et al. 2011).

Yet there is an alternative reading of the social construction of the Holocaust as a supreme evil. Peter Novick (1999) describes this process in terms of capture by Jewish identity politics and its use in building US support for the state of Israel. Alexander initially rejected this account and presented 'bridging' as a fundamental departure from it: 'Whereas Novick describes a particularization of the Holocaust ... I will describe a universalization. Where Novick describes a nationalization, I trace an internationalization. Where Novick expresses skepticism about the metaphorical transferability of the "Holocaust," I will describe such metaphorical bridging as essential to the social process of moral engagement.' (Alexander 2002: 73, n.57) However Alexander (2009) has subsequently acknowledged the depth of the problem of the particularistic pro-Israeli appropriation of the Holocaust.

In reality, both dynamics (nationalization/internationalization, restriction/bridging) are at work simultaneously. Novick and Alexander capture two sides of the same process, evident ever since 'the Holocaust' morphed from Israeli commemorative activity to universal or pan-Western 'sacred evil'. Alexander's examples actually demonstrate not the one-sided extension of the Holocaust narrative, but these more complex dynamics. The comparison of Native American suffering and the Holocaust has been bitterly contested on both sides (Stannard 1992, 2001; Katz 1994), while the encapsulation of Bosnian violence in Holocaust imagery and its description as 'genocide' have been the subject of extensive political battles (Campbell 2001). Many have described the Bosnian violence as 'ethnic cleansing' (the adjective 'mere' or 'only' is usually implicit), in order to *unbridge* it from the Holocaust and genocide, a pattern seen in many other cases. Indeed the politics of every subsequent genocidal crisis, from Rwanda to Darfur, have revolved considerably around the tension between demands for and refusals of the 'genocide' label, understood largely as the acceptance or denial of Holocaust bridging. Refusal has been as common as acceptance.

What these conflicts demonstrate is that in the twenty-first century, the sacred-evil quality of the Holocaust is no longer spread case by case. The idea of genocide itself has gained a similar quality, used to mark off absolute evil from somehow more tolerable violence, and has hence become a *sine qua non* for campaigners for any civilian population which has become a victim of atrocity.

## Competitive, even denialist, politics of victimization

A major problem with the discussion of the Holocaust and genocide is that it often over-interprets them in the light of American politics. Alexander (2002: 73) criticizes Novick's 'tendentious focus' in suggesting 'that the Holocaust became central to contemporary history because it became central to America, that it became central to America because it became central to America's Jewish community, and that it became central to Jews because it became central to the ambitions of Jewish organizations who were central to the mass media in all its forms' (Novick 1999: 207). However Alexander's own perception of a benign, universalized bridging process is also a largely American perception, reflecting the dynamics of US politics in which various ethnic organizations have tried to emulate the success of Jewish organizations. In consequence, Holocaust and genocide discourse has mushroomed hugely in the USA, and from there has rippled to other Western societies and more weakly to the non-Western world. But the non-West is catching up, and the politics of genocide are being generalized in a more contradictory sense than Alexander suggests. Instead of a benign, harmonious extension of genocide recognition from one case to another, one group's victimization experience is often traded against another's in a competitive political struggle. This leads at best to contentious searches for the right historical analogy and at worst to the denial of the 'other's' genocide.

As the archetype of genocide, the Holocaust is at the centre of these tendencies too. Its often shameless political appropriation by Israeli advocates is today countered by Palestinian claims that the Nakba (Catastrophe) of 1948 was a genocide, that the recent incarceration of the Gazans can be compared to the experiences of Jews in the Warsaw Ghetto, and so on. While supporters of Israel refuse to countenance the possibility that the forced removal of Palestinian Arabs could have anything to do with genocide, pro-Palestinian arguments sometimes involve the minimization and even outright denial of the Holocaust (Achkar, 2010: 243–58). Thus twenty-first-century Middle Eastern political conflicts are marked by a sharp instrumentalization of the Holocaust. For example, the pronouncements of the Iranian president, Mahmoud Ahmadinejad, denying the Holocaust have been countered by Israeli claims that Iranian attempts to obtain nuclear weapons pose an 'existential threat' to the existence of the Jewish people in Israel, potentially leading to a 'new Holocaust', and so require pre-emptive bombing.

These contests in the international political arena have sharp reflections in genocide studies. The most obvious manifestations have involved the US-based International Association of Genocide Scholars (IAGS), the original professional organization founded largely by Jewish academics, which has taken strong positions on the Middle East. It was quick to pass a resolution condemning some of Ahmadinejad's rhetoric as threatening new genocide against Israeli Jews (IAGS 2006), although a less dramatic reading was more sustainable. Indeed IAGS sees itself as an activist as well as a scholarly organization, concerned with preventing as well as studying genocide. It sees its academic credentials as empowering its activism, allowing it to rule authoritatively on where genocide has occurred or is likely to occur. It thus tends to align itself with particular political agendas, notably with the idea that the USA can prevent genocide through military intervention, and against official Turkish denial of Ottoman genocide against Christians.

The problem of this politicization is easily seen. Should anti-Turkish resolutions be followed by resolutions recognizing genocidal violence against Turks and other Muslims at the hands of Christian national-ists, also during the disintegration of the Ottoman Empire? Should resolutions of concern for Israeli Jews be countered by resolutions recognizing the Nakba, the 1982 Sabra and Chatila massacres (at the hands of Israeli-sponsored Lebanese Christian militia), or the ongoing dispossession of Palestinians? It is easy to see how this could lead to a scholarly organization constantly racked by controversy, as indeed happened in 2009 when Israel's invasion of Gaza led some members to demand a reversal of IAGS's pro-Israeli stance.

The dead end to which such politicization leads can be seen in a quasi-scholarly work by two left-wing writers, Edward Herman and David Peterson (2010), with a foreword by Noam Chomsky (Herman's long-time collaborator). *The Politics of Genocide* sees 'genocide' as no more than a labelling device adopted by the US establishment and its tame media and intelligentsia, justifying violence committed by the USA and condoning its allies' violence while excori-ating, exaggerating and even fabricating violence committed by the West's enemies. They allege that '[d]uring the past several decades, the word "genocide" has increased in frequency of use and recklessness of application, so much so that the crime of the 20th Century for which the term originally was coined often appears debased' (Herman and Peterson 2010: 103). Ironically, therefore, they join some pro-Israeli advocates in suggesting a unique place for the Holocaust in the history of violence. But this reference serves the authors' own political argu-ment: if it can be argued that 'current [Western] usage' is (as Chomsky puts it, in Herman and Peterson 2010: 7) 'an insult to the memory of victims of the Nazis', then that usage is discredited. Indeed Chomsky concludes that 'As for the term "genocide", perhaps the most honour-able course would be expunge it from the vocabulary until the day, if it ever comes, when honesty and integrity can become an international norm' (in Herman and Peterson 2010: 12).

Yet not content with exposing Western hypocrisy and underlining atrocities committed by both the USA itself and Western allies, these authors engage in comprehensive denial of genocide by Serbian forces in Bosnia and Kosovo, and even in 1994 in Rwanda, on whose 'genocidal' character there is no scholarly disagreement. They suggest that in official Western narratives, 'our victims are *unworthy* of our attention and indignation, and never suffer "genocide" at our hands' (p. 104, italics in original). Yet in anti-Western, Chomskyan narratives a similar process occurs: the West's enemies, whether Serbian nationalist or Rwandan Hutu Power, have never committed 'genocide', and their crimes are always of less significance than those of Western-supported forces. For the celebrated journalist John Pilger, endorsing this volume on its cover, Herman and Peterson 'defend the right of all of us to a truthful historical memory'. Evidently this did not include the massacred Srebrenica men, Kosovo Albanians and Rwandan Tutsis, who are 'unworthy victims' for these left-deniers. The IAGS would throw up its hands in horror at this selective attitude to genocide recognition, but it is the mirror image of its own.

## Implications for genocide scholarship

More serious, however, than the contradictions of particular academic organizations and political positions is the model of understanding and research implied in this politics of genocide recognition. Clearly scholars mostly work individually, but because they work in social, cultural and political contexts, their work often absorbs and reflects the common assumptions of their time and place. This is an unavoidable problem for social and historical research, whose methodological implications were discussed by Max Weber (2011 (1949)), who argued for sociologists to show awareness of their cultural orientations. He proposed that we distinguish between the choice of research topics, in which it is legitimate for our orientations to play a part, and the carrying out of research, from which we should strive to exclude them. Others, however, have suggested that the problems are deeper and more intractable. The sociology of knowledge proposes that theoretical frameworks are often embedded in ideologies, which in turn reflect particular sets of social interests (Marx and Engels 1970 (1846)). Karl Mannheim (1936) famously suggested that 'utopias' (agendas for change) were as likely to bias knowledge as conservative 'ideologies'.

The most obvious manifestation of cultural and political interests is that a considerable amount of scholarship is conducted with the aim of 'proving' that a particular set of events constitutes genocide. The aim of *recognition* displaces explanation or understanding as the primary goal of research. Yet as Donald Bloxham (2003: 189) writes of the Armenians: 'It may be said categorically that the killing did constitute genocide ... but recognizing this fact should be a "by-product" of the historian's work, not its ultimate aim or underpinning.' Yet far too many social scientists as well as historians work within a quasi-legal framework, aiming to prove that certain episodes can be considered genocide. Often the goal is to establish a moral case that the perpetrators of a given set of atrocities can be seen as guilty of genocide, but sometimes there is a more direct aim of stimulating legal proceedings. Daniel Feierstein (2010), making the case that the Argentine military dictatorship's crimes constituted genocide, argues that this was an attempt to eradicate part of the Argentinian 'national group' (since destroying the latter is covered by the Convention) rather than 'political groups' (which are not covered). Feierstein takes his cue from a novel interpretation by Spanish judge Baltazar Garzón in his indictment of Argentinian officers. Rather than resting on a critique of the Convention's restricted definition, Feierstein embraces a doubtful reinterpretation of it, presumably because without this the episode could not count as genocide within the UN definition.

However the influence of cultural and political interests on genocide research is not restricted to recognition strategies, but also affects the main intellectual paradigm within which genocide research is conducted. In this perspective, we need to examine the links between social and political orientations and theoretical and methodological assumptions. As Thomas Kuhn (1996 (1970)) argued, paradigms consist of sets of assumptions which guide particular areas of scientific research. Change in knowledge does not just arise from the accumulation of knowledge leading to the falsification of hypotheses, as positivists such as Karl Popper (2002 (1957)) had claimed. Instead paradigm shifts (even in the natural sciences, but certainly in the fields of social and historical knowledge) involve not only the crystallization of new sets of ideas, but cultural, political and economic changes.

A moment's reflection on intellectual patterns in recent decades will show the significance of such wider processes: the rise of Marxism and critical theory in the social sciences in the late 1960s and 1970s, after the upheavals of the Vietnam war and the student revolt; the emergence of feminist approaches in the 1970s; the 'cultural turn', post-structuralism and post-modernism, which reacted to these trends in the 1980s; globalism and 'humanitarian interventionism' which developed in the 1990s in response to post-Cold War changes; and security paradigms, which prevailed widely in the 2000s, after 9/11. Such trends have been variably influential across the social sciences and humanities, as some fields are deeply influenced and others remain relatively insulated either in general or from particular trends.

In the case of genocide studies, a distinctive pattern emerges. While heavily influenced by genocide-specific politics, it has been relatively immune from many of the general cultural and intellectual trends just described. The field only really blossomed in the 1990s, and 'missed' much of the impact of Marxism, feminism and post-structuralism. The approaches of the founding figures, sociologists such as Leo Kuper, Helen Fein and Frank Chalk and psychologists such as Israel Charny, were not strongly defined by any of these trends (although Irving Louis Horowitz was known as a radical sociologist before his genocide work). The globalism and liberal internationalism of the 1990s were background assumptions for the interventionist, genocide-prevention approach which was one key influence; equally important were the cultural and political commitments of scholars from Jewish and Armenian backgrounds. In the broader field which genocide studies became in the 2000s, influences such as historical empiricism and links to legal practice, if not *anti*-theoretical, helped reinforce a relatively *a*theoretical orientation.

However explaining an important historical phenomenon such as genocide necessarily involves theoretical assumptions. In a relatively atheoretical environment, implicit theoretical commitments will be important if explicit ones are lacking. The case advanced here is that genocide studies developed within a theoretical and methodological paradigm that emerged from the background cultural and political interests which brought genocide to the fore in the 1990s, and which drove many of its early thinkers to work in the field. In particular, genocide has been very much in the shadow of Holocaust studies, which had become an established area of historical studies in the 1970s and 1980s, and had already developed a sophisticated literature. The Holocaust came to be understood as the archetypal genocide, a perception reinforced by the volume and depth of research. At the same time, however, important real-world developments – in Bosnia,

Rwanda, Darfur and elsewhere – have helped push genocide studies to greater academic prominence.

In Chapter 2, I outline this dominant paradigm of the field and its limitations, and suggest the nature of the paradigm shift which is needed. In Chapter 3, I discuss the foundations of a new approach. In the remainder of this book, I explore the potential of this new paradigm, first in re-evaluating the Holocaust, twentieth-century European genocide and the 'post-genocidal' moment represented by the Genocide Convention, and, second, in exploring the worldwide patterns of genocide in the Cold War and the post-Cold War, 'global' era of the twenty-first century.

# 2 | *Fallacies of the comparative genocide paradigm*

Since genocide studies grew in the shadow of Holocaust studies, they have had to struggle to establish their autonomy. Among historians, the weight of Holocaust historiography is so great that genocide remains a poor relation. The necessity of comparison, which might otherwise be seen as normal in historical and social-scientific research, is seen as a hard-won gain over the idea of Holocaust 'uniqueness' (Huttenbach 2009). Each additional 'genocide' has to be painstakingly added to the canon, often after political campaigning as well as scholarship. The recognition of the 1915 Armenian genocide, pursued both by historians (Hovanissian 1987, Dadrian 2001) and campaigners, is a model which advocates of recognizing other genocides have followed.

Thus although genocide studies have generally criticized the sacralized idea of the Holocaust as a 'unique' event – otherwise it would be difficult to talk meaningfully about its relationships to other episodes, and full bridging would be difficult – it still profoundly influences how the field develops. With the Holocaust as the standard against which other genocides must be measured, most predictably 'fail': hence a narrow scope for 'genocide' is confirmed, and euphemistic descriptions such as 'ethnic cleansing' are adopted instead to describe the 'failed' episodes (Shaw 2007: 37–62). Yet this does not exhaust the problematic influence of ideas about the Holocaust. Even if bridging from the Holocaust sometimes works for *recognition* of other genocides, its consequences for *understanding* genocide are mostly profoundly negative. The bridging approach, I shall argue, has been associated with a theoretical and methodological paradigm which has restricted our understanding of the Holocaust as well as of genocide.

The core academic idea which is inspired by bridging is that the understanding of genocide should proceed by comparing one episode to another. Around this, I argue in this chapter, are clustered a number of key assumptions of the principal paradigm in the field, which I therefore call the *comparative genocide paradigm*. That this is not just one of many paradigms, but the dominant approach, is clearly reflected in the way that the field has usually been defined, as 'comparative genocide studies' (Scherrer 1999).

## Comparative method and genocide research

Comparison is normal, unavoidable and necessary in social science and history. Yet the value of comparison depends on its purpose, how its units are defined, and the frame of reference within which it is made. Precisely because comparison is axiomatic, the idea is hardly sufficient to define a field. Therefore genocide studies' self-definition in these terms suggests the weakness of its theoretical goals. Indeed for some practitioners, the purposes of comparison hardly go beyond the essentially political goal of recognition.

The kind of comparative reasoning to which 'bridging' most obviously leads is argument by analogy. This is the most limited type of comparison, understanding new events by reference to established narratives of given events. Not surprisingly there is, writes the sociologist Alberto Toscano (2010: 153), 'a contemporary trend to see analogy as a representational trend that stifles singularity and novelty, reinforcing the standardised prejudices as doxa'. In contrast, meaningful comparison depends on developing theoretical frameworks, which do not depend on narratives of specific events but can make sense of a whole universe of events. As Charles Ragin (1989: 19) puts it, 'it is not difficult to make sense of an individual case ... or to draw a few rough parallels across a range of cases ... The challenge comes in trying to make sense of the diversity across cases in a way that unites similarities and differences in a single coherent framework.'

Even when it moves beyond its analogical starting point, genocide studies still remain a branch of the most common kind of comparative social science which deals with variations between what are seen as discrete national cases. In this sense, comparative study is 'the branch of sociology that uses society as its explanatory unit' (Ragin 1982), where 'society' is understood as a national unit. This kind of sociology and political science compares national societies, seeking to explain variation in the dimension studied in terms of the societies' more fundamental differences. When this traditional comparative sociology is taken seriously, Philip McMichael (1990: 385) points out, 'The logic of comparative inquiry requires independent or uniform cases and formal quasi-experimental designs for comparative generalization.' This kind of work is common in the more readily quantified areas of social science, dealing with regular micro-phenomena such as crime and electoral trends. However comparative genocide studies, like other fields dealing with more irregular macro-phenomena such as war and revolution, has unsurprisingly produced little work of this kind.

This kind of comparative study involves, moreover, what Ulrich Beck (2005: 43–50) calls 'methodological nationalism', which over-privileges national contexts of social relations. In the mid twentieth century, this led to the reification of national peculiarities or 'social science as stamp-collecting' (Shaw 2000: 68–70). The idea corresponds to a division of labour between domesticated social sciences (sociology, politics, etc.) which work largely within national contexts, and Inter-national Relations which deals with interstate relations. At the end of the twentieth century, this division was breaking down because of the 'global' changes associated with the end of the Cold War (Albrow 1997). The idea of global understanding also implied a changed view of earlier history, so that a methodological separation between the study of 'domestic' and 'international' processes was increasingly seen as archaic in historical as well as sociological research. In this context, although comparative social science continued to be practised, its heyday (Armer and Marsh 1982) had passed, and 'the comparative method' was less discussed.

In serious comparative work in genocide studies (going beyond loose, analogical reference to established cases), the dominant approach has comprised integrated sequential studies of a few major episodes within thematic frameworks which allow qualitative comparisons. Numerous major volumes (recent examples include Weitz 2005, Valentino 2004, Mann 2005, Midlarsky 2005, Sémelin 2007 and Kiernan 2007) follow this approach, which has undoubtedly led to enriched understanding, principally of the restricted universe of major cases. Moreover this kind of work has been less tightly bound by the formal requirements of comparative enquiry and has sometimes moved partially beyond 'methodological nationalism'. Nevertheless even these manifestations of comparative genocide have often involved assumptions about the nature of appropriate comparisons which reflect the analogical bridging of Holocaust-inspired discourse, as well as the mainstream understanding of comparative social science. I shall examine these assumptions in turn, explaining the way the comparative paradigm works as an interlocking set. Although no one writer represents this paradigm in its entirety, and many scholars would disagree with some of its elements even if they accept others, these assumptions have real influence in the field, and the ideal type which I present below represents, I believe, an interlocking set of obstacles to fuller sociological and historical understanding of genocides.

## The study of 'genocides' rather than genocide

The starting point for the paradigm has been the assumption that there are stand-alone episodes which can be compared. Here the Holocaust influence is very evident. In constructing it as a paradigmatic evil event, modern Western culture simultaneously emphasized the distinctive features of the Nazi mass murder of the Jews and de-emphasized the ways in which that campaign of atrocity was linked to others (against other populations and by other actors) as well as to their common Second World War context. Holocaust historiography has been framed by the general social-construction processes discussed in Chapter 1. It has generally held fairly tightly to the idea of the Holocaust as a very distinctive set of policies, processes and events, to be studied in their own frame. For Holocaust historians, as Dan Stone (2008) emphasizes, any comparison with other genocides remains a novelty. Yet as we have seen, the Nazi extermination of the Jews was not originally understood as a stand-alone episode, but as part of the wider sets of Nazi and indeed many-sided atrocities in the world war. Lemkin (1944) referred to 'the Nazi genocide' as a multi-faceted, multi-targeted process, rather than separately to Nazi genocide against the Jews, which he saw as only a part of that process. The point is not that Lemkin was right and 'Holocaust' scholars wrong (I pursue the arguments further in Chapter 4) but that labelling a particular set of events a 'genocide' is always a somewhat arbitrary decision. There is always more than one way to define the limits of a particular set of historical processes.

Comparative genocide studies has, however, got badly stuck with the idea that what it is studying are discrete 'genocides' (Armenian, Rwandan, Cambodian, etc.), sharply differentiated from other social processes as well as from each other. In implementing bridging, it recognizes additional distinct genocides even when these occur simultaneously and connectedly with genocides already recognized.

So alongside the Holocaust, the Nazis are widely argued to have committed further 'genocides' of the mentally disabled, Roma and Sinti, Poles, Ukrainians, Byelorussians, Russians, Serbs and other Slavs, etc. The Ottoman Turkish regime is similarly believed to have carried out serial genocides of Greeks, Assyrians and other Christian groups as well as of Armenians (Travis 2010: 173–292). Yet the view of these as separate 'genocides' has more to do with nationalist reclamations of history than with analytical reasoning concerning processes which were highly intertwined.

This approach fails to distinguish the *principal* object of study, which is genocide in general as a type of social action, social relation and social structure, from an entirely *secondary* question, whether, how and when to delimit particular episodes from each other (Shaw 2007: 81–96). Moreover, it answers the latter question in fundamentally inappropriate ways, since there is much to be learned by looking at the common elements of these separated 'genocides', especially when they occur in the same time and context and even more when they are perpetrated by the same actors. These inappropriate answers are the results of further, closely linked assumptions to which I shall now turn.

## Priority of mega-genocides, 'rarity' of genocide

The comparative genocide approach, while allowing recognition of new genocides, tends to prioritize studying the few cases of extremely large-scale and exceptionally murderous genocide which are most easily represented as stand-alone events. Hence the Armenians, the Holocaust and Rwanda take centre-place in most recent grand tomes. The consequence is that genocide studies has been dominated by what Levene (2005a: 163) calls 'mega-genocides'. Smaller-scale and less murderous (but still hugely socially destructive) events, even though far more numerous and indicative of the prevalence of genocide, are often marginalized. In particular, what Kuper (1987: 32) seminally called 'genocidal massacres' have tended to be excluded from the main frame of the field. Indeed, Jacques Sémelin (2007) insists on a categorical distinction between 'genocide' and 'massacre': only large-scale, clearly 'intentional' policy-driven events count as genocide.

Certainly, the mega-genocides can be made to stand out from history as sacred evils. Yet it is more important to appreciate the extent to which even these cases are embedded within histories of war, political competition, religious domination, colonization, etc. The dominance of the field by mega-episodes involves a serious distortion of the overall pattern of genocidal violence, and leads directly to the questionable consensus which Straus (2007: 479) summarizes from his survey of recent literature, that 'Genocide is a rare event.' Genocide is only 'rare' because it has been defined in a way that excludes many smaller and localized cases. Even the UN Convention's specification of five means of genocide is too broad for scholars who redefine genocide simply as 'mass murder' (Chalk and Jonassohn 1990, Charny 1988 and 1991). This reduction to mass murder is a pervasive tendency in comparative genocide research, and can be seen in a range of recent comparative and single-case studies (e.g. Midlarsky 2005, Straus 2006, Sémelin 2007).

Here there is a close coincidence between the dominant academic paradigm and the nationalist political agendas of those who claim to speak for major victim-groups (even if many of the authors cited would distance themselves from these agendas). For Jewish nationalists, if the Holocaust is the prime genocide, then the destruction of Arab society in Palestine a few years later – which manifestly involved far fewer victims, a very much smaller proportion of whom were murdered – cannot be genocide. Likewise, from the point of view of the Rwandan Patriotic Front, because the mass murder of Rwandan Tutsis was a major genocide, smaller-scale massacres of Hutus by the RPF itself cannot be genocide. Such arguments not only sustain dubious political agendas, but also work to block a full view of the scope of genocide in the 1940s and the 1990s respectively. This is a type of argument that would never be entertained if we were discussing a similar question in another field. In war studies, for example, no political interests would block us from seeing major and minor examples of the same phenomenon, in the same period, involving a variety of actors. Yet in genocide studies, the dominant assumptions about the demarcation of genocides work in precisely this way.

## Singular perpetrators, singular victim-groups

A corresponding component of the comparative genocide paradigm is that the social relations of genocide tend to be represented in one-dimensional terms. Perpetrators perpetrate; victims suffer victimization; and, last but not least, bystanders stand by. Certainly, the core meaning of genocide is the destruction of a civilian population or group by armed power, and in this sense the idea involves the qualitatively asymmetrical relationship which is captured by the 'perpetrators/ victims' dichotomy. Yet in the comparative genocide paradigm, much more is generally assumed. Perpetrators are assumed to be single hierarchically organized collective actors typically centred on state power, victims to be socially coherent collectivities typically (in the terms of the UN Convention) ethnic, national, racial or religious groups. Bystanders, in contrast, are sociologically anonymous: this is an empty category indicating no particular type of actor.

There is considerable disagreement on the secondary characteristics of perpetrator organizations. It has been noted that they involve particular types of regime, rather than of state (Dadrian 2001: 155), and require the support of other social actors, such as paramilitaries and social constituencies, to carry out their goals (Mann 2005). But that the organizers of genocide are basically centralized, hierarchical actors is widely assumed, excluding the possibility that diverse arrays of state and non-state actors might be responsible. Empirical evidence that the perpetrators of anti-population violence are often more diverse has even led Christian Gerlach (2010) to reject the genocide concept as irredeemably contaminated by unrealistic assumptions about perpetrators. It is difficult not to share his frustration with the prevailing narrow conceptions, but these should be linked to the comparative genocide paradigm rather than the idea of genocide as such.

Likewise, although many scholars add social classes, political and/or gender groups to the list of victim-group types, few dispute that each genocide involves a singular, specific victim-group deriving from, as Helen Fein (1990: 24) puts it, 'basic kinds, classes, or sub-families of humanity, persisting units of society'. Even if some add the important qualification that victim-groups are defined by the perpetrators (Chalk and Jonassohn, 1990: 23), the idea of a singular target- or victim-group remains fundamental. Underlying this is the idea of 'ownership' of each genocide by a particular group that is targeted, ownership which remains with the descendants and especially the political representatives of such groups decades or even centuries later. This notion is essential for maintaining the links of genocide studies to the commemorative traditions of ethnic, national and other groups, but it blocks conceptualization of the complex and often two- or multi-sided targeting which is normal in genocide. In order to deal with the latter, the singular victim-group concept requires us either to identify a series of simultaneous genocides by the same perpetrators (e.g. Nazi genocides against the mentally handicapped, Roma and Sinti, etc., as well as against the Jews) or to conceptualize 'major' and 'minor' victims (for example, Tutsis and 'moderate Hutus' in Rwanda in 1994).

The idea that particular victim-group identities should define our understanding of genocide is attractive because it pays attention to victim experience. Bartov argues of Nazi genocide that 'listening to the voices of victims, Jewish or not, is crucial to the kind of empathy that brings with it a modicum of understanding'. But this is accompanied by the following assertion, which defends the particularity of Jewish experience against a broader view of the Holocaust and Nazi genocide: 'I am not sure that writing about *many* genocides instead of just one is a moral statement; but I *am* sure that it precludes empathy' (Bartov 2010: 28, emphasis in the original). Here 'empathy' becomes an enemy of an integral approach, even to a particular genocidal history in a given time and space. Apparently we cannot listen to Jewish and other victims at the same time: in Bartov's study of the 'erasure' of Jewish life and culture in Galicia (in today's Ukraine), which occurred simultaneously with the removal of Polish life and culture from the region, the latter is often recognized parenthetically, in references to 'Jews (and Poles)' (e.g. Bartov 2010: 67). A synthetic narrative of genocide in a given historical context, let alone any generalization about genocide in larger historical periods, would appear to be impossible.

In the comparative paradigm, therefore, perpetrators are coherent, organized groups driven by hatred, which is a *sine qua non* of the explanatory thrust since it makes them *purely evil*. Victims are not really actors, but fundamentally passive *pure victims*, since the violence of genocide is by definition 'one-sided' (Fein 1990: 13, Charny 1994: 75). The problem, of course, is that historical reality is more complex. Even in the most asymmetrical conflict, victims are also actors. And while *individual* victim-actors are mostly *not* also perpetrators of anti-civilian violence, the larger ethnic and national groups to which they belong – and especially political movements based on them – often include those who are perpetrators, either simultaneously or at a different moment in time. Moreover, even the most asymmetrical conflict is often embedded in a system of conflicts, in which actors from victim-groups are allied to other actors who are perpetrating violence.

The Holocaust is of course the prototype of pure 'perpetrator/victim' relationships, since European Jews were almost entirely unarmed in the face of the Third Reich. Yet Jews did resist both non-violently and violently, and in their armed resistance allied themselves with Nazism's Soviet enemies. The latter in turn perpetrated their own genocidal violence against various populations before, during and after the Second World War. And after the war, the Zionist movement in Palestine, while rescuing Jewish victims of Nazism, used their suffering as part of a rationale for its own violence against the Arab population. Such complexities do not, of course, render the terms 'perpetrators' and 'victims' redundant, but they oblige us to recognize that no population group is purely perpetrator or victim, but that all such groups, and often individuals within them, have complex and changing roles which these terms only partially capture.

The underlying problem here is that the purity of victims' victimhood is important not only for maintaining a simple 'perpetrator/victim' analytical model, but also for group 'ownership' of genocide. Which ethnic or national group, or movement claiming to speak on its behalf, wants to own a messy, conflicted historical record in which its own members have committed violence against civilians as well as being victims? The integrity of the 'perpetrator/victim' dichotomy is fundamental to the comparative genocide paradigm's fit with nationalist narratives of genocidal victimization. The danger is that the idea of singular victim-groups becomes a device policing our understanding more or less directly in the interests of particular communal identities (e.g. Jewish, Tutsi) and often of political institutions and causes which mobilize them (e.g. the Israeli state, the RPF government). It asserts by definitional or methodological fiat the superior importance of the general targeting of a particular nationality or ethnicity. This in turn fragments our understanding of how genocide develops through combined, sequential and sometimes mutual targeting of different groups. Likewise it blocks recognition of the complex discriminations along lines of class, gender, party and locality which – together with more indiscriminate violence against whole ethnic and national populations – actually characterize genocide.

## Third parties as bystanders

If the way that the comparative genocide paradigm uses 'perpetrators' and 'victims' needs to be rethought, the matching 'bystander' category should be abandoned altogether. This category recognizes that genocidal relations involve people who are neither perpetrators or victims, but it is mainly a residual, catch-all category for those who don't belong to the defining groups. The term 'bystander' wraps up these third parties, moreover, in a particular kind of relationship to the conflict between perpetrators and victims. They 'stand by', observing, perhaps commenting – but, like the victims, characterized by passivity. They are not regarded as actors, and this confirms that only the all-powerful perpetrators are really actors in genocide.

Certainly, passivity is *one* common stance in relation to genocide by *some* kinds of third party. States and other actors who have the power-capabilities to prevent or halt genocide often do not see their interests engaged or develop effective policies to oppose it. Population groups in genocide zones who are not themselves directly threatened often fail to stand up for their neighbours, whether out of hostility, indifference or fear. Global media audiences who are aware of distant genocides may not look for, or find, meaningful ways of showing solidarity. These and many other responses to genocide could be called 'bystanding', in the sense of observing without acting to halt genocide. Yet while this description may be morally enlightening, it is sociologically weak: it tells us little about the different modes of and reasons for 'bystanding' which are apparent in the three different cases. Moreover none of these responses should necessarily be considered 'non-action'. On the contrary, many of these actors may indeed be acting, according to their own perceptions of their interests, values and capabilities, even if in ways which fail to prevent or which even facilitate genocide. From a moral point of view, the only action which counts may be that which helps stop violence; from a sociological point of view, however, actors often have other interests, are involved in other relationships and undertake other sorts of action.

So 'bystanders' and 'bystanding' are inadequate ways of framing the range of third-party actors and actions that impinge on genocide. Just as perpetrators include many different types of actor (states, regimes, parties, armies, armed movements, factions within all of these, and others), and victim-groups are varied (ethnic, national, racial, religious, political, class, gender, etc., together with the organizations which represent them), so third-party actors may include all the types of actors who may be perpetrators and victims, and more. While perpetrators are generally armed power-actors, and targets/victims are basically unarmed civilian social groups, third-party actors may be either.

Moreover, the impact of third-party actions on genocidal situations is not restricted to 'bystanding'. Most obviously, there is also 'intervention', not only in the military form in which it is often advocated, but also through political, ideological, social and cultural action designed to impact on genocide.

However even the 'bystanding/intervention' dichotomy utterly fails to illuminate the full scope of third-party action. This conceptualization assumes that third parties are simply oriented towards genocidal situations, and must adopt one of these alternatives. In reality third parties, *simply because they are third parties*, are partially or mainly *oriented towards other situations* as well as to genocide. Yet their non-genocide-oriented actions may have as great an impact on the genocidal situation as any deliberate 'intervention'. For example, neither the Soviet Union nor the Western Allies developed a general policy of intervention to halt the Holocaust; yet in the end, their military campaigns against Nazi Germany achieved that result. Of course when they liberated the camps, they applied policies to help the survivors; this shows how genocide-oriented actions may develop out of policies not primarily designed as intervention. Bystanding and intervention were both components of Allied policies towards the Holocaust, but neither was really the main driver of the policies which actually had the greatest impact on it.

## Regime and ideology

The comparative genocide paradigm's other core assumptions are the closely linked ideas that totalitarian and authoritarian regimes are typical perpetrators, and that racist ideology is the root cause of their violence. These assumptions reflect the origins of the genocide idea in the Nazi context, and the belief that perpetrators will normally resemble the Nazis to some degree. It is widely believed, as Geoffrey Hartman (2009: x) claims, that 'What we do know clearly is that genocides are incited by a demagogic leader who lends credence to a scapegoating myth and reinforces that "narrative".' Contemporary leaders implicated in genocide, such as Slobodan Milošević and Saddam Hussein, are assimilated to a Hitlerian stereotype, although their systems of power and their rationales for genocidal policies are significantly different from Hitler's. Thus the 'regime' assumption not only blocks recognition of the complex and varied nature of perpetrator actors, reinforcing a fundamentally statist conception of them which is belied by the evidence. It also tends to minimize the differences between genocidal states (and indeed among dictatorial and authoritarian regimes), and embeds as a general understanding something which belongs to a specific time and place.

This approach gels easily, of course, with the assumption that Western democracies and international organizations are the 'answers' to genocide, not part of the problem. It marginalizes troubling issues such as the involvement of more-or-less democratic settler governments in colonial genocide, the role of Western democracies in promoting national homogenization in the era of the world wars, the role of the Western powers and the UN in producing genocide-prone partition plans as solutions to ethno-political conflicts, and the role of democracy promotion in stimulating genocidal violence in the twenty-first century.

The assumption that the root cause of genocide is a racist or similar exclusive ideology, which designates a particular group for destruction, is closely related to the regime assumption. If genocide is defined by a particular victim-group, then perpetrators' *attitudes towards that group* are easily assumed to be the primary cause of violence against them. Once again, the Holocaust is the model: if the Holocaust was about the Jews, then it is easily concluded that Nazi anti-semitism was its driver. The general approach that is derived from this looks for 'race-hatred' towards particular groups. A recent example is John Hagan and Wynona Rymond-Richmond's (2009) attempt to explain attacks on 'African' groups in Darfur in terms of racist labelling, downplaying factors such as counter-insurgency and competition for land (Shaw 2011).

An obvious weakness of the assumption that racism against a given target group must drive the genocide against them is that genocidal actors have complex ideologies. Even at the level of ideology we need to ask how racist attitudes fit with other ideas the perpetrators hold. Nazi attitudes towards Jews were conditioned by the belief in the superiority of Germans and Aryans over *all* other peoples: they were part of a hierarchical racist world-view which also regarded Slavs, blacks, homosexuals and others as inferior. This comprehensive racism, in turn, was linked in Nazi ideology with nationalism, eugenics, patriarchy, and other strands. To understand the ideological sources of Jewish persecution we need to understand the linkages between these sets of ideas. The salience of this point is underlined by the fact that genocidal actors often have multiple targets, either simultaneously or sequentially: we need to investigate the common frame which drives a collective actor to attack several population groups. In these cases, it is hardly likely that the specific attitudes towards the groups will be unconnected.

In any case, we cannot assume that perpetrators' ideologies are coherently or consistently developed, or that ideology drives genocidal policies in a simple way. Even the most ideological genocidists hold fantastic, pseudo-scientific ideas that are significantly incoherent. Genocidal policies often represent more pragmatic situational responses to threats, difficulties and the actions of others, including the target groups as well as third parties. We must take seriously the idea that genocide often constitutes *policy* and like all policy develops situationally, rather than as some sort of unbending implementation of an original idea. In the Nazi case, historians have long moved beyond the idea that anti-Jewish policy resulted from a singular intention on Hitler's part, to look at the dynamics of a field of policy implemented by complex party, state and military bureaucracies, which was constantly changing as Nazi Germany expanded its control of the European continent and faced new challenges in the world war.

The inbuilt tendency of the comparative genocide paradigm towards ideological explanation derives from a deep-rooted paradox of the 'perpetrator–victim' dyad. Because victim-group experience is regarded as 'sacred' and perpetrator 'intentions' as extraordinarily evil, the focus is on the most 'evil', racist ideas rather than on more mundane ideas that they may share with other political actors. The definitionally criminal character of genocide also works in this direction, pushing towards indicting perpetrators for their ideological beliefs as well as their particular decisions. Thus, as I have explained elsewhere (Shaw 2007: 81–96), genocide studies tend to get stuck at the first stage of sociological explanation, examining the subjective orientations of the actors (indeed really only the perpetrators). They fail to move sufficiently to the more complex causal and contextual explanations that are normally sought for social phenomena. This reflects the 'sacred-evil' quality of genocide: if it is not a normal social phenomenon, it cannot be explained by normal sociological means.

## Domesticated genocide

Linked in the comparative genocide paradigm to the emphasis on regime is the assumption that genocides are produced primarily in domestic rather than international relations, and become of international significance mainly because they offend against the Genocide Convention and demand international intervention. These assumptions are reflected in influential explicit claims for the domestic character of the most important genocides. Thus the political scientist Robert Melson (1992: 18) refers to 'total domestic genocides like the Armenian Genocide and the Holocaust, including the extermination of the Gypsies, ... the destruction of the Kulaks and the Cambodian "autogenocide"'. Christian Scherrer (1999) also distinguishes 'foreign' and 'domestic' genocides – putting the Holocaust in the 'domestic' category – while René Lemarchand (2002) remarks that both Jews and Rwandan Tutsis 'have been the target of a "total domestic genocide", to use Melson's phrase' (501). As I have argued (Shaw 2007: 149), such 'domestic' characterizations cannot be sustained. All these and other major cases involved populations targeted across borders or for reasons connected with international conflict, and had intimate relations with international politics and war. Yet such 'domestic' categorizations are strongly linked to the conceptions of perpetrators, victims and bystanders which we have discussed. Perpetrators and victims are assumed to be locked in an essentially 'domestic' conflict, of which international actors are essentially 'bystanders', or in which they 'intervene'.

Of course despite such 'domestic' claims, many scholars actually treat the production of genocide at least partially in international contexts, since these are difficult to avoid in the rounded historical treatment of almost any episode. Indeed Melson (1992) argued that when international and civil wars occur together, there is the strongest chance of the onset of genocide – an argument which has been seen as among the most relevant claims for the international production of genocide (Krain 1997: 348). Yet the core of the 'domestic' mindset remains even when some international context is recognized, because it is embedded in the dominant methodological assumption that genocide consists of a series of *discrete* cases which must then be compared.

## A restricted view of international relations

The comparative genocide paradigm allows international relations a particularly restricted role. An international dimension is recognized in almost all genocide research: typically, international context is incorporated ad hoc in accounts of the genesis even of supposedly 'domestic' genocides. But the main role of international relations is seen not in the *production* of genocide but in *responses* to it once it has occurred. It is assumed that the largest global and world-regional contexts of international relations do not produce genocide, and the great (especially Western democratic) powers and international organizations are not responsible for it. Rather, legitimate states and international institutions respond, it is assumed, to the domestically generated genocide of local authoritarian and totalitarian regimes.

These assumptions are simply the other side of the way methodological nationalism has embedded itself in genocide research. Yet they are also articulated and reinforced in the way that International Relations has approached genocide. Most IR literature has explored the responses of the the great powers (mainly the USA) and the UN to genocide, chiefly in the context of 'humanitarian intervention'. IR literature did not initially identify genocide, however, as the necessary condition for such intervention. For example, Nicholas Wheeler's influential survey (2000) saw only one (Rwanda) out of seven cases of humanitarian intervention as raising questions of genocide. Indeed even Rwanda was not immediately analysed in genocide terms. One of the best IR books on genocide is Michael Barnett's *Eye-Witness to a Genocide* (2002), about his secondment to the UN during the Rwanda crisis: only afterwards did he realize fully what they had been dealing with. Barnett's ringside experience may be unusual, but his absorption of the ideological reflexes of the practitioners was typical. Just as political leaders had been reluctant to use the 'g-word', so IR scholars were (and often remain) too willing to use practitioner euphemisms like 'humanitarian crisis' and 'ethnic cleansing' for situations which involved genocide.

Rwanda did eventually raise the profile of genocide issues in IR, for example in Alan Kuperman's (2001) critique of the limits of intervention in 1994. In recent normative and policy-oriented developments, notably around the Responsibility To Protect, genocide issues are increasingly salient (Bellamy 2009). This literature shares, however, the assumption that the IR issues concern responses to genocide rather than its production, assumed to be largely domestic. Certainly, among authors critical of 'humanitarian intervention', we find arguments that reject this 'production–response' dichotomy: for example, that intervention helps to produce the genocide it is supposed to prevent (Gibbs 2009), and that genocide is 'provoked' by attempts to bring about intervention (Kuperman and Crawford 2006). Yet while the former argument leads us to consider the roles of great powers and international organizations in producing genocide, the latter continues to ascribe primary responsibility to local actors.

In this it aligns with older IR discussions of how genocide is produced. The pioneering analysis of Barbara Harff and Ted Robert Gurr (1988), for example, identified forty-four 'genocides and politicides' between 1945 and 1988 (yet they classified only six of these as genocides, an attribution which should be questioned in the light of the broader definition advocated above). However, they classified these episodes not according to international context, but according to the types of relationships between states and target populations, in line with Harff's (1986) earlier concept of genocide as involving the domestic form of 'state terrorism'. The types in terms of which they classified the 'genocides' ('hegemonial' and 'xenophobic') indicated relationships that could have international dimensions, but they did not highlight these. Moreover although they also classified their episodes regionally, they did not analyse the role of regional international relations in their genesis. And while their analysis covered exactly the Cold War period, this context was not problematized (the term 'Cold War' does not even occur in the article), although in many of their cases it was germane. In this sense, the article typifies the omission of international contexts of genocide. Even in Harff's later statistical study (2003), genocides and politicides are still seen as a product of 'isolated states' that could 'eliminate unwanted groups without international repercussions'. She concludes that alongside domestic 'political upheaval' and 'prior genocides', 'exclusionary ideology' and 'autocratic' regimes are major predictors of genocide and politicide. International relations are seen as necessarily constraining, rather than enabling, genocide: 'The greater degree to which a country is interdependent with others, the less likely its leaders are to attempt geno-/politicides'. Thus although Harff (2003: 64–5) acknowledges that '[i]nternational context matters for geno-/politicides', this is only in terms of effects on 'international responses'.

Subsequent work has certainly indicated 'international' production more explicitly. Matthew Krain (1997: 335), using Harff and Gurr's data, criticized the argument of Rudy Rummel (1997) that the structure of states and the distribution of power within them explained genocide or 'democide'. Instead, Krain argued, changes 'in the political opportunity structure' were key to adoption of genocidal or politicidal policies by states, and 'changes in the international political opportunity structure (often caused by war) have important structural effects on the national political opportunity structure' (Krain 1997: 330, 331). So while Krain continued to see genocide/politicide as fundamentally a 'national' phenomenon, concluding (1997: 355) that 'civil war involvement is the most consistent predictor of the onset of genocides or politicides', he agreed (as we saw above) with Melson that when international and civil wars occur together, there is the strongest chance of genocide onset. Yet the argument that domestic situations are most potent is still asserted: Harff has argued (2003: 57) that 'almost all genocides of the last half-century occurred during or in the immediate aftermath of internal wars, revolutions, and regime collapse'.

The post-Cold War era has seen more wide-ranging comparative work by IR scholars. Benjamin Valentino (2004) argues for seeing 'mass killing' (he eschews a specific genocide focus) as 'strategic' political action. In a wide-ranging survey, Valentino's 'motives/types' (including 'territorial', 'counterguerilla' and 'imperialist'), and his 'scenarios' (including colonial enlargement, expansionist wars, guerrilla wars, terror bombing and imperial conquests and rebellions) obviously indicate international relations. Yet Valentino draws no particular attention to the relationships between 'international' and 'domestic' in delineating his types and scenarios, and the central focus of his 'strategic' argument is the implicitly 'domestic' focus on regime–population relations. Like Harff and Gurr he sees mass killing as a problem of localized political conflict, and his 'strategic' conception, although enlightening in its own terms, remains centred on perpetrators. Genocidal actors are understood in simplified unified-state terms: he gives little indication of the messiness of genocidal situations, in which civilians are often not only victims but also participants in violence (for this he is criticized by Stathis Kalyvas (2004)).

The focus on 'response' is not a purely academic choice. It reflects the dominance of US scholars in both IR and comparative genocide studies, and their attachment to US power. As Michael Desch (2006: 108) points out, 'it is an article of faith among American elites that the United States has a moral responsibility to shut down virtually any mass political violence, but especially to stop genocides in the making'. Although Samantha Power's (2002) historical critique suggests that mostly it has failed in this task, Desch (2006), David Hoogland Noon (2004) and Jeffrey Record (2005) have shown that 'genocide' analogies have a powerful rhetorical function for US policy makers. For example, President George W. Bush justified Operation Iraqi Freedom by the fact that in 'the 20th century, some chose to appease murderous dictators, whose threats were allowed to grow into genocide and global war' (quoted by Record 2005: 17). Yet policy making by analogy in general, and through the Holocaust analogy in particular, is highly flawed (Desch 2006). These critiques of the function of 'genocide' in US policy making are important steps towards a critical approach to the international relations of genocide. As David MacDonald (2009) has shown in a wider survey, how violence comes to be represented as genocide is a complex and contested process with powerful implications for international politics. Yet we need to move beyond studies of genocide representation and rhetoric to the role of international relations, including Western powers and international institutions, in producing genocide.

## An ahistorical paradigm

I have argued that the discreteness of genocidal episodes and their contained characters are powerful assumptions, even when there is no explicit assertion of domesticity. Almost all the major synthetic works that have been produced – from the pathbreaking survey of Chalk and Jonassohn (1990) to most of the studies in what Straus (2007) calls the 'second wave' of genocide research – deal with a certain number of major genocides considered as discrete phenomena. Comparisons can be made as broadly as one wants across historical time, so that Christopher Powell (2011), for example, compares cases ranging from thirteenth-century Languedoc to 1994 Rwanda. Episodes are typically treated successively and compared across their discrete situations but without systematically drawing connections between them. The literature is more interested in *transhistorical comparisons* between these cases than in *historical connections*, prioritizing domestic and local environments rather than larger contexts. Thus the comparative method in genocide studies is understood in a fundamentally ahistorical sense, if we understand history as being about sequences, linkages and development.

This tendency prioritizes domestic and local environments rather than systematic investigation of international contexts. For example, one can find many comparisons between the Holocaust and Rwanda (e.g. Lemarchand 2002, Miles 2003, Sémelin 2007), but fewer systematic discussions of the connections between Nazi policies and those of the USSR, the Western Allies and eastern European states allied to both, in the Second World War; or of the connections between what happened in Rwanda in 1994 and preceding genocidal violence in Burundi and Uganda or succeeding violence in the Congo. Yet prima facie these two specific 'international' contexts have more to tell us about the Holocaust and Rwanda respectively than comparisons between them.

What is at stake here is the integrity of a historical understanding of genocide. In part, the trans- or ahistorical tendency reflects the disciplinary origins of genocide studies in sociology, and the influence of comparative social science. Yet even historical research has been heavily influenced: a recent survey of the historiography of genocide (Stone 2008) is largely an accumulation of case studies, with little more than an aspiration to comparison. Certainly we need close, particular research in order to construct synthetic studies, but the empiricist bias of historiography and its suspicion of approaches such as 'world history' which attempt to synthesize broad panoramas in single narratives, probably also play roles here. Even Mann's study of 'ethnic cleansing' (2005) mostly fails to sustain the macro-historical framework proposed in his major work, and falls into a comparative approach.

The result is that there are historical studies of genocide, but there is not really *a history* of genocide, in the sense of work which seriously interrogates the tendencies of genocide over time and the variation between different periods. Promisingly entitled volumes such as Weitz's *A Century of Genocide* (2005) turn out to be the usual comparisons of four or five major episodes, through a thematic prism (in his case, 'utopias of race and nation'): they almost never offer a comprehensive, developmental history of genocide in the given period. Even Ben Kiernan's (2007) 'world history of genocide' offers an uneven combination of extensive surveys of genocide in key regions of Western imperial expansion with fairly conventional, discrete case studies of the largest recognized genocides of the twentieth century. The linkage between the two is established entirely through transhistorical themes – cults of antiquity, a fetish for agriculture, ethnic enmity and imperial and territorial conquests – illustrated by comparing cases across recorded history. So Kiernan's book is primarily about continuities in the history of genocide: although it also offers some clues to its discontinuities, historical *change* is not its main theme.

## Conclusion

It is the contention of this book that the comparative genocide paradigm blocks the understanding of genocide, in which historical change is central. In the next chapter, I outline a different paradigm of international historical-sociological understanding, within which transhistorical comparison no longer plays the defining role, although comparisons continue to be made on the basis of a different set of assumptions.

# 3 | *World-historical perspectives: international and colonial*

The comparative genocide paradigm, I have argued, is an inadequate intellectual framework, which in turn reflects the cultural and political demands placed upon genocide studies. It reifies 'mega-genocides' as stand-alone events, exaggerates their discreteness and their domestic character, blocks view of the complex range of genocidal violence, and makes it difficult to pose meaningfully the question of the history of genocide. In this chapter, I argue for an alternative, looking at the phenomenon in world-historical terms, its variation between periods, and its connection to changing international contexts, and leading to a specification of the *discontinuity* of contemporary genocide with that of earlier periods. Before laying out my own approach, however, I discuss how the foundations of a different perspective have already been laid by a range of contributions, and I discuss their strengths and limitations. I focus on the 'international' and especially 'colonial' frames which have been the main foci of serious alternatives.

## The international system

I have suggested that IR scholarship has accommodated to the comparative genocide paradigm, by limiting the significance of international relations to the response to domestically generated genocide. However there is explicit dissatisfaction with this focus. The political sociologist Jacques Sémelin comments that 'Too many studies of genocide limit themselves to analysing factors at work inside a country ... This kind of closed-cell analysis is untenable.' However, he argues, 'there is no standard explanatory framework that we can propose. Trying to arrive at an understanding of relationships between "massacres" and the "international system" would ... appear well-nigh impossible.' Nevertheless, he continues, two types of interpretation are possible: 'The first looks closely at the foundations of the international system itself, particularly the history of a region, to show in what ways certain types of observable facts (state sovereignty, former massacres, movements of refugees, rivalries between powers-that-be) are likely to be propitious to outbreaks of violence. The second shows how this escalation into violence – within a particular country – can always go further because, on an international scale, there is no breaking system, no serious obstacle to its ineluctable progression.' Sémelin calls these 'structural' and 'functional' (or conflict-dynamics) approaches, respectively, and sees the two as complementary (2007: 107–8). However, perhaps in line with his view of the near-impossibility of a systemic explanation, Sémelin lists only a series of ad hoc 'structural' factors: the enabling character (for domestic geno-cide) of international norms of sovereignty; conflict over territory; legacies of ethnic violence; instability caused by population flows; and state collapse.

Manus Midlarsky similarly claims to 'reverse the understand-able tendency to see genocide as mainly a domestic enterprise'. He introduces the crucial idea that the 'international context' can be 'critical in either promoting or abetting genocide, or preventing it altogether ... Events occurring within a single country are not suffi-cient for genocide to occur ... It is the regional or international context that is crucial' (2005: 18). However Midlarsky does not directly or systematically examine 'international contexts' from the point of view of their potential for violence and the ways in which, within such contexts, multiple actors may be involved in related genocidal violence. Rather he emphasizes the interstate logic which produces 'state inse-curity', leading specific states to genocide, highlighting 'realpolitik' ('management of threats to the state') and 'loss' ('signals of state vulnerability') as drivers of mass killing (2005: 85). Thus Midlarsky examines international contexts only situationally, from the point of view of how they impact on specific genocidal actors. In this sense, he still remains close within the comparative genocide paradigm. This is true in other ways, too: although he acknowledges that genocide 'is not a one-size-fits-all happening' (2005: 18), he focuses mainly on the mega-genocides.

Perhaps the most ambitious arguments on the role of international relations are those of the historian Mark Levene. Unlike Sémelin, he locates genocidal continuities in the logic of the competitive inter-national 'system' of nation-states. 'The system is itself a root cause of modern genocide,' Levene argues (2005a: 156), suggesting two main ways in which it is causative:

1 'all modern genocides [are] perpetrated with an eye to the integrity of the state vis-à-vis other competitor states'; this 'linkage regularly manifests itself in the way that regimes repeatedly accuse the targeted communal population of being collective agents of outside, extra-state forces whose alleged aim is the undermining of the state's own efforts towards covering up, or rectifying, its international *weakness*' (Levene, 2005a: 156, emphasis in original); and

2 although 'the system, in principle, has been committed to a repudiation of genocide [in the Genocide Convention] ... The system has colluded with genocide because to do otherwise would have been massively to destabilise the sophistry upon which the system rides: namely that it is a global family of bounded but equally sovereign states' (Levene, 2005a: 158–9).

It is apparent that here Levene refers to two different kinds of international reality – power competition in interstate relations and the normative framework of international institutions which regulates these relations – and how they interact in the production of genocide. It is the first which international scholars generally identify with the idea of 'international system' (Waltz 1979): the second, often called 'international society', was originally identified as a tendency within the system (Bull 2002 (1977)), but is increasingly understood as dominant (Buzan 1993), so that 'society' becomes an alternative concept of international order. Since Levene does not make this distinction, his concept of international system combines these two ideas in a way which is not entirely clear.

With his second argument, Levene starts to recognize differences between states within the system: 'while ... acts of genocide are mostly committed by states challenging or defying the system ground rules, the system leaders themselves – that is those with the power to respond – have either condoned, or turned a blind eye, or in some cases, even covertly abetted such acts in complete contradiction of their own UNC [United Nations Convention] rhetoric' (Levene 2005a: 159). Therefore despite systemic drivers, Levene notes significant diversity in the political entities that commit genocide. Indeed he qualifies his system argument to acknowledge relationships between states and non-state 'loci of power' (parties, militaries, etc.); the 'specific contexts' ('crisis conditions') from which genocide emanates, including war, state instability and revolution; and variations in political geography (the importance of 'regional clusters' in places such as the African Great Lakes and Balkans). In fact Levene insists on 'the dynamics of uneven historical development' (2005a: 174), and particularly on a 'three-tier system profile' of relations between core, semi-periphery and periphery (2005a: 178). He also argues that 'genocide states are likely to be ones obsessed by their "strong–weak" contradictions ... [and] whose anxiety on this account are [*sic*] often unfolded in an "old state–new state" dichotomy or discrepancy' (Levene 2005a: 187).

It will be apparent that Levene's argument shifts to and fro between strong generalizations about 'the system' and recognitions of diversity in contexts, regimes, etc. Although he starts from a determined 'system' perspective, he is heavily drawn back into a focus on units within the system. This suggests that Levene recognizes that his strong version of the 'system' argument cannot be sustained: if genocide is a tendency of the modern international system, it clearly doesn't occur at all consistently across all its periods, regions, units, etc. Yet he returns to 'a broad chronological plot ... geared towards drawing parallels between the emergence and changing contours of the international system and the actual incidence of genocide'. And since both old colonial empires like Britain's and 'radically reformulated entities' like Communist Russia and China have been notable perpetrators, he is drawn back to genocide as 'an essential continuity of state geo-strategic policies ... regardless of the radical change of regimes' (Levene, 2005a: 162). Levene's theorizing therefore reproduces the tendency of realist IR, echoed in different ways in Anthony Giddens' historical sociology and Immanuel Wallerstein's 'world system' theory (the theoretical reference points of his discussion), to emphasise the most general 'system' properties of modern international relations.

The idea of a continuous system based on the principle of 'sovereignty', supposed to have originated in the Treaty of Westphalia in 1648, has been comprehensively critiqued in the IR literature (Teschke 2003). Indeed if exclusive ideas of the 'nation' are central to high-modern genocide – here there is a convergence between Levene, Mann and others – their origins are more plausibly located in French Revolutionary nationalism and its 1794 assault on the Vendée (Levene 2005b: 103–61) than in Westphalia. Thus Levene's reversion to actor-analysis tends to blunt more historically specific system-questions: what have been the historical tendencies in the forms and incidence of genocide, how have international relations in general changed over the modern period, and what are the relationships between these trends?

## Colonialism and genocide

The problem of the international relations of genocide is best encapsulated, therefore, not by abstract 'system' analysis, but by theorizing *specific* types of genocidal context in the context of constantly *mutating* international politics. As Levene himself shows (2005b: 5–100), a more obvious beginning to the history of modern genocide is colonial conquest and settlement, not European interstate relations as such. Chronologically, Europeans committed extensive genocide during colonization before, as well as simultaneously with, genocide in Europe itself.

Indeed the most substantial body of work that studies genocide in an international context has grown up around colonization, stimulated by critical reflection in Australia, the USA and elsewhere on its effects on indigenous populations. Although relations between colonizers and colonized are manifestly international, genocide has chiefly been studied in a historical rather than an IR frame. Here the concerns have been relations among imperial centres, colonists and indigenous peoples, rather than interstate relations in a 'systemic' sense. Genocide is linked more obviously to 'empire' and 'race' than to the master concept of 'nation' suggested by Levene and Mann. Nevertheless, the 'colonial' genocide literature raises many fundamental issues of a larger international approach. (The term 'colonial genocide' is disputed by Palmer, 2000, because genocide had many different colonial manifestations. However, many writers suggest that there was at least a general colonial framework which makes it plausible to look for common patterns. For the sake of convenience, I shall also refer to 'colonial genocide'.)

This field does not escape the general norm of bridging from the Holocaust. Thus David Stannard (1992) entitled his book about the destruction of indigenous peoples in the United States *American Holocaust*, and argued that the destruction of the Jews did not have an exclusive claim to the word 'holocaust' (Stannard 2001). Yet whereas Armenian scholars focused on similarities with the Jewish fate, colonial genocide writers have had to deal with manifest differences from it. Within each region of European colonization in which genocide has been identified (the Americas, Asia, Africa and Australasia), there were at least hundreds of different indigenous peoples, several different colonial powers, and many local colonial authorities and groups of colonists. Violent confrontations, involving complex combinations of protagonists and varied outcomes, occurred not within a single decade but over several centuries. Manifestly colonialism was not universally genocidal in the maximal, Holocaust sense: to understand its destructive aspects calls for different models and, some have argued, a broader definition of terms.

Although colonial genocide also involves the political claims of victim-peoples, the issues in each region concern many original peoples. The very conception of 'indigenous' is a construction of the colonial encounter, and indigenous identities like Native American transcend the original identities, rather than simply consolidating them in nationalist guises. Moreover, despite a few prominent indigenous writers such as the Native American Ward Churchill (2001), most of the major figures in the field come from the colonizing societies, expressing critical engagement with their nations' or civilization's pasts rather than the claims of particular victim-peoples. Thus a different idea of Holocaust connection has inspired the colonial genocide literature. Whereas the focus of comparative genocide studies has often been on the similarity of other genocides with the Holocaust, Moses (2008: 152) speaks for a group of scholars when he calls for 'the critical reflection needed to rethink the relationship between the Holocaust and the indigenous genocides that preceded it'.

The most important idea of colonial genocide studies has been that empire and colonialism contained a potentially genocidal *structure* centred on *settler* colonialism. Early in the development of the field, Tony Barta (1987) questioned the exclusive concern with the 'intentions' of perpetrators as the criterion of genocide, argued that Australia is a 'genocidal society' and that Australians live in objective 'relations of genocide' with Aborigines. From a definition based on intention, in the light of settlers' complex confrontations with the approximately six hundred indigenous peoples in the continent, Moses (2004: 19) suggests that 'many genocides took place in Australia, rather than being the site of a single genocidal event'. However Moses (2004: 24–5) argues that the 'radically voluntarist' intentionalist view has little to say about colonial genocide – with perpetrators difficult to identify and most deaths resulting from diseases – and that it is blind 'to the structural determinants' in colonization itself. These, according to Patrick Wolfe (2001: 867), lie in the settler-colonial drive to annex the land but not the labour of indigenous peoples: 'Thus the primary logic of settler colonialism can be characterized as one of elimination.' However, Moses (2004: 32) argues, 'As it stands, the structuralist schema is too static. It needs to be supplemented by an account of how and why the settler-colonial system radicalizes from assimilation to destruction.' Settler colonialism was not always and everywhere genocidal, and it is not clear that saying that it involved 'structural genocide' (Wolfe 2008: 121) answers this problem. From a general methodological standpoint, it is no answer to radical voluntarism to introduce one-sided structuralism. In this sense, the agency/structure dilemma is a problem for genocide studies in general (Shaw 2007: 81–96).

Mann (2005: 70–110) addresses these problems by identifying different kinds of colonial economy, from those based on trade, plunder and tribute taking which do not involve significant settlement, to settlement involving dispersed (farming) and concentrated (mining, plantations) indigenous labour, to 'settlement not requiring native labour' which alone he regards as a context prone to 'murderous cleansing'. Thus he argues that in colonial unlike other genocide, 'underlying the ethnic conflict was a direct economic conflict over who should possess and use the land' (Mann 2005: 71). Moreover Mann identifies the key to colonial genocide in the character of political rule: colonial rule was more genocidal the more settlers controlled local power. But even the most 'instrumentally rational settlers did not perpetrate murderous cleansing as a single premeditated plan'. Settler violence had much to do with the 'loose and fluid', insecurely institutionalized, character of rule on the frontier. Mann's preferred terms are 'rolling genocides' or (of the USA) 'a mixed rolling ethnocide/genocide of many rolling waves, breaking westward over the country' and involving 'perpetrators in different localities drawn from different generations' (Mann 2005: 84). Each wave involved a new radicalization, after the failure of other plans to displace indigenous peoples or subdue their resistance. Even the frontier itself, the 'most obvious core constituency' for this violence, was 'rolling' (Mann 2005: 109).

The emphasis on settlement and frontier as 'structural determinants' illuminates a broad swathe of European violence against indigenous peoples over several centuries, but highlights one economic type of settlement and one tendency in colonial rule. Yet colonial settlement was always part of larger systems of empire. Settlement was not only for settlers: it was part of how empires consolidated their holds over distant territories, even if there were other methods too. However much settlers, their local authorities and militias ruled in remote locales, they depended on imperial centres and later, as colonists gained independence, on new central governments. Mann (2005: 92–4) provides an illuminating discussion of the roles of the five most famous pre–First World War US presidents (Washington, Jefferson, Jackson, Lincoln and Theodore Roosevelt) in the 'cleansing' of Native Americans. Thus the 'structural logic' of settler colonialism was played out in larger geopolitical contexts which changed over the centuries of expansion, not least in the transitions from empires to settler states. The settler-colonial paradigm has been deployed to explain settler–indigenous relationships from seventeenth-century New England to twentieth-century Palestine, but the huge economic and political transformations in between these cases point to its insufficiency as an explanatory framework.

The settler-colonial theme has been supported by reference to Lemkin himself, notably his statement that

Genocide has two phases, one, the destruction of the national pattern of the oppressed group: the other, the imposition of the national pattern of the oppressor. This imposition, in turn, may be made upon the oppressed population which is allowed to remain, or upon the territory alone, after removal of the population and the colonization of the area by the oppressor's own nationals. (Lemkin 1944: xi)

As Moses comments, 'Lemkin hints that genocide is *intrinsically colonial* and that therefore settler colonialism is *intrinsically genocidal*.' However *non*-settler imperialism is different: 'not all imperialisms are genocidal. The British occupation of India, for example, was not a project of settlement, and the fact that the colonizers relied on the labour of the locals was an impediment to physical genocide' (Moses 2004: 27, emphases in original).

Yet analysing Lemkin's much-quoted statement, it seems less clear than this interpretation implies. In his first scenario, the 'imposition' of the oppressor's pattern may also occur where 'the oppressed population is allowed to remain'. Yet in this case, it is not clear that the prior destruction of the population's previous national pattern is required.

A population may survive 'imposition' and maintain its customs and traditions, at least underground: for example, if its language is banned in public, speaking it in private, in the home, in concealed religious ceremonies and other local settings not monitored by the oppressor. Two national patterns may coexist, even if not peacefully or equally. If the national institutions, values and language of an oppressor are imposed in a way that leaves the population and its way of life largely intact, the imposition cannot really be seen as involving the *destruction* of the indigenous society (in terms of which genocide is defined). Thus this seminal quotation actually bares the contradiction, at the heart of Lemkin's ideas, between institutional and cultural 'imposition', on the one hand, and group 'destruction', on the other. Only the latter should, consistently, be regarded as genocide: the former is genocidal only when accompanied by the latter. This is no small point since, I have argued, the difference between socially destructive and non-destructive coercion is a key limit of genocide, and it renders the idea incoherent to regard all cultural imposition as genocide.

It is important, moreover, to recognize imperialism's broader genocidal effects: 'it is not only cases of settler colonialism that are potentially genocidal' (Moses 2008: 25). First, where a new order was imposed through conquest, it often involved killing native elites and weakening indigenous populations through overwork, hunger and sexual exploitation. These genocidal processes often combined with the unintended effects of imported diseases. Second, where imperial imposition led to resistance, genocidal violence often followed. Wars of imperial subjugation rarely respected the distinction between enemy combatants and the civilian population. Resistance to conquest, occupation and the imposition of rule was generally a popular cause among indigenous populations: imperial violence was often meted out to the population as a whole.

While violence may sometimes have been limited to reinforcing the imposition of colonial rule, very often it involved the partial or even total destruction of indigenous society. Counter-insurgency has remained notoriously brutal even into the twenty-first century. Insurgents often melt into the population, and governments and armies find it difficult or do not bother to distinguish between the two. Both insurgency and counter-insurgency draw civilians into the struggle as suppliers of information and as they use civil war to pursue their own local conflicts (Kalyvas 2006). Counter-insurgency often leads to destructive anti-population measures (Gerlach 2010: 177–234). Even the most extreme twentieth-century episodes generally identified as stand-alone 'genocides' can be seen as substantially motivated by counter-insurgency 'security' considerations, such as the Rwandan genocide (Straus 2006) and even the Holocaust (Moses 2011). Nevertheless John Darwin argues that

> Resistance and rebellion by indigenous or first peoples against *settler* states and communities were … more dangerous. Settlers had much stronger motives to impose total defeat and demand total subjugation. They had less need to rely upon local power-brokers and make the concessions they sought – or so they believed. And once their settler community had reached a critical size, the settler mentality crossed a psychological threshold. The land they had occupied became home (if not Home). It was now, or should be, a white man's country, whose indigenous people were at best a resource to exploit, at worst a menace to crush. (2012: 258, emphasis in the original)

So while resistance and rebellion were generally catalysts for genocidal violence by empires, they were particularly so in settler colonies.

Another reason for the genocidal tendency of imperial wars is highlighted by the idea of 'subaltern genocide'. The straightforward meaning of this concept is that indigenous resistance sometimes takes the form of destructive violence. This idea partly explains how non-settler forms of imperialism and colonialism may involve genocide. The extremes of colonial imposition, its generally racist character and deep inequalities clearly facilitated holistic views of Europeans in 'native' eyes, so that when indigenous peoples rebelled they often wreaked vengeance on the entire colonizing population. The slave rebellion in Haiti at the beginning of the nineteenth century was directed genocidally against the colonizers as a whole, and French retaliation in turn engulfed the slave population in genocide (Girard 2007). The Great Rebellion against British rule in India in 1857 notoriously attacked the entire European population: 'A grim logic dictated that the sepoys' best chance to escape retribution was to kill every white who might bear witness against them' (Darwin 2012: 246). But when the British eventually crushed the rising, they were even more sweeping in their violence against the Indians (Dalrymple 2006: 346–92). In Delhi, the Mughal emperor's sons were shot and his courtiers were hanged, while '[t]he city itself was given over to killing and plunder. In one quarter, about 1,400 were murdered as British troops took revenge for their

losses' (Darwin 2012: 252). The dynamics of resistance here are the
same as in much settler-colonial violence, so 'non-settler' as well
as settler colonization could be implicated in two-sided genocide.
(However the 'subaltern genocide' idea has a second layer of meaning,
the general tendency of genocidists to see their own peoples as colonized. The Nazis even thought of Germans as colonized: 'When Nazis
set out to annihilate Jews, it is . . . likely that they thought of themselves
as native, and Jews as settlers': Mamdani 2002: 13).

Thus the equation of settler colonialism and genocide creates twin
dangers for critical genocide research: the simplification of settler
colonization itself, and unwarranted narrowing of the scope of
genocide in modern imperialism. Settler colonialism's underlying
agricultural-pastoral logic – the 'false notion that the land was
previously empty' combined with 'an equal determination to fill it full',
which Ben Kiernan (2007: 167) attributes to American colonists – was
only one of the drivers of imperial genocide. As Kiernan remarks
(2007: 168), 'the idyllic images of pastoralism and the economics of
expanding and intensive agriculture often accompany genocide but
cannot fully explain it. Along with violent religious or racial prejudice,
genocide usually requires territorial conquests, frequently based on
classical models.' The classical model associated with settler colonization is imperial expansion, but imperial contraction and retreat,
accompanied by nation-state formation, have also been powerful
contexts of genocide, as we shall see later.

The interest of critical genocide researchers in Lemkin's argument
about the imposition of one 'national pattern' on another has had
another driver. Nazi genocide itself can be re-envisioned as a project
of colonization in eastern Europe (Zimmerer 2007), chiming with a
trend in the historiography to emphasize the imperial character of
the Nazi project (Mazower 2009). The strengths of specific connections between German colonial genocide (especially the 1904–5
destruction of the Herero and Nama in German South-West Africa:
Zimmerer 2009) and the Holocaust can be debated. But this literature
has introduced the powerful idea that there were historical *relations*
across time and space, not just between different colonial episodes,
but also between colonial and European genocide. Both can be seen
in the larger international context of European imperialism, which
profoundly affected European as well as colonial politics and
society. Such 'relational' arguments are potentially of much wider

significance, opening up the question of whether we might look not just at *specific* relations between genocides, but at the *wider complexes* of social and international relations in which these are embedded. Thus 'relational' arguments are a route to an 'international relations' of genocide.

The colonial genocide literature has greatly advanced the genocide debate. It shows that genocide is associated with the inherently *international* relationships of colonization and imperial expansion. It emphasizes that genocide is manifested not in a few isolated and exceptional catastrophes but in *extensive* patterns of violence during colonization and resistance to it. It utilizes Kuper's idea of 'genocidal massacres', smaller-scale incidents in which local populations belonging to larger groups are targeted. It shows how genocide is implicated in complex state–society relations between settlers and imperial centres, and international relations between empires. Yet the emphasis on settler colonialism has also sometimes led to an emphasis on regime type – as when Mann (2005: 4) says that the link between settler control over local institutions and murderousness 'is the most direct relationship I have found between democratic regimes and mass murder' – rather than the larger structures within which settler regimes developed. In this way the idea of the inherently 'colonial' character of genocide may narrow the general significance of imperial and international relations for genocide.

## Historic specificity in the international relations of genocide

These difficulties in a strong version of the 'settler colonial' perspective, like the issues which arise from a strong version of the 'international system' approach, underline the complexities involved in an alternative to the comparative genocide paradigm. In both cases, the danger is of reifying an important explanatory element so that it becomes a new transhistorical super-explanation. If modern genocide is always and everywhere a product of the international system, then everything else becomes no more than a secondary gloss on the 'fundamental' explanation. If it is ubiquitously 'colonial' in character then we need attend only to the specific circumstances and forms of colonization. The danger is that important insights substitute for full, rich and variable explanation, and block rather than aid historical synthesis. For although we must always guard against historical empiricism, a developmental account of genocide needs to be guided by a sharp sense of historical specificity.

Thus while we can read genocide as inherently international, colonial or imperial, we must be aware of the difficulties involved in each of these prisms. The study of genocide compels us, for example, to remember two distinct meanings of 'international' (as 'interstate' and 'between nations') which do not necessarily coincide (even in so-called 'nation-states') and which are fluid and changing. For example, genocide may involve relations between a state, whether or not formally an empire, and subordinate nations, as in the Ottomans' extermination of the Armenians. Constitutionally this appears as a 'domestic' (but evidently also 'imperial') relationship since the Armenian population had long lived within the Ottoman empire, yet the identification of the Armenians as an enemy was premised on the rulers' belief that they were *not* part of the emerging Turkish nation-state, but constituted another, incompatible nation. In this sense genocide, with its declaration of profound and irreconcilable otherness, may not only *presuppose* but also *construct* a relationship which is 'international' in the antagonistic sense. Genocide may be part of the process of reconstructing the 'domestic' relations between emergent nations in an old empire as 'international' relations between nation-states in a post-imperial context. Indeed, genocide may not be the product of the fixed structures of an international system so much as of the fluid circulation of sentiments, or a 'political economy of affective dispositions' as Andrei Gómez-Suárez (2011) argues.

This brings us to an important argument for both IR and genocide debates. Categories such as 'international' and 'domestic', 'nation' and 'ethnic group' are not fixed and given, but fluid and constructed. This idea has been particularly difficult in the genocide field. The genocide concept emerged from the Second World War era in which the principle of nationality was at its strongest in world affairs: in Lemkin's mind there was little doubt as to the meaning of 'nation'. The Genocide Convention then inscribed this and related categories ('ethnicity', 'race', 'religion') as though their meanings were fixed and self-evident. Some legal scholars such as William Schabas (2000) still defend this notion and resist a fluid interpretation, let alone replacement, of these categories. Yet Frank Chalk and Kurt Jonassohn's (1990: 23) insistence that the target group of genocide is *subjectively* defined by the perpetrators has been highly influential. Even in international law there has been increasing recognition of the need to understand categories such as ethnicity flexibly, and to move partially beyond them. Thus the International Criminal Tribunal for Rwanda argued that the destruction of the Tutsis constituted genocide although they were not an ethnic group in the given sense of the term (Schabas 2000: 131–2).

The idea that genocide, whether committed during formal colonization or not, is *inherently* a colonial relationship has the advantage that 'colonial' necessarily suggests inequality and imposition. In contrast 'international' is neutral as to the content of the relations between nations or states, and can be understood in both equal/unequal and cooperative/antagonistic senses. However it is not evident that a history of colonialism, any more than of international relations in a narrow sense, will inscribe the full range of genocidal experiences, including for example the destruction of religious-, political- and class-defined populations. Just as neither perpetrators nor victims always see themselves as national in character and operating in an international relationship, so they may not see themselves as colonizers and colonized. Rather, on either side, other markers of identity may be used. Therefore genocide forces us to think of categories such as 'colonial' as well as 'international' in a broad, open sense. If genocide occurs whenever any organized, armed actor defines a civilian social group or population as an enemy and aims to destroy that group or population, then defining genocide as an inherently colonial or international phenomenon is only one way of encapsulating the 'othering' involved. The justification for seeing genocide as involving these types of relationship is, first, that 'national' and the closely related 'ethnic' are typical markers which may partially stand for a wider range of experience; but also, second, that even class, religious and political targeting is generally framed by international relations in a wider sense.

The case for an international understanding of genocidal relations does not concern only the direct relations between perpetrator and victim actors. These are only the most immediate layer of the structuration of genocide. International, colonial and imperial relations constitute larger structural contexts which generate genocidal relations. These are larger complexes of relations, constituted largely on axes other than genocide, in which a range of international actors including third parties operate and relate to each other. As Midlarsky and Levene recognize, actors in genocidal conflicts operate simultaneously in interstate and state–society relations. However this description does not exhaust the international relations context of genocide. As much work in IR since the 1990s has shown, international relations comprise (increasingly) many layers of relations across as well as between states – 'global', 'transnational' and 'regional' as well as strictly 'international' or 'interstate' – and involve many different types of non-state as well as state actors. Moreover, where states are concerned, although some definitions of genocide (e.g. Chalk and Jonassohn 1990: 23) refer (like Realist IR) to 'the state' as an actor, it is often not states as such, but regimes and particular elements of state apparatuses, which organise genocide (Dadrian 2001: 140). The 'unity' of the state-as-actor is something which needs to be established empirically, rather than assumed. Interactions between various 'state' and 'non-state' actors are often crucial (Gerlach 2010). Therefore an international relations of genocide does not need a fixed conception of the 'international system', 'colonialism' or 'imperialism', so much as a concept of complex, multi-layered relations (economic, social and cultural as well as political and military) involving many types of actors and of linkage with 'domestic' contexts.

These relations and contexts are constantly reconfigured in dynamic genocidal processes, so that a historical approach is essential to an international understanding. The failure to develop a fully developmental historical approach is evident also in colonial genocide studies. As I noted in Chapter 2, Kiernan (2007) links genocides across times primarily in terms of continuities of agricultural fetishism, ethnic enmity and imperial and territorial conquests. However the briefest of introductory notes to the twentieth-century part of his study provides a clue to a possible *discontinuity* in the history of genocide: 'By 1910 the world had become smaller, the great powers greater, and contests for territory more closely fought. A new phenomenon emerged: genocides perpetrated by national chauvinist dictatorships that had seized control of tottering, shrinking, or new empires, aiming to reverse real or perceived territorial losses or conquer new regions from established powers' (Kiernan 2007: 393). The looseness of this thesis is evident in the alternatives 'tottering ... or new', 'reverse ... or conquer'; its location within the established comparative literature rather than IR is suggested by the emphasis on regime type ('national chauvinist dictatorships'); and in any case, the book fails to systematically pursue the argument.

Nevertheless the sense that there was a major *shift* in genocide, from the era of settler colonialism to that of radical party-states, is also implicit in Mann (2005). He adds a further disjuncture: the shift from the era of nationalist genocide, perpetrated primarily by radical party-states, to the post-colonial era, in which maximal forms of mass murder are tending to give way to less murderous forms of 'ethnic cleansing'. William Rubinstein's (2004) three modern eras of genocide – the colonial age, the age of totalitarianism, and the era of 'ethnic cleansing' – constitute a similar periodization. But none of these writers develop a theoretical exploration of the historical transitions involved.

The aim of an international relations of genocide should therefore be to place these questions of *historical transformation* at the centre of analysis, and to formulate more precise theories of changing inter-national and social contexts. If genocide is not a general feature of international relations in all periods and regions – even if it is also not as rare as some think – the task is to identify particular temporal and geographical clusters of genocidal violence, the specific international conditions in which they are located, and the larger international dynamics involved. Any adequate 'international' theory of genocide must offer a complex understanding of the changing relations across and between societies, as well as between states, in the historical transformations of modernity. In this sense an international theory of genocide must be framed not only sociologically, but in historical-sociological terms.

In what follows, I develop an international historical account. In Chapter 4, I re-examine the classical locus of genocide in early twentieth-century Europe. In succeeding chapters I examine genocide in the Cold War and post-Cold War periods, with special reference to the 'transitions' from the Second World War to the Cold War and in the end of the Cold War. These discussions will involve different types of comparison from those which are normal in comparative genocide studies. I compare the historical periods themselves and different world regions within each of these periods, as well as specific episodes of genocide. In so doing I situate the latter in their international-historical contexts. In other words, I re-envision the comparative work of genocide research along the lines described by

Philip McMichael (1990: 385): 'Global conceptions of social change violate formal comparative requirements, necessitating an alternative form of "incorporated comparison", that takes both multiple/diachronic and singular/synchronic forms ... The fixed units of comparison used by modernisation and world-systems theories yield to an alternative strategy of grounding the analytical units of comparison in the world-historical processes under investigation.'

# PART II

# Twentieth-century genocide

# 4 | European genocide: inter-imperial crisis and world war

This chapter revisits the classical modern sites of genocide in twentieth-century Europe and explores the scope for international-historical explanations. An alternative to the comparative genocide paradigm should not only expand the range of genocide research beyond the mega-genocides: it also needs to reframe these episodes, above all the seminal Holocaust and Armenian cases. These archetypal 'stand-alone' genocides are assumed to be state-centric and based on a particular regime type, and are often seen in a domestic frame despite their roots in international wars. They need to be reinserted in a larger historical narrative of nationalist population-politics in the crisis of the European imperial system. However this requires a theoretical reorientation, with which I begin this chapter.

## The 'nation-state-empire' and the 'inter-imperial' international system

The major problem in 'international' explanations of genocide to date has been an over-generalized understanding of the international 'system' as a Westphalian, sovereignty-centred structure. To understand how genocidal war in Europe in the first half of the twentieth century was implicated in internationally systematized relationships, we need to specify historically our concept of the 'system', focusing on the particular character of statehood and interstate relations in the period that culminated in the Second World War. We need to move away from the abstract concept of sovereignty and examine the content of power relationships within as well as between states. In particular, we need to integrate two core aspects of statehood – nationality and empire – into our understanding of interstate relations.

I noted that the interstate system did not become truly international in the modern sense until the era of the French Revolution. States after Westphalia were almost all dynastic monarchies, ranging from small principalities to large absolute states, in which the people played little or no political role and ideas of nationality were still weak. The popular nationalism which emerged from the era of revolutions transformed the state system; moreover the idea of 'nation' was linked to 'democracy', and it is this link, as Mann (2005) argues, which lay behind the development of exclusive nationalism. We can never understand genocide as a simply interstate development, yet without understanding how nationalism was implicated in interstate relations in the nineteenth and twentieth centuries, we cannot fully understand European genocide.

If it is essential to integrate nation-formation dynamics and nationalist politics with interstate relations in explaining genocide, it is at least equally essential to grasp the significance of empire. As we have seen, empire has sometimes been reduced in genocide research to a particular settler type of colonialism. I have argued that European imperialism involved more general tendencies towards genocide, especially during conquest and counter-insurgency. Here I go further: the structural feature of the international system that was crucial for genocide was its *inter-imperial* character. The interstate system of the last half-millennium should be understood as a competitive system, not simply of sovereign or nation-states, but above all of empires.

The Westphalian concept allowed (and still allows) a great number of entities, many of them relatively insignificant, to be regarded as sovereign. From the nineteenth century there was a strong momentum towards identifying states with nations. However the central power-dynamics in the European and world state-system in the last half-millennium were between states that extended their rule across large territories and multiple societies. World history from the end of the fifteenth to the middle of the twentieth century was dominated by imperial conquest and rivalries, culminating in the decisive conflicts of major empires in the two 'world' wars. In the final two centuries of this period, the principal states – and indeed almost all European states, since even minor states had their colonial possessions – did not simply become 'nation-states'. They could just as easily be called 'empire-states', and perhaps the best terminology, if slightly cumbersome, is 'nation-state empires', since this captures the dual reality of world empires and core nation-states that characterized all the more important states in this period. The challenge for genocide research is to grasp the significance not simply of conquest and colonization, but of inter-imperial rivalries as well, and to integrate with these the roles of nations and nationalism, in an understanding of how 'nation-state empires' and the inter-imperial international system as a whole generated anti-population violence.

There were, I propose, six major ways in which the European inter-imperial system was implicated in genocide. First, *the core Western European 'nation-states' of the global inter-imperial system were formed through imperial relationships of capitals with provinces, which at critical moments involved genocidal violence.* In an age when belief systems were entirely framed by religion, this was the key determinant of loyalty to rulers and the principal means of homogenizing populations. Genocide in European history from the Middle Ages until the eighteenth century was carried out primarily along religious lines (Rubinstein 2004: 29–38). Major examples include the murderous war against heretics in medieval Languedoc, massacres of Jews in many countries, expulsions of Muslims from Spain and of Catholics from parts of Ireland, and violence against Protestants in France. However the Westphalian system of sovereignty, as such, did not cause this genocide, much of which pre-dated it. Indeeed, the Treaty of Westphalia of 1648 involved a settlement of the religious issues in European politics: while enshrining the principle of *cuius regio, eius religio* (the ruler's religion was also that of the state), it also embedded principles of religious toleration and minority protection, paving the way for secular definitions of minority rights a century or so later. Westphalia marked the beginning of the end of religion's dominant role in defining anti-population violence, even if there were notorious cases afterwards, such as the persecution of the Protestants in the Cévennes at the beginning of the eighteenth century. Population homogenization was based increasingly on ideas of nationality rather than religion, reflecting the entwining of nationalism with imperialism that dominated in the nineteenth and early twentieth centuries.

Second, *the strong centralized states that formed the bases of global empires were formed by consolidating new types of national society.* Through central control based on internal cultural, ideological and political homogenization, European states could mobilize the power which they would project externally in world empires. Despite the ease with which the term 'nation-state' is often used to describe modern states, few states arose directly out of pre-existing nationally homogeneous societies. A higher level of homogeneity had to be achieved, via assimilation, coercion or destruction of populations not seen as fitting with the dominant nationalism (Rae 2002, Mann 2005). These populations are usually thought of as 'minorities' but they often constituted majorities within contested regions or even within the full territory of the projected nation. These processes involved what has been called 'internal colonialism' (Hechter 1999) vis-à-vis the highly segmented, localized societies of pre-modern Europe. Some dynamics involved more or less consensual arrangements among elites, such as the alliance of English and Scottish ruling classes that formed Great Britain in the eighteenth century (Colley 2009). Some involved cultural coercion of populations, such as the policies through which the 'Parisian empire' (Robb 2009) turned 'peasants into Frenchmen' (Weber 1977), imposing the French language and French institutions in place of myriad local forms of speech and social organization. Yet others were deeply destructive (or as Rae 2002 puts it, 'pathological'), eliminating historic communities from states' territories.

As Levene and Mann argue, the genocidal developments involved in forming strong, centralized states were linked generally to the new forms of nationalism that were so decisive in European history after the French Revolution. The seminal case is the revolutionary violence that destroyed the 'counter-revolutionary' Vendée in the 1790s (Levene 2005b: 103–61). Yet the Vendée was not quickly followed by a wave of similar large-scale genocidal events in Europe; its closest counterpart was a 'colonial genocide', the violent uprising in Haiti and the French repression of it (Girard 2007). In the perspective of earlier 'religious' genocide, nationalist genocide could be seen as more of an alteration in the ideological terms of destruction than a new type of violence, but the changing terms were clearly important, as amply demonstrated in the twentieth century. National Socialist anti-semitism, for example, was not just a modern political form of older Christian anti-semitism, however much it drew on the latter. It involved a monstrous escalation in violence, reflecting the expanded mobilization capacity of the modern state as well as modern nationalist, totalitarian political ideology. In the perspective of European history, the Vendée appears as an early warning of the genocidal escalation of revolutionary and counter-revolutionary totalitarianism in the twentieth century.

Third, *the internal homogenization of empires' 'national' cores fed into the often genocidal processes of settler colonial settlement in empires' global expansion.* Social constituencies that experienced discrimination and even genocide in the national core often provided the basis for settlement in the 'new' world, where they were implicated in the coercion and genocide of indigenous populations. Examples from the British empire give an idea of the range of ways in which this could happen: persecuted religious minorities such as Puritans established new communities in North America at the expense of indigenous peoples; landless labourers who fell foul of draconian property laws were transported to Australia where they helped displace the indigenous; and Highland clansmen who were cleared from their lands filled the imperial armies which suppressed colonial rebellions. In ways like these, the 'colonial' genocides of settlement and counter-insurgency followed from the homogenizing coercion and genocide of the core nation-states.

Fourth, *conflicts brought from European societies contributed to the contradictory relations of settlers and empires, leading to both autonomous colonial nationhood and new potentially genocidal conflicts with indigenous populations.* Settlers whose ancestors had clashed with imperial authorities in the core nation developed new conflicts with them over relations with indigenous peoples, as the colonial genocide literature attests. European settlement was, moreover, a highly multinational process: in all the regions of European colonization, settlers came from many different original nations. The process of independent state formation, which freed settler colonies from imperial control, involved a homogenization of new post-European nations somewhat resembling the earlier homogenization of the original western European nations. Yet just as many core European nation-states were left with internal imperial contradictions – such as the Irish conflict which affected Great Britain to the end of the twentieth century – so the colonists' new nations burdened themselves from the outset with internal imperial contradictions in relations with indigenous peoples.

Fifth, in central and eastern Europe the pattern was different from western Europe. *Here genocide has been seen as a reactive product of imperial disintegration, but it is more accurate to see the process as one of nation-state formation in the context of imperial decline.* While in western Europe national homogenization and imperial expansion developed through the merger, expansion and consolidation of existing kingdoms, here the same processes occurred by forging new states out of the Habsburg, Romanov and Ottoman dynastic empires which survived into the twentieth century. Genocide studies have mainly noticed the Ottoman empire's genocide against Christian minorities.

But this genocide arose in the last years of the Ottomans not from an attempt to maintain an old empire, but from a determination to recast the state in a more Turkish national form, removing incompatible minorities. This, of course, is why the Turkish nation-state of Kemal Atatürk continued the process begun under Ottoman rule, and why the modern Turkish state denies the Armenian genocide to this day as well as suppressing Kurdish identity.

This is also why genocide in this region was not a one-sided process. The territories sought by new nationalist movements, and the nation-states formed in the nineteenth and early twentieth centuries from the declining Ottoman empire, *generally* contained extensive national minorities, *generally* sought national homogenization within as expansive territories as possible, and *generally* pursued exclusionary policies against minorities. These policies were often repressive and coercive rather than directly destructive, but (especially during wars) they led to violent population removals on many sides. Therefore like the new settler-colonial nation-states formed out of the west European empires, the newly independent eastern European nation-states inherited, in revised forms, the imperial contradictions of the old empires. Like the settler states, they were miniature nation-state-empires, inheriting 'minority' problems and often a tendency to genocidal solutions. Moreover genocidal violence was generally stimulated, as Bloxham (2007) has shown, by international conflict between the Ottoman/Turkish state and its enemies. As H. Zeynup Bulutgil (2010: 57, 59) argues, 'once the minority group is allied with a rival during a war, ethnic cleavages gain relative importance and majority politicians turn to more hostile policies ... ethnic polarization and ethnic cleansing are outcomes of international factors, rather than deep ethnic divisions'.

Sixth, finally, and not least, *inter-imperial relations between the major formally constituted empires constituted the larger 'international' context in which all other national–imperial contradictions were played out*. So far I have explored the imperial characteristics of the states which make up the system, and their connections with nations and nationalism. However I have defined the international system as an *inter*-imperial system, and this dimension of empire needs to be accorded the importance it deserves. Inter-imperial relations are the most general framework of all imperial relations.

During European colonization of the 'new world', competition among western European empires conditioned their strategic orientations, but it was not mainly a direct driver of genocide. Rather it was the interactions with indigenous polities that more directly determined the extent of genocidal violence. However inter-imperial competition within Europe became more decisive in the twentieth-century crises of the inter-imperial international system. As the western European empires became ever more globally dominant, their territories in Africa and Asia continued to expand, the USA and Japan emerged as imperial powers, and the older eastern European empires (Habsburg, Romanov and Ottoman) entered a period of terminal crisis. Rivalries between western European empires over the colonization of Africa were overtaken by deeper conflicts over European and Asian political space, coinciding (especially in east-central Europe) with nationalist conflicts during the break-up of old empires. It was in this context that the most notorious European genocides of the first half of the twentieth century occurred, but these were the nadirs of wider patterns of genocidal violence, as inter-imperial rivalry led to European and world war and nationalisms were radicalized.

Some general conclusions can be drawn from this preliminary discussion. Empire is not simply or mainly a process external to the modern state, but also an internal relation. The modern state in the second half of the last millennium was typically national and imperial at the same time – a nation-state-empire. Population politics in general and genocide as their extreme expression were simultaneously external and internal to states, related to imperial relations of both kinds. In this sense, genocide was the product of 'international relations' in two main senses, between nations and emergent states within empires, and between national-imperial states. It was the product of the 'international system' in the full sense of a system that combined relations between nations and between states, where the units were primarily empires. The international system of the second half of the second millennium was at its core inter-imperial: this was the defining context of its genocides.

## Nineteenth-century roots of twentieth-century genocide

It is time to approach the specific problem of twentieth-century European genocide. Recent historical work suggests that nationalism became increasingly widely – although never universally or constantly – genocidal towards the end of the nineteenth century, first in south-eastern Europe and later across eastern Europe as a whole, with increasingly large implications for the wider continental order. Bloxham (2007, 2009a and 2009b) and Weitz (2008) demonstrate important shifts in population politics from the 1870s or even 1860s, in the disintegration of the Ottoman, Romanov and Hapsburg empires. Insurgent as well as post-imperial nationalisms were implicated in anti-population violence. Although the Ottomans perpetrated the largest genocide, Turks and Muslims were also victims of genocidal expulsions and massacres at the hands of Christian nationalists.

It was in war contexts that nationalism was most genocidal. Although there had been earlier large-scale massacres of Armenians in the Ottoman heartland, Anatolia, it was several-sided massacres in the 1912–13 Balkan Wars that generalized genocide across a significant region of south-eastern Europe. The general European war that broke out in 1914 then implicated the Armenians and other Christians in the Ottoman war with the Russian empire, which served as the catalyst for the 1915 genocide. Thus the dynamics and forms of inter-imperial conflict increasingly conditioned the development of genocide. Moreover the fallout from the war brought further large-scale genocidal violence, not only in the former Ottoman lands (where Greek and Turkish armies marauded in 1918–21, expelling, often murderously, the 'other' population: Bloxham, 2007) but further north too, in the civil war following the Russian Revolution, most notoriously in the massacres of Jews in the Ukraine in 1918–20 (Midlarsky 2005: 45–53). Bloxham (2007) captures how western European and US as well as Ottoman and Tsarist empires were implicated with his idea of 'the great game of genocide'.

The international settlement following the war, dictated by the victorious US, British and French empires, was based on the Wilsonian principle of national self-determination. Since, in mixed societies, one nation's self-determination was invariably another's subordination, this principle provided incentives for exclusion. The self-determination idea, influential to the extent that even social revolutionaries like V. I. Lenin adopted it, reflected the extent to which nationalist thinking was dominant even as the rights of minorities were reasserted. Indeed Weitz (2008: 1,316) points out that even 'the origins of human rights standards are not so pristine and pure … A major part of their history lies in a way of thinking about populations – group protection and group rights – that entailed the very same thought patterns that enabled and promoted forced deportations.' The same leaders advocated both. Although the settlement was accompanied by measures for minority protection, the latter served to irritate 'majority' nationalists as much as to genuinely protect. The culmination of the post-Ottoman violence was the 1923 Treaty of Lausanne, internationally sanctioning the destruction of historic Greek and Turkish communities in Turkey and Greece respectively. Nationalist population politics, legitimated at Paris and in the League of Nations, became only more central to the international system. Indeed Howard Adelman and Elazar Barkan (2011) go so far as to claim that forced population exchange became a 'norm' of the international system until 1950. The idea of minority protection was a source of Lemkin's first conceptualization of genocide (Shaw 2007: 24), but it was also part of the rationale for Nazism's revisionist approach to the post-First World War settlement. Hitler's first international aggression, the annexation of the Sudetenland from Czechoslovakia, invoked the principle of minority protection in favour of that region's German population.

Another consequence of the First World War was a sharp polarization of class politics across Europe, peaking in the revolutionary wave of 1917–19 in Russia, Germany, Hungary, Italy and elsewhere. This had far-reaching consequences for European politics in the following decades, leading to the Bolshevik regime in the former Russian empire (1917), the rise of counter-revolutionary fascism to power in Italy (1922) and Germany (1933), and consequent conflicts of communist and fascist movements across Europe. Melson (1996) sees the revolutionary ideologies of such movements – and the earlier Young Turk movement – as an important factor in the development of genocide. While revolutionary Bolshevism came to power in the Soviet Union with an ideology of council democracy, in principle supporting pluralities of both parties and nations, civil war quickly led to more repressive policies, culminating in Stalin's internal counter-revolution of the late 1920s. Counter-revolutionary fascism was repressive from the outset, suppressing all competing parties and movements as well as (especially in the Nazi case) population groups that were seen as hostile to the national project, notably Jews.

For genocide, the key question is the point at which the repression common to these regimes mutated into group destruction. Chronologically, Stalinist preceded Nazi genocide. As Norman Naimark (2010) summarizes, three episodes of Stalinist rule in the 1930s have been discussed as genocide: dekulakization (the destruction of the so-called 'kulaks' or 'rich' peasants before and during forced collectivization of agriculture in the early 1930s), the 'Holodomor' (the regime-exacerbated 'terror-famine' in Ukraine, Kazakhstan and elsewhere in the mid 1930s), and the deportations of many whole 'unreliable nations' (which began in the late 1930s and peaked in the Second World War). To these Naimark rightly adds the 'Great Terror', the purges, peaking in the late 1930s, at all levels of the ruling party, state and many areas of society.

Clearly Stalinist genocide was not the product of a simple nationalism: historically Communism had subverted nationalism, and Lenin's endorsement of 'national self-determination' was a strategic rather than an ideological choice. However under Stalin, despite the nominal self-determination of national groups, the USSR was treated as a single nation represented by the Communist state, whose interests were regarded as threatened by both non-proletarian social classes (notably the peasantry) and many non-Russian national or ethnic groups. Moreover, all Stalin's genocidal policies were conditioned, directly or indirectly, by Soviet rivalry with Western capitalist states and international threats, perceived from the late 1920s and actual in the Second World War. Behind forced collectivization, the 'liquidation of the kulaks' and the terror-famine lay Stalin's belief that the USSR needed to industrialize rapidly if it was to compete with Germany in a future war. Deportations of nationalities were directly linked to the perception that they were internationally 'treacherous', potential or actual supporters of the Soviet Union's international enemies.

It was not only in the Stalinist case that nationalism was entwined, as Mann (2005) suggests, with class politics and conditioned by international conflict. In the polarized context of the 1930s, 'right-wing' as well as 'left-wing' violence was directed against class as much as ethnic and national enemies. In the early phases of fascist rule in Italy and Germany, working-class organizations (the Communist and Socialist parties and the trade unions) and their linked communities were destroyed, in Germany simultaneously with the repression of the Jews. In Spain, the Nationalist movement of General Franco launched its military rebellion to destroy the parties of the left and their social bases, and continued its 'holocaust' (Preston 2012) after victory in 1939, at the same time as repressing minority nationalities in Catalonia, the

Basque Country and Galicia. For 'nationalists', internal social enemies were therefore class as well as national, just as for 'Communists', they were national as well as class.

International rivalry was most often the decisive factor in the escalation to radically genocidal policies. Just as international security concerns lay behind Stalin's genocides, Hitler's were ratcheted up as his international expansion began. Anti-Jewish policies became more generally violent during the March 1938 Austrian annexation, while Kristallnacht (the anti-Jewish pogrom across Germany on 11 November 1938) followed the annexation of the Sudetenland. In September 1939, as Germany invaded Poland, the Nazis began to liquidate the mentally handicapped in Germany itself, ostensibly to free resources for the care of anticipated military casualties (Aly et al. 1994). In an era of international polarization, genocide had many different kinds of targets. However exclusive interpretations of national principles, which permeated Stalinist and democratic as well as fascist thought, were central to most genocidal processes, and it is these that were to define national groups as the main targets of genocide as polarization turned to international war.

## The Holocaust and the wider pattern of genocide

The Nazis were the most internationally important instigators of genocide during the Second World War. Germany's war in east-central Europe was a genocidal war, its objective to establish a racial empire while destroying the Soviet Union and the Slavic states and peoples in general. As a result of the war that Germany unleashed, genocide became widespread in the east-central European theatre. These were 'the bloodlands', as Timothy Snyder (2010) calls the region between the Nazi and Soviet empires and which included, as Bloxham (2009b) shows, much of south-eastern Europe too, where widespread bloodletting had already occurred over half a century before 1939. So ultimately it is the *general* character of genocidal violence in these regions, rather than its Nazi-centrism, which is most important. The Nazis were central not just for what they themselves did – theirs were the most ambitious and ultimately most murderous campaigns – but because their population-inspired military aggression and territorial expansionism were catalysts for a wider pattern of genocide by many of the states involved.

To an academic literature saturated with the idea of the specificity if not 'uniqueness' of the Holocaust, this may seem a radical reorientation. Yet the destruction of Europe's Jews, rather than being exceptional, was the most murderous element of Nazi Germany's generally genocidal war in eastern Europe against Slavs as well as Jews, which in turn was the most comprehensive and aggressive of the *many* destructive campaigns of the states and armed movements involved in the war in Europe and Asia. Most of Germany's European allies and client states developed their own genocidal objectives against unwanted minorities (Croatia to murder Serbs, Romania to remove Turks, Italy and Hungary to 'nationalize' annexed Yugoslav territories, and so on), as well as participating in Nazism's overall anti-Jewish programme, sometimes (as in Romania) developing their own lethal anti-Jewish initiatives (Ahonen et al. 2008: 43–60).

Moroever, Second World War genocide was not confined to Nazi Germany and its allies. In the context of the European war that Hitler began with the invasion of Poland, Stalin's USSR, already responsible for domestic genocide, became an international genocidal actor too. There were three main phases of wartime Stalinist genocide. First, in alliance with Nazi Germany (following the Molotov–Ribbentrop pact), the USSR engaged in large-scale ethnic removals in the eastern part of Poland (Ahonen et al. 2008: 23–6) and the Baltic states, while the Nazis carried out their better-known expulsions in western Poland. Second, in response to the German invasion of the USSR in 1941, Stalin's internally genocidal policies deepened with the expulsions of the Chechens, Crimean Tartars and other peoples deemed unreliable in the war (Werth 2008: 405–6). Third, as the USSR began to throw back the German invaders and to conquer Poland, Czechoslovakia and other countries in which German populations lived – including the eastern part of pre-war Germany itself – the Red Army began forcing German populations westwards through a combination of direct coercion, terror and mass rape, while Stalin began to plan the general territorial-cum-population reorganization of eastern Europe.

In the conclusion and aftermath of the war, the USSR and the restored Czechoslovakia, Poland, Hungary and Yugoslavia forced the removal of 10 million or more Germans. In addition, the USSR expelled Poles from the areas of former Poland it annexed and carried out further deportations from the Baltic states, while the Yugoslav Communists expelled Italians from their reconquered territories.

All the expulsions can be considered genocidal because their aims were to wholly or partially destroy unwanted populations as presences in their homelands. The implementation of these policies invariably involved violence – in the case of the Germans at high levels (at least half a million civilians died, according to Bloxham 2008: 122). The continuity between events often seen as categorically opposed is summed up when Bloxham notes (2009b: 106) that 'the eviction of more than 200,000 ethnic Germans from Hungary from 1945 [was] conducted by many of the same Hungarian personnel as had targeted Jews in 1944'. That the USSR began destroying Polish communities in pre-war western Poland through its understanding with Nazi Germany in 1939–41, and completed the process – albeit with Germans as the main target – with the collusion of the Western powers and even the re-emergent Polish state in 1944–5, is a striking illustration of the general character of population expulsion in the war.

'Counter-genocidal' plans for the expulsions of Germans were not purely Soviet policies. They were first developed by the non-Communist, London-based governments-in-exile of Czechoslovakia and Poland, the prime mover being the social-democratic Czechoslo-vak leader, Eduard Beneš. These plans were approved by the Western Allies, Great Britain and the USA (Ahonen et al. 2008: 61–9, Brandes 2009). Indeed the British Foreign Secretary, Anthony Eden, informed Beneš in July 1942 that 'his colleagues agree with the principle of transfer' (Ahonen et al. 2008: 65). At Potsdam in 1945, the Allies gave their imprimatur to Stalin's more ambitious plans, and in due course received many of the expelled Germans into their occupation zones. The generally genocidal character of the Second World War in eastern Europe is underlined by these roles of non-Communist eastern Euro-peans and the Western Allies in the removal of German populations. If Britain and the USA did not pursue directly genocidal policies of their own, they sanctioned the plans for genocidal reprisal by the Czechoslovak and Polish governments, and later by Stalin. Moreover the genocidal Zeitgeist played a role too in the Allies' own policies. City-bombing, considered in terms of its aims, constituted degenerate war rather than genocide (Shaw 2003); however a 'genocidal mentality' (Markusen and Kopf 1995) can be seen, for example in 'Bomber' Harris' goal of erasing German cultural centres (Grayling 2006).

It was not only in Europe, of course, that the Second World War was genocidal. Before the Nazis began their aggressions in central and eastern Europe, the Japanese empire had begun its own ambitious programme of expansion with the annexation of Korea in 1910. In 1932 Japan invaded Manchuria, in 1937 China as a whole, and after 1941 much of South East Asia, regarding the populations it conquered as inferior and systematically exploiting them through forced labour (Kratoska 2005), much as the Nazis did in eastern Europe. Although the 'rape of Nanking' in 1937 has come to represent Japanese wartime genocide (Chang 1997, Yoshida 2006), this was only one of a number of large-scale massacres carried out by Japanese armies. Smaller-scale atrocities were widely committed, with systematic brutalization, best known through the organized rape of 'comfort women' and biological experimentation on prisoners, but also reaching deep into the daily lives of the occupied peoples. As with the Nazis in eastern Europe, it makes sense to identify a generally genocidal element in the Japanese conquests in Asia, even if extreme atrocities were mainly linked to phases of conquest and resistance. Japanese racism towards the occupied peoples was partly mirrored in American attitudes towards the Japanese, which facilitated the GI-saving calculus of the atomic bombings.

## Explaining genocide's internationally systemic character

The new historiography, emphasizing the wider character of Second World War genocide, raises fundamental questions about how various genocidal policies and actions were related and how they should be explained. Comparative studies can deal with them only partially, for example by incorporating 'Stalin's genocides' as a distinct set of domestic regime-driven genocide alongside Nazism's (Mann 2005: 318–30; Werth 2008; Naimark 2010). But Stalinist policies, against 'treacherous' nationalities during the war and against Germans and Poles at the end, particularly demonstrate the limits of explanation in terms of nationalism, or indeed ideology, alone. Soviet policies show how 'nationalist' policies could be framed in terms of real or imagined security considerations, driven by the perceived demands of international military competition as much as by ideology.

Many deaths occurred, in Snyder's words (2010: 381, emphasis in original), 'as a result of the *interaction* of the two systems', rather than simply because of the characteristics of each. Thus although recent research partially reinforces the emphasis on nationalism, it shows that this was not only an ideology, still less an exclusively domestic phenomenon. Rather international relations stimulated the development of exclusive-nationalist, racist and genocidal policies, and we cannot understand the latter without the former. To summarize, early- to mid-twentieth-century European genocide involved the following international–national dynamics:

1. *Changing international relations increasingly stimulated nationalist population politics, which in turn became increasingly embedded in international relations from the end of the nineteenth century.* The weakening of old empires in east-central Europe stimulated nationalisms, which in turn generated conflicts with new nation-states, in which 'other' national populations became enemies and were targeted for expulsion or worse. The general character of this process meant that even liberal-democratic and Communist leaders, whose politics were ostensibly not nationalist, thought in terms of the equation of nation and territory. Great powers supported, intervened in and attempted to manage these conflicts through international institutions and law.

2. *International armed conflict played a central role in the coming to power of radical nationalists for whom violent expulsion was an acceptable means of solving population 'problems'.* International war and conflict often helped radicalize domestic politics, bringing to power more radical nationalists – particularly but not only the rise of the Young Turks (in responses to Ottoman losses in war) and of the Nazis in Germany. The latter should not be regarded as a mainly 'domestic' phenomenon: it was clearly conditioned by the international results of the First World War (militarism, resentment at Germany's treatment) and the subsequent international economic crisis. In German-allied Europe, the accession of extreme nationalists to power was largely a direct result of the international war which Germany unleashed. Indeed some of the states involved, such as Croatia and Slovakia, were creations of the expanding Nazi empire.

3. *International war radicalized nationalist population policies, providing opportunities for deportation and mass murder.* Throughout the period, it was above all international war which enabled 'solutions' which were not previously politically possible. For many nationalists, genocidal population policies were a large part of what

the 1939–45 war in eastern Europe was about. International war provided the opportunity for territorial expansion, fed moves towards population expulsion and enabled increasingly murderous policies. Moreover the genocidal policies of Nazi Germany and Stalinist Russia led to a pattern of imitation by their allies. Thus not only extreme nationalists and Communists but also 'democrats' embraced deportation and mass killing.

4. *Genocidal expulsions were conditioned by international armed conflict in the sense that they were responses to enemy military campaigns, which created real and imagined security concerns in which minorities were seen as implicated; and also in the sense that they were sometimes limited by these campaigns.* The Ottoman campaign against the Armenians can be seen partly in this light, as a response to the Russian and Allied threat and putative Armenian complicity. However the clearest positive case is probably the expulsions of nationalities inside the USSR which – although with precedents including ethnic deportations during the civil war as well as the campaigns against the peasantry in the 1930s – were responses to the German war campaign, mediated by Stalin's own genocidal ideology. Negative cases can also be found, however, particularly in the increasing reluctance of Germany's allies to accede to its demands for action against the Jews once it became clear that Germany might lose the war – not to mention the impact of Allied action in ending Nazi genocide even as it enabled Soviet population policies.

5. *Some genocidal expulsions can be seen partly as international 'counter-genocide', i.e. responses, facilitated by international victory, to enemy genocide.* Thus 'revenge' expulsions of Germans were conditioned by Nazi genocide, as well as more generally by their aggressive war and its atrocities, against Poles, Czechs, Russians and others (but less by their anti-Jewish policies, of which many counter-genocidists did not disapprove). However genocidal population policies were also important international war aims for the USSR in its annexations of the Baltic states and Poland in 1939, and for the USSR, Poland, Czechoslovakia and the emergent Tito regime in Yugoslavia in the later stages of the war, and so can be seen only partly in revenge terms. In this perspective, it might be more accurate to say that international victory enabled genocidal

policies, driven by a combination of exclusive-nationalist and security goals, which were partly legitimated by 'revenge'.

6. *The development of international law and agreements after wars, although intended to produce peaceful relations between nations as well as states, often stimulated or at least permitted genocidal conflict.* After the First World War, the Western powers' 'Paris system' served to stimulate as well as limit genocidal expulsions; and the Allies' Potsdam conference, which led to the United Nations, also approved the destruction of German communities after the Second World War. International treaties ratified as well as limited expulsions and violence, most notoriously in the Greco-Turkish 'population exchanges' of 1923.

## Limits of genocide in the inter-imperial crisis

We have seen that inter-imperial international relations play an essential part in explaining the wider development of genocide in Europe in the first half of the twentieth century. Yet these interstate relations contributed partly by stimulating 'domestic' nationalism and authoritarianism, underlining the need for a type of IR explanation which bridges the 'international–national' divide and recognizes the linkages of intra- and interstate relations. Levene's question remains: in what sense did genocide become internationally systemic?

To answer this we first need to acknowledge the *limits* of genocide in this period. International relations never became generally or universally genocidal, even during the Second World War. Genocide was primarily a regional phenomenon of east-central Europe, becoming concentrated finally in the 'bloodlands' between Russia and Germany, and of parts of Japanese-occupied Asia. In western Europe, even the Nazis' war was not generally genocidal against the major national populations – although of course it was against Jews, Roma, the mentally handicapped, etc. – and some 'Aryan' nationalities were integrated into the Nazi system of power. (Lemkin's 1944 argument that German policies and laws were generally genocidal in occupied Europe is valid only in the sense of 'cultural' genocide, since clearly not all societies were subjected to deeply destructive policies.) Soviet policies were even more selectively genocidal, and US and British policies not directly at all, despite their complicity in their allies' acts of genocide. In Asia, some Japanese policies might be qualified as genocidal, but not all. So overall genocide was partial even in the Axis campaigns – it was only sometimes and in some places what they were about – and it was *not* what the war as a whole was generally about.

Why did not the inter-imperial international system become more generally genocidal? While ideologies and political systems are clearly part of the explanation for the variation (genocide was mainly a policy of fascist, Stalinist and authoritarian states), this discussion has emphasized specific regional dynamics, particular historic crises of state forms, the conflicts these set up, and above all war interactions. The wider conflicts of the European and world inter-imperial system helped produce a *regional system* of international relations, in east-central Europe, in which genocide was increasingly endemic. War interactions repeatedly produced genocidal responses from actors, and even sometimes led 'counter-genocidally' from one genocide to another. For the most part genocide was developed – and also constrained – because of how the policies of regional actors changed in the context of pan-European and worldwide military–political interactions.

What does this tell us about relations between genocide and inter-national relations in a longer historical perspective, and in particular how should it influence the framing of genocide production in contemporary global politics? First, it suggests a narrower formulation of the relationships between genocide and international 'systems' than proposed by Levene. Genocide has been shown to be complexly implicated in the inter-imperial system, and more particularly in regional sub-systems and systems of armed conflict, rather than in the modern 'international system' in general. Second, it suggests that we should see the relations of global great (including Western) powers, international institutions and law to genocide not only in terms of 'response' but also in terms of how they enter into the production of genocide.

From a historical point of view, we need to recognize the greatly changed characters of global social and power relations since the period discussed in this chapter, and changed articulations of regional with global relations in the post-Second World War world. For the approach developed here to have purchase in explaining contemporary genocide – for example in regional political systems and systems of armed conflict in former Yugoslavia and the African Great Lakes – it will have to take into account the different international relations of the late twentieth and early twenty-first centuries. This account of the role of international relations in genocide, and genocide in international relations, in twentieth-century Europe does not offer a universal model, but a starting point for the analysis in the following chapters.

# 5 | The 1948 Convention and the transition in genocide

Twentieth-century European genocide developed within an inter-imperial international system that had already produced colonial genocide. However the latter happened episodically across several continents over five centuries, out of repeated but often discrete clashes of Western European empires with indigenous polities and societies, conditioned by inter-imperial rivalry but not a direct outcome of it. In contrast the high-genocidal period in Europe was packed into roughly three-quarters of a century, from the 1870s to 1949, concentrated chiefly in the eastern parts of the continent, and came to a head during the two pan-European wars resulting directly from the rivalries of the major empires. As we have seen, the Second World War generalized genocide in parts of Europe and Asia.

In this chapter I explore how genocide changed again with the ending of that war, which produced the most radical changes in world politics of modern times. I argue that incidence and forms of genocide changed as the international system changed in the 'post-war' era. The imperial system changed in two crucial directions. First, complex multi-imperial rivalries were replaced by the competition of two Cold War blocs, which after the Sino-Soviet split became three-way rivalry between the West, the Soviet bloc and China. Second, European colonial empires were replaced by a large number of independent post-colonial states. And if the new world international context changed the patterns of genocide, particular interest lies in the 'transition' period at the end of the war – not least because this was when the new United Nations Organization drafted and adopted the Convention on the Prevention and Punishment of the Crime of Genocide. In this chapter I locate these key years in the history of genocide, and develop a more general discussion of the changes in the international system and how they impacted on it. In Chapter 6, following, I outline a longer survey of genocide in the era of Cold War, decolonization and the consolidation of post-colonial states.

## 1944–49: the Convention and a new pattern of genocide

In genocide scholarship, the period 1944 to 1949 is best known for Lemkin's naming of 'genocide' and the adoption of the Genocide Convention on 9 December 1948. Among the lofty ambitions of the early UN was the outlawing of the newly named horror widely practised by the defeated powers. This was first expressed in General Assembly resolution 96(1) of 11 December 1946 and brought to fruition, after a lengthy drafting process, two years later. It is doubtful that it would have been possible at any other point, before or since, to gain the agreement of most major states to such a broadly and in many respects powerfully framed agreement. It is all the more amazing that this was done less than five years after the word 'genocide' was invented. These years were manifestly a period of change, sometimes seen as a movement from a period of high genocide to one of law, but more conventionally seen in international history as the interval between the end of the world war and the full onset of the Cold War. I shall argue that these few years were indeed transitional, not from a genocidal to a non-genocidal world but from one period in the history of genocide to another.

Today the Genocide Convention – signed over six and a half decades by 142 of the UN's 192 member states – has two main international functions. It is the foundation of the international law of genocide and a political benchmark for the UN, states, NGOs, media and social movements in dealing with genocide. It has also been widely adopted as a framework for academic study. In each of these contexts the Convention is treated, if not with awe, largely as a given. Certainly, case law has begun to modify some of its original understandings and the need for legal interpretation is better understood. Likewise its political uses are recognized, both by those who want it more widely enforced and by those who wish to narrow its remit, as involving interpretation. Scholars have widely pointed out limitations such as the exclusion of political groups and social classes, and have modified and even radically overhauled its definition for academic purposes. However, conservative legal and political readings (e.g. Schabas 2000) remain dominant; even scholars who are aware of the Convention's conceptual limitations sometimes find it convenient to use it as an benchmark, fearing that further conceptual dispute will obscure analytical issues.

All these approaches take more or less at face value the Convention's commitment to 'preventing' and 'punishing' genocide, and therefore see it as a basis for the understanding necessary to achieve these tasks. But acceptance of these claims also implies a *historical* interpretation in which its adoption marks a rupture in the history of genocide, between the period in which the crime was unnamed and unprevented and perpetrators went unpunished, and an era in which genocide is named and criminalized and international organization is harnessed to prevent and punish it. However the Convention's adoption did not genuinely represent such a rupture. Or rather, this is not the kind of rupture in the history of genocide that the Convention represents.

What is lacking is a historical treatment of the Convention, which understands its context, and interprets its possibilities and limitations in the light of the histories from which it came and in which it has subsequently been used, neglected and interpreted. Certainly, its immediate drafting history has been rehearsed several times (Kuper 1981, Schabas 2000, Cooper 2008) and is reasonably well understood, together with some of the political constraints which it created – for example, the omission of political groups, seen as a function of the Soviet interest in self-protection. What is less clear is how the Convention should be viewed in the larger historical contexts out of which it came and in which it has functioned, and how it should be seen in the history of genocide. An uncritical attitude to the Convention means we are likely to take at face value the assumption of a *progressive* development in which genocide, previously rampant, was outlawed and prevented. When reinforced by an overwhelming focus on the mega-genocides, of which those conventionally assumed to be the most important (the Holocaust, Armenia) occurred before the adoption of the Convention, critical questions about the Convention moment in genocide history are unlikely to be asked. And yet, prompted not just by the occasional recurrence of mega-genocides (Cambodia, Rwanda) but by the wider ocurrence of genocidal violence, these questions remain: Is the problem of genocide really less now than it was before the Convention? Has it changed in scope, scale or form since the Convention's adoption? If there is a turning point in the history of genocide around this time, what kind of turning point was it? Was it actually the result of the Convention – or of larger historical changes which also produced the Convention?

The standard view sees the Convention as a response to the Holocaust. On this view, there was a simple movement from the unprecedented evil of Nazism to the moral and legal norms of the Convention. And if the reality that the Convention has *not* led to a genocide-free world in the following sixty years is recognized, this is put down to the Cold War and failures of political will by major powers. However such a perspective sets up a simple tension between given norms and current reality; it does not *investigate* the reality out of which the Convention's norms came. Such an investigation will invest the Convention with a rather different meaning.

The immediate post-war years from 1945 to 1949 were the period in which the UN was consolidated. As Mark Mazower argues, it was not envisaged by its founders as the idealistic guardian of a new and peaceful global order, but as a world organization to protect the interests of the major empires – even if this imperial vision was decisively reshaped by the unanticipated rise of India and other post-colonial powers. Mazower (2009: loc.55) remarks: 'A great deal is assumed about the UN's past by both supporters and critics on the basis of cursory readings of foundational texts, and there is very little acknowledgement of the mixed motives that accompanied their drafting.' At the time, many commentators saw the rhetoric of the UN founders as 'shot through with hypocrisy. They saw its universalizing rhetoric of freedoms and rights as all too partial – a veil masking the consolidation of a great power directorate that was not as different to the Axis powers, in its imperious attitude to how the world's weak and poor should be governed, as it should have been.' It is in this light that we should understand the raft of conventions and declarations drafted and approved in this period – the 1945 UN Charter, the 1948 Universal Declaration of Human Rights, the 1949 Geneva Conventions which enhanced the rights of civilians in war, and the 1951 Refugee Convention, as well as the Genocide Convention. All these agreements, which still provide much of the official normative framework of world order, corrected, *in principle and for the future*, the horrors of the recent world war for which Allied as well as Axis powers had been responsible. But they were very far from representing unqualified commitments to the implementation of principles: they could also be read as 'promissory notes that the UN's founders never intended to be cashed' (Mazower 2009: loc.87).

Although Lemkin emphasized the advantage of the Genocide Convention, as law, over the Declaration of Human Rights, it is clear that even documents with potential for enforcement were actually largely declaratory in significance. The Geneva Conventions did not inhibit the permanent members of the UN Security Council from developing atomic weapons, although their use could only contravene the conventions. The Universal Declaration did not abolish Soviet unfreedom or racial segregation in the Southern USA. As for the Genocide Convention, it did not abolish genocide or greatly inhibit the major powers or the UN itself from practising, facilitating or condoning it. Mazower (2009: loc.238) goes so far as to say that the Convention, 'often hailed as a stride forward, was in fact a last genuflection to a past in which international law had been accorded more weight than could be allowed in the late 1940s'. It 'cannot escape our notice that precisely as the Genocide Convention was wending its way through the various organs of the UN in the late 1940s, the prewar minority rights treaties were quietly and unobtrusively laid to rest'. The removal of the 'cultural genocide' clause from the Convention's draft was of a piece, he argues, with the ending of minority protection.

The continuity of the UN order, including the Genocide Convention, with *past genocide* is encapsulated by an event on 26 November 1948, just twelve days before Soviet representatives in the UN voted for the Convention that they had helped draft. On this date, the Supreme Soviet of the USSR ratified the continuation of much of the wartime Soviet genocide, ruling that the Chechens, Ingush and Tartars (whose societies Stalin's regime had destroyed through brutal deportations and extensive loss of life) should be punished 'in perpetuity' (Werth 2008: 413). The probability of *future genocide* in the new 'genocide-free' order was indicated by another event that occurred on 29 November 1947, in the middle of the drafting process: the UN's adoption of Resolution 181 for the partition of Palestine. By the time the Convention was adopted in December 1948, this partition proposal had already contributed to the removal of 750,000 Arabs from their homes through violence and terror.

In fact, at least four major genocidal episodes were under way during the drafting period of the Convention, in eastern Europe, China, Palestine and India, with varying forms of complicity of the UN itself and UN powers. Between them these cases show different ways in which genocidal dynamics continued to operate in the immediate post-war years. They tell us a considerable amount about the history of genocide, for although this period showed continuity with the inter-imperial, Second World War system of genocide, it was also one of new beginnings, pointing the way to a mutation of genocidal patterns in the future. In short, 1945–9 was a period of transition, not from a genocidal to a post-genocidal world, but *in* the history of genocide.

## The expulsion of German populations

Of the four main episodes of this transition, the expulsion of the Germans concluded the Second World War pattern of genocide in east-central Europe. This was the direct continuation of policies developed during the war and first implemented during the Soviet advance in its final stages. The Germans had been, before the war, among the most scattered (along with the Jews) of all the European nationalities. Slated by Hitler to provide the backbone of his new racial empire, with its demise they were the main losers, shunted often murderously into the occupied rump Germany. As I have noted, the Western Allies ratified and helped implement this campaign. The expulsion of the Germans was a key part of the reorganization of nationalities within eastern Europe in line with Stalin's programme. It underlined the fact that the result of the war was the victory of one set of genocidal policies and actors over another, not of anti-genocide over genocide.

For this reason, and because no new German state yet existed (let alone was represented in the UN), it appears that the forced removal of Germans made no direct impact on the debates leading to the Convention. It was assumed on all sides that the defeat was that of Germans as a people, not just of the Nazi state, and that the recently defeated were not entitled to the full protection of the new norms. The absence of the expulsion of the Germans from the genocide debate, moreover, was striking even in Lemkin's own work – as Melchior Palyi (1946) commented at the time in his review of *Axis Rule* in the *American Journal of Sociology* – and his campaigning (Cooper 2008).

Indirectly, moreover, the fate of the Germans may have been significant for the narrowing of the Convention's definition compared to Lemkin's original. The proposal that the forced removal of populations should be considered within its scope received short shrift during the drafting debates, since it was recognized that this was so common and was still being practised. Yet by the same token, forced removal (or as it is now euphemistically described, 'ethnic cleansing') was, of course, the *most common method* of the 'destruction' of population groups that not only Lemkin, but also the Convention, defined as a genocide. This was a very significant, indeed fundamental, lacuna, of which the Convention's drafters were clearly aware. Schabas notes (2000: 196, quotation abbreviated in original): 'There is no doubt that the drafters of the Convention quite deliberately resisted attempts to encompass the phenomenon of ethnic cleansing within the punishable acts. According to the comments accompanying the Secretariat draft, the proposed definition excluded "certain acts which may result in the total or partial destruction of a group of human beings . . . namely . . . mass displacements of population".' This absence also bears strongly on the three other main cases of genocide in the post-Second World War transition.

## Anti-population violence in the Chinese civil war

The second area of widespread genocide was another continuation of wartime violence, but linked also to emerging Cold War polarization. In China, the Japanese defeat in 1945 set the stage for the final phases of the civil war between Chiang Kai-shek's nationalist Guomindang (GMD) government, which allied itself with the USA and Britain, and Mao Zedong's Communists, linked to the USSR. This last Chinese civil war – like the Japanese war and previous civil wars in the 1920s and 1930s and of course much of the Second World War in Asia as well as Europe – was highly degenerate, with endemic genocidal violence, as social opponents were treated as enemies in themselves as well as proxies of armed enemies. Both Nationalists and Communists targeted civilians amid death tolls of millions. Until recently, this war has been neglected by historians: it is far less well documented than many smaller conflicts, and much of the existing analysis focuses on the political struggle rather than the atrocities that accompanied it.

Like its enemies, the People's Liberation Army (PLA) pursued its war ruthlessly, often disregarding civilian life: large numbers of civilians are claimed to have starved to death in its 1948 siege of Changchun. In the crucial northern region, from 1946 to 1949, the Communists waged a 'struggle to the death' in the countryside, targeting 'counter-revolutionaries', GMD supporters, landlords and 'rich' peasants, and encouraging 'popular revolutionary forces' to carry out their own violence against these presumed 'enemies' (Zarrow 2005: 357); as in all civil wars, this involved much settling of private scores. 'Land reform', intended as a means of mobilizing the peasants to support the Communist campaign, 'meant the complete economic and political destruction of the landlord class'. This involved indiscriminate beatings, killings, and mutilations as a form of punishment, although these methods were also periodically reined in, as random violence alienated many peasants (Westad 2003: 137). The GMD responded by killing presumed pro-Communist peasants in recaptured districts: 'The killing of these peasants was conducted in as brutal a fashion as the executions of tyrant landlords. Live burial was a common punishment.' The Communists supported the peasants in their demand for revenge, with the most violent treatment of landlords occurring as the PLA pushed back GMD reconquests (Pepper 1999: 284, 302, 311).

## The forced removal of the majority of the Palestinian Arabs

Other 'transitional' cases concerned expulsions of Arabs from areas of Palestine incorporated into the new state of Israel, and of Hindus and Muslims from areas of the new states of Pakistan and India respectively, during the Indian Partition. Unlike the German and Chinese cases, neither was a direct continuation of wartime dynamics, nor directly related to the emerging bipolar conflict of the Cold War. Yet both were indirectly connected to effects of the world war, including in the case of Palestine the results of the Nazi genocide.

The Zionist project of creating a Jewish state in Arab-majority Palestine was half a century old by the 1940s. Like many nationalist projects in eastern Europe, where Zionism originated, it had long been envisaged as involving the need for 'transfer' of at least part of the 'other' population, although until the 1940s this had usually been qualified – in public at least – as a 'voluntary' process. However the Holocaust had created a new demand from Jewish refugees to emigrate to Palestine, in part because of the unwelcoming policies of governments in the USA and other possible destinations. It had also altered the political dynamics, creating an opening for the Zionists and increasing the receptivity of the West and the USSR to their demands.

The problem of Palestine was, moreover, the responsibility of both Britain (the administrative power under the mandate of the League of Nations) and the UN itself (as successor to the League).

Hence in Palestine both the Western powers and the new international institutions were implicated directly, rather than indirectly as in eastern Europe, in the development of the crisis. The UN's 1947 plan for the partition of Palestine between Jewish and Arab territories favoured the minority Jewish population and was rejected by the Arabs. In the circumstances of the 1948 war, it provided in effect a charter for the expulsion of many Palestinians from Jewish-allocated areas. When Arab armies intervened to prevent Israel establishing itself on the expanded UN basis, the emergent Israel expelled sections of the Arab population, often brutally, killing around 5,000 civilians, while terrorizing many more into flight and refusing to allow those who fled to return. Although Morris (1989, 2004) suggests that Israeli forces took advantage of the opportunity offered by the war to achieve these population changes, Pappé (2006) demonstrates that Zionist leaders had considerably pre-planned the detailed destruction of Arab society, and extended the expulsions to territory previously allocated to the Arabs (see also the discussion in Levene 2007). International ramifications included, over the following decade, the removal of most of the Jewish populations of the Arab countries to Israel, as a result of a combination of the polarization caused by 1948, repressive policies by Arab states, and encouragement of migration by Israel itself.

Palestine can be seen as the reflection of three international patterns of genocide: a late case of settler-colonial genocide (Wolfe 2008), the exclusivist expression of a European nationalism (Sand 2009, Shaw 2010), and a case of decolonization, as the UN and the British divested themselves of colonial responsibilities, handing the greater share of post-colonial power to the European colonists rather than the indigenous population.

## Two-way genocidal violence in the Indian Partition

However, the prime case of genocidal decolonization in these years, and the most serious pointer to the post-colonial future, was in India. The violence of the Partition (1946–8) was an indirect consequence of the Second World War, which had weakened Britain, finally undermined the Raj, and made the demand for Indian independence irresistible. Yet the war also strengthened communally based politics, already evident in provincial elections in 1937 when the (mainly Hindu) Congress and the Muslim League had divided the provinces. In 1940, with the British empire threatened, the League's leader Mohammed Ali Jinnah demanded a separate Muslim state of 'Pakistan'. When Britain emerged victorious in 1945, India's participation in the British victory raised expectations of independence and deepened the contest between Congress and League. Increasingly Congress and the British accepted the inevitability of the division of the subcontinent, which in turn sharpened the stakes for all involved, especially the mixed populations of potential border areas.

Conflicts over the control of border provinces, and of local areas within them, led to a drastic radicalization of political rivalry. On both sides, militias were organized and large-scale violence was targeted against 'enemy' civilians during 1946 and early 1947, leading the retreating British to propose a rushed partition, with severe, unthought-out consequences. As in Palestine, the imminence of partition only increased the incentives to violence in order to homogenize territory. In this case, the national leaders of both League and Congress, like the British, abjured anti-civilian violence. Yet murderous expulsions, massacres and mass rapes were carried out by militias linked to the main parties' local and regional leaders and organizations, and condoned by state and local authorities and courts which they controlled (Khan 2007, Talbot 2008). Overall, more than 10 million were forced from their homes, at least a quarter of a million were killed, and many women were raped. Effectively the British and the new ruling parties of the successor states condoned the violence as an unavoidable price of the political changes they had agreed upon.

More than any of the other cases, India pointed to a new 'post-colonial' pattern in which genocidal violence – although in line with nationalist goals set centrally – would be wholly or partially carried out in a decentralized fashion by local politicians, paramilitaries and mobs. A key factor, prefiguring conflicts in the post-colonial world during the rest of the twentieth and early twenty-first centuries, was the role of electoral politics. A widely based suffrage created the conditions for deadly rivalry between the main parties and the mobilization of religious and other communal differences. The fear of majority rule in an independent India underlay both the national-level secession of the Muslim League and the state and local rivalries that directly precipitated destructive violence.

## The character of the transition

So the 'post-war' period began in a genocidal, not a post-genocidal manner, and the UN drafted its Genocide Convention in the context of ongoing genocide in which several of its principal members were involved, and which in one case it played a part in enabling. The Palestinian and Indian cases did make appearances in the drafting debates: Arab states complained about Israel's treatment of the Palestinians and Pakistani delegates complained about violence against Muslims. Yehonatan Alsheh (2012: 271–91) shows how states' attitudes to concepts such as 'national groups' and 'religious groups' were influenced by their positions on the situation in Palestine. Alsheh argues that '[t]he inability of representatives in the drafting discussions to properly define what was the violence in Israel-Palestine' predicted the future failures of the Convention to prevent genocide. Yet even Lemkin, campaigning indefatigably for the Convention, aimed to ensure that these events did not seriously disturb the drafting process, and failed to demand that the UN deal with the human catastrophes which they produced (Cooper 2008). Thus the Convention failed its first tests even before and as it was agreed.

The adoption of the Convention coincided however with a drastic reduction in the incidence of genocidal violence in Europe. Here genocide had become more and more pervasive in the previous half-century, but for almost four decades beginning in 1949 it effectively disappeared from the continent. Straus (2007) argues that genocide scholars should pay more attention to the non-occurrence of genocide, and this seems a case in point. Genocide was pushed out of the European region, which continued to be the central arena of the the Cold War even if the superpowers were outside the European core. Yet this was not because the powers pursued the spirit of the Convention. Rather, in eastern Europe, the Second World War had secured the definitive victory of one set of genocidal interests over another. The more ambitious and murderous Nazi programme for reordering the region's population was defeated, and the less ambitious and murderous but still far-reaching Stalinist proposals prevailed, with the consent of the West. The Convention was *one* effect of the post-war settlement: others included, in Europe itself, this consolidation of the results of the unprecedented period of genocide.

Outside Europe, there were new genocidal conflicts. Nor were these new genocides merely transitional phenomena that would disappear once the Cold War international system stabilized. On the contrary, the post-1945 transition also pointed the way to a future of genocide. While the expulsions of the Germans were the last phase of the old genocidal period in Europe, conflicts over boundaries, ethnicity and minorities spread to the rest of the world in the post-colonial era. As the Indian events showed, conflicts resulting from the break-ups of West European empires – like those of the East European empires in the previous period – could radicalize the empires' inter-communal contradictions, leading to genocide during the transition. Moreover, many post-colonial nation-states were in reality new nation-state-empires, which transformed the political meaning of the inherited contradictions and created new forms of domination. While new nationalist rule in post-colonial states was no more generally genocidal than European imperial rule, like the latter it would generate repeated genocidal episodes in various parts of the world in subsequent decades.

# 6 | Cold War, decolonization and post-colonial genocide

In this chapter I explore transformations of the international system during the Cold War period and their implications for genocide. The transition in genocide in the 1940s reflected significant changes in the international system itself. One was the United Nations, conceived by the victorious powers as a more ambitious replacement for the defunct League of Nations, and the raft of global economic institutions developed by the USA and Western states after 1945. There had been a secular growth of international institutions during the inter-imperial era (Murphy 1994), but the post-1945 world saw their qualitative expansion, despite Cold War rivalries. Neither bloc could dispense with them and soon they provided fora for the many new independent states. Nevertheless, there were tensions from the very beginnings of the UN in the wartime alliance, as the incipient superpowers combined ambitions for a new international order with preparations for rivalry. Relations both among major imperial powers and between them, other states and societies were drastically changed in what came to be seen as a Cold War international system. These changes and the processes of change had profound consequences for the pattern of genocide.

## The changing international system: the Cold War and genocide

The 'world' wars that had produced extensive genocide represented two quickly succeeding crises of the inter-imperial system, which radically changed its composition and dynamics. The First World War led to the end of the old East European empires and the emergence of smaller nation-states in central, eastern and south-eastern Europe. The Second led directly to the end of the German, Japanese and Italian empires and indirectly to the end of the British, French and other European empires, which except for the Portuguese were dismantled by the mid 1960s. Thus the first war left a large number of rival empires – Britain, France, the USA, Japan, Germany (although it lost its colonies) and the USSR (which quickly restored much of the Tsarist empire) – intact as autonomous centres of military-political power. The second war, in contrast, subordinated not only the defeated German and Japanese but also the 'victorious' but indebted British and French militarily and economically to the USA. The latter became the centre of a gigantic Western political, military and economic bloc, while the USSR established its own (repressively quasi-imperial) bloc among its 'satellites' in Eastern Europe.

The post-1945 changes represented, therefore, a more radical transformation of the international system than the post-1918 changes. Inter-imperial military competition was largely transformed into inter-bloc competition. Nation-states mostly lost the 'territorial monopoly of violence' that Max Weber classically described. The control of violence, the core of sovereignty, was increasingly exercised at the bloc level. The reconstituted West German and Japanese states were militarily neutered and, like most of the smaller Western European states and Canada, thoroughly subordinated to the USA. Even Britain and France, which maintained great-power ambitions, lost much of their military sovereignty: the limits were dramatically demonstrated in the Suez debacle of 1956. Within the Western bloc, nation-states retained a reduced, domestic sovereignty, with administrative control over their territory and borders, enhanced through new economic powers. In the Soviet bloc, the USSR was the only major power after the ending in the late 1950s of the short-lived alliance with Maoist China; the smaller states' domestic sovereignty even in the economic sphere was weak.

Bloc competition centred on the military-political rivalry of the two 'superpowers'. At a world level, this 'bipolar' system can be seen as the rivalry of two 'ultra-imperialisms' (in the terminology prophetically coined by Karl Kautsky in 1895: Salvatori 1979), with China as a lesser third contender. This transformation of interstate power relations was more radical than the surface bipolarity suggested. Although the USSR managed to compete militarily with the West, economically and politically it was far weaker; China was much weaker still. In reality, the West dominated the world economy and politics: its regional alliances with non-Western states were stronger than Soviet alliances, and its core political model (democracy) possessed more cohesion and legitimacy. Although Western supremacy was offset by the appeal of Soviet 'socialism' in the post-colonial Third

World, the collapse of the Soviet empire and the USSR in 1989–91 dramatically exposed their underlying weaknesses, allowing the West to triumph.

The outcome of the Second World War represented, therefore, a more definitive resolution of the crisis of the inter-imperial international system than that of the First. It also involved, as we have seen, a more or less definitive resolution of the empire–territory–population issues in east-central Europe that had produced genocide over the previous three-quarters of a century. The USSR's successful expansion stabilized this situation in the coming decades, and its control over the 'satellites' ensured that no Eastern European state could revive its own population agenda in the new order. In Yugoslavia, the independently victorious Josip Broz Tito imposed his own territory–population solution in the federal structure of the new Communist state. The West accepted these outcomes, and in the ensuing Cold War, the balance of nuclear terror underwrote the stability of the settlement. There is no small irony in the fact that further genocide was partly prevented by the threat of unprecedented mass killing.

In European terms the four decades from the late 1940s to the late 1980s are easily seen, therefore, as a period of Cold War military, political and ideological competition, suppressing historic rivalries and potentially genocidal fractures. However, the Western and Soviet blocs pursued their rivalries through alliances and interventions in political and armed conflicts across the world. Odd Arne Westad (2005: 5) therefore sees North–South power relations in the Cold War period in terms of the competition of Western and Soviet neo-imperialism and neo-colonialism, the 'continuation of European colonial interventions and of European attempts at controlling Third World peoples'. Indeed Westad (2005: 396) claims that 'the most important aspects of the Cold War were neither military nor strategic, nor Europe-centred, but connected to political and social development in the Third World . . . In a historical sense . . . the Cold War was a continuation of colonialism through slightly different means.' Yet if in one sense this period can be seen as part of 'the longue durée of attempted European domination', it can also be seen – as the very ideas of the 'Third World' and 'global South' suggest – as the period in which the colonized regions began to regain strong, independent roles in world history. Many post-colonial states had substantial autonomy, and some saw considerable economic development, whether industrial (recognized in the idea of the 'newly industrializing countries') or commodity-based (especially the oil-producing states). The period was one in which some of the great non-Western economic powers of the twenty-first century (including what are now called the BRICS countries, after Brazil, Russia, India, China and South Africa) first became significant forces.

Thus although the Cold War certainly had huge effects outside Europe, *it is fundamentally insufficient to understand the international system in this era on a world scale in these bipolar, inter-bloc terms.* Outside Europe, major new centres of state power were forming, offsetting the two-way concentration of power in the Cold War, and (as we can see from the perspective of the twenty-first century) laying the foundations for a later transformation. The decline of West European empires led to a great proliferation of independent states, which was to more than triple the UN's membership during this period. Many of these new states were small and weak, rather like the principalities of the Westphalian era, and remained dependent on great powers: either one of the superpowers and/or former colonial powers such as Britain and France. Others, however, such as Communist China, India, Pakistan, Indonesia and Nigeria, were large, populous, multi-ethnic countries – in some cases inheritors of historic empires from the period before European world domination as well as of the European empires. In these massive states, central elites mobilized substantial power and often ruled in a quasi-imperial manner themselves, suppressing peripheral nationalities and ethnicities as well as subordinating masses of poor peasants and labourers. Many medium-sized and even small new 'nation-states' were likewise quasi-imperial entities, in which elites based their power on one population group to the detriment of others. Even in less developed regions such as sub-Saharan Africa, most post-colonial state and military elites had enough autonomous power to enrich themselves, suppress minorities and coerce populations, even if they remained dependent on Northern states.

Therefore we should recognize that the international system in the Cold War period simultaneously saw great *concentration* of state power in the two ultra-imperial blocs (especially the West) and its systematic *diffusion* among a hundred new, post-colonial but often also quasi-imperial states and their elites. Moreover the nationalisms that developed in the multi-ethnic societies of the non-Western world, like those of Europe, would often have exclusive tendencies, which in crises would frequently reproduce genocide. In what follows, I outline the Cold War, decolonizing and post-colonial parameters of genocide in the second half of the twentieth century.

## The Asian Cold War, Maoism and genocide

Of the four transitional genocides of 1945–9 (Chapter 5), only one led more or less directly into an escalating series of genocidal processes in the Cold War era. In Europe, it would be almost forty years before genocide reappeared in the Soviet and Yugoslav break-ups. In South Asia after 1948, violent Indo-Pakistani conflict was mainly confined to Kashmir; it would be over twenty years before the next great genocidal crisis in Bengal, although the Indian state also violently repressed the Naga people in the north-east of the country from the early 1960s. In the Middle East, Israel would not be challenged again for two decades: its remaining Arab minority settled into an uneasy existence within the Jewish state while other Palestinians remained in exile. All these episodes of the late 1940s would reverberate in international politics even beyond the Cold War, but they did not lead immediately to new cycles of genocide. In East Asia, in contrast, from the late 1940s there were three decades in which genocide was repeatedly committed, in the context of international conflict, war and radical Maoist projects. The idea of the Cold War international system as Eurocentric and bipolar is belied by the significance of East Asia as a crucial theatre and of China as a third pole of conflict in the system. Although Europe was seen as the central theatre of the Cold War, it was East Asia where 'hot' war first erupted, often with a genocidal edge, and which was the main region of genocide in this whole historical period.

China in the middle of the twentieth century was a poor peasant country, which had been subordinated (but not generally colonized) by European empires since the mid nineteenth century, had long lacked a strong central state, and had been racked by decades of civil war and occupation. It was not in a position fully to rival the superpowers, but Mao Zedong's Communists, who had fought a long and often murderous campaign to seize and recentralize state power, were determined to raise China up and reassert its role in the world. This led rapidly to new conflicts not only with the USA (which had resisted their rise) but also with the USSR (their erstwhile ally). The international priorities of the new Communist state were to restore the territorial scope of Chinese imperial authority, by incorporating the island of Taiwan and other offshore islands that remained under GMD rule, together with Tibet, then de facto independent but regarded as part of China (by the GMD as well as by the Communists). Mao moved to assert partial control over Tibet in 1950, beginning a process that would eventually destroy much of traditional Tibetan society.

However it was the support of China, together with the USSR, for the Communists in Korea that led to its involvement in major war in the same year, and here genocidal violence was initiated by right-wing Korean nationalists. After liberation from Japanese rule, Korea had seen civil conflict between Communists led by Kim Il-Sung who had resisted the Japanese (in China as well as in Korea itself) and the right wing, many of whom had collaborated. The country was arbitrarily divided by the USA and USSR in 1945, leaving the North under the control of the Communists and the South under US military occupation, under which a right-wing Korean regime led by Syngman Rhee was installed. Each regime suppressed its opponents, but after the North invaded the South in 1950, Southern forces massacred thousands of leftists and burnt hundreds of villages on Cheju island off South Korea.

US forces – who were able to operate under the banner of the UN because the USSR had boycotted the Security Council when Korea was discussed – succeeded through a highly destructive campaign in expelling Northern forces from the South. Most Korean cities were completely levelled and around 2 million civilians died, mostly from extremely degenerate warfare in which civilian casualties were normalized. The war was driven on both sides by the aim of destroying the political enemy, including at times the sections of the population deemed to support it. Populations were frequently moved because they were seen as actual or potential supporters of the enemy, and violence frequently escalated to genocidal massacres of civilians. Both South and North Korean forces (and in the South, police and right-wing political groups) were responsible for mass killings at various stages of the conflict, and the USA was not only complicit in many Southern massacres but committed its own atrocities, notoriously when soldiers killed refugees at No Gun Ri in 1950. The Korean Truth and Reconciliation Commission, which investigated massacres on all sides, estimated that Communist forces were responsible for only one in six of massacre victims (Cumings 2011). In this, the biggest war directly involving major Cold War adversaries during four decades of inter-bloc conflict, the Soviets and Chinese both supported the North, but it was not long before the two Communist powers fell out. By the late 1950s, tensions dating from the earliest days of the Chinese movement in the 1920s led to a decisive breach, so that China now faced hostility from both superpowers.

These international conflicts in which Mao's regime was involved helped sharpen the sense of crisis inside the Chinese party and state, stimulating genocidal policies. Just as Stalin had imposed forced collectivization and industrialization when he felt the USSR threatened by a resurgent Germany, so Mao launched his Great Leap Forward in 1958, seeking rapid industrialization through the fantastical means of forced collectivization and backyard industries in rural communes. The resulting famine between 1959 and 1962 was probably the largest episode of policy-driven mass death in world history. Although estimated death tolls range upwards from 16 million (Wemheuer 2010), Dikötter (2011) presents a strong case for 45 million. While Mao did not initially intend to cause mass starvation, his policies *were* designed to destroy peasants' autonomy and subordinate them to the state, squeezing their labour for breakneck development. The intentional elements of the famine were the regime's prevention of access to grain supplies for starving populations, subordinating consumption to exports, violent suppression of resistance, and refusal to change direction even after millions had died. The famine clearly demonstrated the genocidal mentality ingrained in Maoism, in which huge numbers of peasants were considered physically dispensable and catastrophic mass death an acceptable price to pay for policy goals. It also showed how this was institutionalized in the Communist Party, preventing challenges to Mao: those who criticized, even afterwards, were removed from power or physically liquidated. The extent of this man-made disaster was concealed from the world. Partly this was because food shortages in the cities were not allowed to become as bad as those in the countryside, where even cannibalism became widespread. But it was also because China was a highly closed society, from which only foreign Communist propagandists were allowed to report. (Becker 1998, Dikötter 2011)

Just as the Stalinist terror-famine hit hardest in the Ukraine, where the regime perceived nationalism as an enemy, so the effects of the Great Leap Forward were particularly severe and combined with national repression in Tibet. Here land reforms had already provoked rebellions, leading in 1959 to a major uprising and an extensive military crackdown, massacres and the widespread suppression of Buddhist monasteries, which struck at the core of Tibetan culture. Mao's famine deepened this destruction of traditional Tibetan society. Within China proper, although the Great Leap Forward was abandoned after 1961, this terrible crisis created instability in the party that appeared to threaten Mao's control later in the decade. In response he launched the Great Proletarian Cultural Revolution in 1966, attacking 'bourgeois' and 'revisionist' elements in the party and state machines, and mobilizing youth in the Red Guards to physically attack these enemies. The Cultural Revolution was directed not only at party leaders but also at whole sections of the educated, urban middle classes in Chinese society, whose social milieux were destroyed through dismissal, dispersal to labour camps in remote rural areas, indoctrination, intimidation and killing. Although this attack on urban society did not repeat the mammoth death toll of the Great Leap Forward, it was another great phase of violence in China, in which over a million probably died.

The Cultural Revolution ended definitively only with the arrest of Mao's allies the Gang of Four and his own death, both in 1976, but by the early 1970s he had begun to seek an end to China's international isolation. In 1972 US President Richard Nixon famously visited China, a visit which led to a partial rapprochement that for both sides balanced their competition with the USSR. In 1979, tensions with the latter led to a Sino-Soviet border war and China briefly invaded the USSR's ally, Vietnam – the nadir of international relations within the Communist world. Inside China, however, Deng Xiaoping attempted the kind of bureaucratic normalization achieved in the Soviet Union after Stalin's death. From the 1980s he opened the Chinese economy to capitalism and world markets, leading to unprecedented development in subsequent decades. The Chinese regime remained brutally repressive, but Deng's reforms marked the end of the long period in which it regularly produced genocidal violence.

Internationally, Maoism remained implicated in its allies' genocide. China represented from the 1960s not just a third international pole but an alternative model of Communism, which was divided worldwide between pro-Soviet and Maoist movements. Since Vietnam was a Soviet ally, the Cambodian Communists (Khmer Rouge) under Pol

Pot, in rivalry with the Vietnamese, aligned to China. Under the impact of a destructive US bombing campaign against Cambodia, the Khmer Rouge underwent an extreme radicalization and, after seizing power in 1975, embarked on a genocidal restructuring of society. In a policy even more radical than Mao's Cultural Revolution, they emptied the cities, attacked Buddhism and traditional rural society, and turned the country into a giant labour camp, in a multi-targeted destructive process involving extensive killing and torture. Ethnic minorities, especially the Vietnamese who were linked to the international enemy, were disproportionally targeted (Kiernan 1996). The Khmer Rouge was overthrown and genocide was ended by Vietnam's invasion in 1979; however, for Cold War reasons the USA and Britain as well as China continued to support the Khmer Rouge's retention of Cambodia's UN seat in the 1980s.

### Genocide in wars of decolonization

If the overarching structure of the international system after 1945 was the Cold War rivalry of Northern powers, the underlying process was the decline in European empires and their replacement across large parts of the South by independent nation-states, of which Mao's assertion of Chinese power was also an example. Genocide was a recurring feature of the world-historical process of decolonization, in many places part of armed conflicts between European empires and independence movements. Where open warfare broke out, insurgents often attacked colonists and sections of the indigenous population loyal to the colonial power, while imperial counter-insurgency targeted sections of the population believed to support insurgents. In these conflicts, the line between degenerate war – in which civilians were attacked as a means of defeating the armed enemy – and genocide – in which they were attacked as an enemy in themselves – was often unclear. The truth about 'national liberation' wars is therefore that, despite the myth of liberating anti-colonial violence (Fanon 2004), they were often experiences of oppression and destruction for many indigenous people as well as colonists. Despite the inclusive ideas of nationality of some nationalists, one group's liberation often meant a new form of subordination or even destruction for others.

The fundamental reason for this was the same as it had been in eastern Europe: society within any given set of state boundaries was almost always complex and plural, so that nationalists could only create homogeneous nations by attacking and removing groups whose presence did not fit their projects. European empires had generally practised 'divide and rule', setting up or accentuating conflictual political understandings of social and cultural differences. These were deepened both through insurgency and counter-insurgency and later through the struggle for control of the post-colonial state. Despite the general association, especially in the earlier part of the Cold War period, of nationalism with 'socialism' of one kind or another, nationalists often based themselves mainly on certain communal groups in the population and built particularistic bases after they achieved power, leading to the subordination of excluded groups. In this sense, independence often involved the formation of quasi-imperial statehood.

Although from the vantage point of the twenty-first century it is easy to see European colonial empires as doomed, few government leaders, colonial officials or colonists understood this clearly at the time. The historic changes in the international system resulting from the Second World War were not quickly or universally grasped: Mazower (2009) even argues that the Allies originally saw the UN as a means of maintaining empire. When nationalists began to contest the continuation or reimposition of western European colonial rule (in countries in Asia and North Africa overrun by Axis powers this can be traced to their defeat in 1944–5), the empires almost always resisted in the first decade after 1945. Moreover in cases where there were enough colonists to provide – at least in their own eyes – the basis for the settler states achieved earlier in the New World, the defence of the old order was often reinforced by the colonists' own determination to rule. Even in countries without large colonial settlement, European powers were reluctant to concede independence: some like France and Portugal had invested in the fictions that their colonies were integral parts of the home nation. Even Indian independence was not widely expected until very late and, when it happened, was hardly recognized as entailing the liquidation of the British empire elsewhere. In Africa, more than a decade of nationalist agitation would be needed before a British prime minister, Harold Macmillan, famously acknowledged in 1961 the 'winds of change' sweeping the continent.

Thus genocide had structural roots in processes of decolonization as it had had in European imperialism and colonialism, although no more than in the earlier case was it a general or universal accompaniment. Most nationalists recognized the need to keep at least some colonists for their productive expertise, as well as to maintain continuing relationships with former colonial powers who protected their colonists. But colonists who were identified strongly with imperial counter-insurgency became targets of violence. Usually there was a strategic or tactical lure in this process, but it could also become an end in itself, so that forcing out masses of colonists together with the imperial powers became at times an insurgent goal. On the other side – as earlier in the German genocide in South West Africa in 1904–5 – colonial administrations, armies and colonists often perpetrated atrocities against sections of the population assumed to support insurgents. All European empires were involved in important cases of this kind, from the Dutch in their attempt to foil the independence of Indonesia after 1945 (Luttikhuis and Moses 2012), to the Portuguese in their late defence of empire in the 1970s.

The three major Western powers were involved in key cases. In French-ruled Algeria, symbolic nationalist demands during the commemoration of Victory in Europe on 8 May 1945 had been met by a massacre in Sétif by the colonial authorities; Algerian reprisals brought around a hundred deaths among the surrounding French *colons* (Vétillard 2008). Jean-Paul Sartre (1968) wrote: 'The Nuremberg Tribunal was fresh in the memory when the French, to make an example, massacred 45,000 Algerians at Sétif. This was such a common occurrence that no one then thought of judging the French government as the Nazis had been judged.' Sartre's figure is contested and he mistook the sequence (Nuremberg began a few months after Sétif), but the point that colonial massacres were internationally unremarkable is well made. The subsequent war of national liberation (1954–62) was marked by direct attacks on populations by both sides, the Front de Libération National (FLN) attacking *colons* and pro-French Algerians, while the French counter-insurgency collectively punished many villages with the *regroupement* (concentration) of around 2 million villagers in camps. In 1961, police also massacred Algerians in Paris itself.

Britain too was involved in genocidal counter-insurgency, notoriously in Kenya during the insurrection of the Land and Freedom Army (known to the British as Mau Mau) from 1952 to 1960. British forces detained 160,000 'suspected terrorists' in camps, while concentrating almost the entire Kikuyu population of one and a half million in villages ringed with barbed wire. Counter-insurgency tactics included summary executions, electric shocks, mass deportations, slave labour, the burning down of villages, and similar collective punishments, starvation and rape. Tens of thousands died from the combined effects of exhaustion, disease, starvation and systematic physical brutality. In contrast, the 'savage' insurgents killed about eighteen hundred Kenyan loyalists as well as thirty-two settlers out of a total of ninety-five 'Europeans' (Elkins 2005: 366).

The USA went down the same road in Vietnam. By the 1950s, nationalist movements usually adopted some kind of 'socialist' ideology and colonial authorities equated their challenge with Communism, so merging decolonization war with Cold War. In South East Asia, the anti-colonial struggle *was* dominated by Communists, so that when the French empire was no longer able to withstand Vietnamese nationalism, the USA took on the challenge of defeating it on behalf of the 'free world'. The US war, attempting to bolster the anti-Communist regime established in Saigon after the French departure, was generally degenerate in the sense of using methods that indiscriminately affected the civilian population: aerial bombing, chemical defoliation and mass concentration of population. Its genocidal aspect became explicit in atrocities such as the massacre of hundreds of Vietnamese civilians by US forces at My Lai in 1968.

The violence of wars of decolonization also sometimes continued, or took new forms, in the post-colonial aftermath. Regimes and militaries forged in liberation struggles turned their armed forces on domestic enemies. Indonesia was formed in the late 1940s out of the independence war to prevent the reimposition of the Dutch East Indian empire, after the expulsion of the Japanese. The new state had to struggle from the outset to assert its control over the far-flung archipelago, suppressing local nationalisms fostered by the Dutch in their attempt to retain control, and containing social antagonisms, one expression of which was the Indonesian Communist Party, the largest non-ruling party in the world in the 1950s and early 1960s. The armed forces played a key part in the consolidation of the new state, and in 1965 a military group seized power, possibly in response to the threat of a Communist coup, suppressing the Communist Party. The military and their varied 'coalition' of local allies (Gerlach 2010: 17–91) killed an estimated half a million presumed party members, supporters and family members, the largest anti-Communist mass murder of the Cold War. They forced a million more into camps (Cribb 2010: 450–4). Similarly, the Zimbabwean government of Robert Mugabe, which came to power in 1979 after a bitter liberation war against Rhodesian colonists, deployed North Korean-trained army units to massacre Ndebele supporters of his political opponents in Matabeleland in the mid 1980s.

## Post-colonial states, contested power

In cases of decolonization without armed struggle, power usually passed from European empires to local elites without the genocidal violence seen in India, but genocidal violence often occurred in subsequent power struggles. Nearly all post-colonial states contained ethnically, religiously and linguistically diverse populations, and in many cases central state power was monopolized by groups that ruled in the interest of one section of the population over others. Political opposition often mobilized social differences, leading to conflicts and civil wars in which sections of the population were treated as enemies to be destroyed. Political conflict, war and genocidal violence were not, however, simply processes that occurred within states. They were often linked to conflicts between neighbouring states and larger international power struggles, not only between the Cold War blocs but also involving great regional powers such as China and India.

There were two basic patterns of conflict, each of which could produce genocide. Oppositions could challenge for control over the existing state in its entirety, changing the dominant population-balance, or they could seek to partition the territory through secessionist war. The most important cases of the former were in the Great Lakes region of central Africa, especially the former Belgian territories of Rwanda and Burundi – where movements based in the Hutu and Tutsi sections of the population contested power – and neighbouring formerly British Uganda. In Rwanda, independence in 1961 was accompanied by the so-called Hutu Revolution, in which nationalists based on the Hutu majority overthrew the Tutsi monarchy and ruling elite sustained by Belgian rule. This led to the massacre of tens of thousands of Tutsi in 1963, prompting mass emigration to Uganda. In Burundi, rivalry between parties based in the same groups led to the killing of over a hundred thousand Hutu in a 1972 genocide (Lemarchand 1996: xii). These genocidal conflicts were reflected in

Congo-Kinshasa (later Zaire, currently the Democratic Republic of Congo or DRC) where the civil war of 1960–4 led to the little-known 1963–6 Kanyarwanda war in the east of the country, involving large-scale massacres of Hutu and Tutsi (Lemarchand 2009).

In Uganda, the 1972–9 government of Idi Amin massacred political opponents, often identified with enemy ethnicities. After Amin over-reached himself by invading Tanzania, it repulsed Ugandan forces, leading to his overthrow in what Nicholas Wheeler (2000) sees as an early 'humanitarian intervention'. Amin's predecessor Milton Obote was restored, but his forces too carried out large reprisal killings against population groups presumed to support Amin and later the rebellion led by Yoweri Museveni (Kasozi 1994, Harff 2003: 60). After Museveni took power in 1986, civil war continued, including large-scale population removal by the regime's army in the late 1980s, and the emergence of the Lord's Resistance Army which continued extensive violence against civilians across the region into the 2000s. The linkage of Uganda and Rwanda proved very important for the subsequent history of genocide: exiled Tutsis who fought with Museveni went on to form the Rwandan Patriotic Front which invaded Rwanda in 1990, initiating the events leading to the 1994 genocide. Connections between political violence in Rwanda, Burundi, Congo and Uganda showed the importance of regional international and transnational linkages in generating patterns of genocide (Chapter 9).

## Quasi-imperial states: territorial conflicts and secessionist wars

Most genocidal post-colonial conflicts were linked, however, to crises of territorial control, where ruling elites sought to expand a state's territory or opposing elites sought to break it up. Many of these conflicts centred on the larger colonial entities with disparate populations created by the European empires. Post-colonial states inherited their unwieldy agglomerations of power and developed new quasi-imperial rule. States' territorial integrity was not underpinned by social cohesion, so political conflict often took the form of secessionist wars by movements based on regional majorities. Genocidal violence arose in many territorial conflicts between the 1950s and the 1980s. This type of genocide is often represented by minority nationalists as one-sided violence by the dominant state nationalism, but this simple narrative does not work in many cases. Secessionists as well as central powers were involved in anti-population violence, and conflicts were often messy with numerous genocidal actors.

In Pakistan, created as a state in two parts in 1947, conflicts between East Pakistan (Bengal)-based parties and the preponderantly West Pakistani state erupted into open war in 1971. The Pakistani army committed extensive violence against Bengali civilians, mainly targeting presumed secessionists (assumed, moreover, to be collaborating with the international enemy, India) rather than Bengalis as such. However, significant anti-civilian violence was also committed by Bengali nationalists, themselves divided into a variety of forces. Sarmila Bose (2011: 403) notes that even in 'commentary that acknowledges some violence by Bengali nationalists against non-Bengalis, it is often assumed that not only was this violence sporadic and exceptional, but that violence committed by non-state actors such as Bengali rebels had to be insignificant compared to that perpetrated by the organized forces of the state. In other words, non-state actors are assumed to be able to do less harm, for instance, killing fewer people.' But Bose concludes: '[i]n the case of 1971, such distinctions and assumptions do not hold': 'it is clear from available evidence that the "non-state" actors killed significant numbers of people and drove out many more' (Bose 2011: 404). While Pakistani forces at times targeted Hindus, so did many Bengali nationalists, who drove many Hindus and non-Bengali Muslims over the border into India. Thus this was not a one-sided genocide by Pakistan; rather, like the genocidal violence of Partition, some of which had occurred in Bengal, this was many-sided violence. Gerlach (2010) sees it as an example of an 'extremely violent society'; it can also be seen as a complex political and armed conflict with a combination of civil and international war and multi-targeted genocide. Levene (1999) has argued, moreover, that genocide continued in independent Bangladesh, against hill peoples in the Chittagong region.

In Ceylon, renamed Sri Lanka in 1972, the emergence of majority (Buddhist) Sinhalese nationalism led to the growing exclusion of the minority (Hindu) Tamil population (Rotberg 1999: 41–2, shows how 'ethnic' and 'religious' markers are entwined). Several waves of 'cleansings' of 'plantation Tamils', as well as urban political discrimination, escalated periodically to direct anti-Tamil violence. In response to increasing repression, Tamil opposition radicalized into the full-scale insurgency of the Liberation Tigers of Tamil Eelam (LTTE), partly in the expectation of Indian support in the aftermath of Bangladeshi independence. When the Sri Lankan military began to gain the upper hand against the LTTE, Indian peacekeepers were introduced, but as they were defeated by the LTTE, India withdrew in 1990. The LTTE's assassination of the Indian prime minister Rajiv Gandhi ended Indian involvement; the LTTE's rule within its zone was draconian, and it carried out its own expulsions of Muslims (Sivanandan 2009).

In Indonesia, conflict arose from the ambitions of Suharto's regime (formed through the mass murder of Communists in 1965) to annex areas of the archipelago that remained under European colonial control. Western New Guinea (Irian Jaya), under Dutch rule, was seized after a military-controlled consultation exercise in 1969. In Portuguese East Timor, the colonial power abdicated after the 1974 revolution in Portugal, and the Fretilin movement declared Timorese independence in 1975. Indonesia's response, under the pretext of preventing a 'Communist' regime from being established, was a full-scale invasion. When Fretilin resisted the occupation, the Indonesian counter-insurgency caused many civilians to flee their homes, destroyed food stocks, and interned large numbers in camps where they were inadequately fed. At least 100,000 civilians are estimated to have died, the majority from hunger and illness caused by the 'starvation strategy' of the Indonesian army (CAVR 2005).

Similar conflicts arose in Africa. Nigeria, the most populous African state, was a British imperial creation uniting diverse peoples that had previously had separate political systems. After independence in 1961, Nigeria quickly saw sharp political conflicts, expressed in rivalries between different sections of the military linked to the main peoples, the mainly Muslim Hausa and the largely Christian Yoruba and Igbo. An attempted coup and counter-coup led to genocidal massacres of thousands of Igbo civilians in the mainly Muslim North, which in turn led the military governor of the Igbo-dominated south-east, Colonel Odumegwu Ojukwu, to proclaim the secession of the south-eastern region as the Republic of Biafra in 1967. In the subsequent war, both Nigerian and Biafran forces killed members of minority populations, causing hundreds of thousands to flee in both directions, and the Nigerian drive to crush the secessionist state caused extensive hunger and disease from which large numbers of civilians died.

Similarly, modern Sudan was a British imperial creation, formed only in 1946 from two previously separate colonial territories, each containing very mixed populations. After independence in 1953, opposition emerged in the south, where the people were mainly Christians and animists, to the rule of northern Arab Muslim elites. Insurgency produced a devastating civil war from 1955 until 1972, when an agreement for autonomy was reached. However the conflict revived in 1983 after the formation of the Southern People's Liberation Movement and lasted until the early 2000s. This was one of the most destructive of all civil wars in the second half of the twentieth century, with over 2 million casualties and 5 million people displaced. Although most deaths and displacements were indirect consequences of the fighting, Alex de Waal (2007) argues that 'at least half a dozen episodes in the Sudanese civil war would be genocide' in terms of the definition of the Convention, in the sense of an 'attempt to inflict harm on members of a racial, religious or ethnic group, with the intent to destroy them in whole or in part'. The Khartoum government repeatedly mobilized paramilitary militias to destroy the crops, farmlands and homes of the populations assumed to support rebels, a modus operandi that was to be repeated in Darfur in the 2000s.

In the Middle East, the main case concerns Iraq, a state with a very mixed population, created under British auspices after the First World War following the defeat of the Ottoman empire. The British-installed monarchy was overthrown in a 1958 coup, leading in turn to the seizure of power by the Arab-nationalist Ba'ath party in 1963. The Ba'athist regime aimed to 'Arabize' the population in the Kurdish-dominated north, partly because of security concerns related to regional conflicts, as Human Rights Watch (2009) summarizes:

In the 1970s, 80s, and 90s, Iraqi central governments attempted to change the ethnic composition of northern Iraq by expelling hundreds of thousands of Kurds and other minorities from their homes, and repopulating the areas with Arabs transferred from central and southern Iraq. The government policy, known as 'arabization' (*ta'rib*), intensified in the second half of the 1970s with the aim of reducing minority populations whom authorities considered to be of questionable loyalty in this strategic area. The government responded to Kurdish insurgencies by mounting a concerted campaign to alter the demographic makeup of northern Iraq, especially in areas bordering Turkey and Iran. The government used military force and intimidation as the primary methods. These policies completely depopulated entire non-Arab villages that authorities then bulldozed. By the late 1970s the Iraqi government had forcibly evacuated as least a quarter of a million Kurds and other non-Arabs.

After the rise to full power of Saddam Hussein in 1979 – with apparent support from the US Central Intelligence Agency (CIA), and in the same year as the revolution in neighbouring Iran – the Ba'athist regime's international and domestic policies radicalized. Saddam took advantage of Iran's internal instability to attack it, which led to the 1980–8 war, the bloodiest of the late Cold War period. Iraq was supported and supplied with arms by Western and Soviet bloc as well as Gulf Arab states, since all feared the dominance of a (Shia) Islamist Iran in the Middle East and the wider political effects of the revolution. However Kurdish nationalists' control of parts of northern Iraq led Saddam to massacre Kurds and other minority groups in 1983. In the Anfal campaign of 1986–9, thousands of Kurdish villages were razed, tens of thousands of civilians were killed – most notoriously in the chemical bombing of Halabja (Hiltermann 2007) – and hundreds of thousands were displaced. Violence was also directed at Shia, Assyrians and Yezidis. Western states showed little concern at Saddam's policies, but this was to change with the end of the Cold War (Chapter 7). In the same period, Kurds were increasingly repressed in Turkey – where three thousand villages were wiped off the map and hundreds of thousands were displaced – and Iran. Turkish armies expelled Greeks from Northern Cyprus after their invasion in 1974 (Anderson 2008). The Syrian regime killed many thousands in the city of Hama in 1982.

Not all the quasi-imperial states in which genocidal episodes took place were simple inheritors of colonial empires. Ethiopia was a historic empire never colonized by Europeans, although it was brutally conquered by Fascist Italy in 1936–41, and later annexed the Italian colony of Eritrea after the liquidation of the Italian empire. After the Marxist-Leninist Dergue movement led by Mengistu Haile Miriam overthrew Emperor Haile Selassi in 1974, it faced armed opposition from the Tigrayan People's Liberation Front (TPLF) as well as the Eritrean People's Liberation Front (EPLF), which sought to separate Eritrea from Ethiopia. The Dergue, supported by the Soviet bloc, carried out a 'red terror' against its enemies: according to Edward Kissi (2006: xxii–xxiii) 'it was the revolutionary regime's ideology of national unity that tempted the Dergue to convert particular groups into enemies to be destroyed'. Kissi argues that 'the extent of the Dergue's atrocities against political groups are clear', but he is sceptical of 'an overall intent of the military regime to completely or partially annihilate the ethnic groups from which its opponents came' (2006: xxiii). Eventually, military pressure from the regime's opponents and reduced support from the USSR in its terminal crisis led to the collapse of Mengistu's regime and the independence of Eritrea.

## Consolidation of settler states and the special case of apartheid

Amidst wars of decolonization and secession in Asia and Africa, the earlier waves of settler-colonial independence continued to have ramifications. Settler colonies in the Americas and Australasia had already overwhelmed indigenous populations in the nineteenth century; their independent states faced few real indigenous challenges in the second half of the twentieth. Therefore new genocides were not common, but measures consolidating earlier episodes continued: in Australia, indigenous children continued to be transferred to European families until the 1960s; in North America, indigenous people were confined to reservations; and in Israel, where the partial destruction of indigenous society was much more recent, additional territories were occupied after 1967 and the gradual 'legal' confiscation of Arab land would last into the twenty-first century. Israel also had responsibility for the massacre in the Palestinian refugee camps in Lebanon in 1982, carried out by its (Christian) Phalangist militia allies. (Phalangists had previously massacred Muslims in 1976, provoking a retaliatory massacre of Christians by the Palestine Liberation Organization, during the Lebanese civil war.)

In South Africa, a European settler minority had long ruled over a black and mixed-race majority, in a state unified in 1910 from British colonies and the settler republics of Dutch origin defeated in the 1899–1901 war. In 1948 the Afrikaner-based Nationalist party came to power and formalized long-standing racial segregation into the system of apartheid. To an extent not matched except in Nazi Germany, this involved a complex, pseudo-scientific, rigidly delimited hierarchy of racial 'groups' (Dubow 1995), proscribing interracial contact except under defined, unequal conditions. In theory, unequal 'separate development' represented a mode of rule over rather than destruction of the non-white population, and so was not intrinsically genocidal. However in the given conditions of mixed South African society, its implementation had genocidal consequences. In the radical form envisaged by the Nationalists, its prime aim was the extinction of the Black political presence in the country. There were to be 'no more Black South Africans', as the Nationalist minister Connie Mulder put it in 1978 (Platzky and Walker 1985: 17).

Apartheid therefore involved 'a programme for the removal of as many Blacks from the White zone of South Africa as possible'. So-called 'black spots', pockets of Black-owned land in the territory zoned for the White state, were 'to be expunged from the map', while the practices of labour tenancy and sharecropping, through which black labourers used land, were abolished. Over 1.7 million rural blacks considered surplus to the needs of White farmers were 'resettled': rounded up with dogs and guns, they were trucked to distant, barren zones in the Black statelets or 'bantustans' that the apartheid regime established. Here they were frequently dumped in tented camps among the poorest communities, generally without access to land for either grazing or cultivation (Christopher 2001: 66, 73, 82). From the cities, too, there was mass displacement. Frequently 'only the unemployed, the women and children, the elderly and the disabled, were moved, leaving the workers to live in single-sex hostels'. Sometimes there was a slow whittling away of Black and mixed communities; sometimes, as in the Johannesburg suburb of Sophiatown in 1955, 'a dramatic uprooting and relocating of people in a single swoop. One week there is a community, with its own particular life and institutions. The next week it is destroyed, the people gone, the buildings in ruin, its history wiped out' (Platzky and Walker 1985: 33, 326).

Thus although apartheid involved 'an extremely sophisticated ... system of *control* over the African population' (Platzky and Walker 1985: 18, emphasis added), it was predicated on the ruthless *destruction* of a large number of black communities. The policy produced many deaths, but direct physical casualties were fewer than in most genocides because the regime's goal was removal, there was little violent resistance, and the regime always retained overall control. Nevertheless, the consequences for blacks' physical survival were severe, especially since in many relocation areas 'the struggle [of the dispossessed was] fought on the very boundaries of life. It [was] about the most basic requirements for mere existence' (Platzky and Walker 1985: 132).

Apartheid became embedded in the Cold War international order. Although it was abjured by Western states and the UN as well as the

Soviet bloc, Western investment in the South African economy continued on a large scale throughout the almost half-century of apartheid. The state was a 'bulwark against Communism', effectively a regional extension of the Western bloc, as it had been earlier of the British empire. The main political and military resistance organization, the African National Congress (ANC), depended on the USSR as well as Western civil-society support, and so the international politics of apartheid were partly polarized in Cold War terms. The system survived, indeed, until the end of the Cold War: only then did the Nationalists and the ANC begin to seek – as their respective Cold War support systems dissolved – a compromise to end apartheid. However, as in some other transitions of the end of the Cold War (Chapter 7), the contested process of change produced a low-level civil war involving multi-sided violence against opposing politically and ethnically defined populations.

## Anti-leftist genocide: Latin America

In Latin America, states formed as a result of colonization over several hundred years, mostly independent since the early nineteenth century, continued to see 'frontier' expansion in the second half of the twentieth. In the Amazonian region of Brazil, new settlement partially or wholly eliminated indigenous communities such as the Yanomami through the characteristic mixture of economic displacement and degradation, coercion and violence, including small massacres, seen throughout the history of modern colonization. However new genocidal issues, more closely connected to the Cold War, were also posed in Latin America. In several countries, military dictatorships allied to the USA targeted sections of the population presumed to support leftist movements, in episodes of mass killing, 'disappearances' and child-stealing from the 1970s to the 1990s.

In Chile after General Pinochet's military coup in 1973 and in Argentina during the 'dirty war' between 1974 and 1983, presumed members and supporters of left-wing organizations were targeted, together with their families, with death tolls of around five thousand in Chile (Hiebert and Policzer 2010) and thirty thousand in Argentina (Feierstein 2007, 2010). In Colombia between 1985 and 2002, those viewed as associated with the left-wing party Unión Patriótica were attacked by a 'bloc' comprising right-wing paramilitaries and drug cartels as well as elements of the military, which led to several thousand deaths (Gómez-Suárez 2007, 2010). In Guatemala, decades of political violence climaxed between 1981 and 1983 in a more extensive campaign of violence targeting the indigenous Mayan population generally, as well as supporters of rural social movements and left-wing organizations. In 1999 a UN-sponsored truth commission counted 669 massacres (over 90 per cent of which were attributed to state forces) and estimated a loss of over 200,000 civilian lives between 1960 and 1996; many more were displaced (Drouin 2010: 87). Likewise in El Salvador and Honduras, counter-insurgencies of the 1970s and 1980s saw targeted mass killing, while earlier in Haiti the notorious regime of 'Papa Doc' Duvalier used death squads against its presumed opponents. In Peru during the 1980s, the Maoist group Sendero Luminoso massacred peasants in its brutal war against the Peruvian state.

In all these Latin American cases (as in Korea, Indonesia, Iraq, etc., discussed above), local powerholders defined their enemies as Communists and invoked the anti-Communist ideology promoted by the USA. The emerging scholarship of late twentieth-century Latin American genocide attributes a crucial role to US 'hemispheric hegemony' (Roniger 2010) and US-backed counter-insurgency programmes (McSherry 2010). However Marcia Esparza (2010: 13) argues that 'extreme class, race and ethnic polarization in the region' lay behind the resort to genocidal violence, leading to 'the construction of *el pueblo* as an entity that can be considered as the "hostage group"'. Esparza's analytically interesting implication is that, rather than there having been a single type of polarization, common but complex and overlapping cleavages, rooted in colonial as well as post-colonial history, produced in the ruling classes a 'neocolonial mentality ... transmitted from generation to generation', which informed the specific violence of the Cold War period conditioned by 'US-led geopolitical projects'.

## Conclusion

In the four decades from 1949 to 1989, genocide continued to be widespread. Yet comparative genocide studies does not generally include even the largest episodes of this period among its paradigmatic cases. The Khmer Rouge campaign in Cambodia, although widely considered a major genocide, is still considered atypical because the regime had a wide range of targets. Indeed the Khmer Rouge attacked Cambodian society as a whole, the majority of whose members belonged to the same Khmer ethnicity to which the perpetrators themselves belonged. This led some who consider genocide necessarily ethnic in character to produce the bizarre idea that this was an 'auto-genocide', in the sense of an attack by members of a group on their fellow members. This notion is truly the *reductio ad absurdum* of the assumption that genocide is predicated on given ethnic identities. The Khmer Rouge were not, after all, attacking the Cambodian people because they *shared* their identity, but because they saw the people's various class, religious and ethnic identities as *incompatible* with the new Cambodian society that they were building. And their multi-targeting, far from being unusual, has certainly been the norm not only for classically totalitarian regimes such as those of Hitler, Stalin and Mao, but also for many other genocidal actors, from New World colonists to recent Sudanese and Iraqi regimes.

If we overcome the prejudices that classify out Cambodia from the core genocidal canon, and understand genocide broadly as purposeful destructive action against civilian populations, then Mao's campaigns jump out from the record of this period. Mao was probably responsible for more civilian deaths than any other ruler in modern times, and the Great Leap Forward was probably the largest single such episode in modern world history – surely 'mega-genocidal' if the idea has any meaning. Other events in this period involved hundreds of thousands of deaths, but have similarly failed to register strongly in the canon of comparative genocide studies. For example, the Indonesian military-led campaign against the Communists in 1965 is generally accepted to have caused around half a million deaths, a toll of a similar order to that in Rwanda in 1994, yet unlike the latter is never considered a prime case of genocide because its targets were 'political' rather than 'ethnic'.

Yet if the Cold War record makes one thing clear, it is that such thinking is an obstacle to understanding genocide. Without improbably full knowledge of the mental processes of perpetrators we shall never know in very many cases how far they saw their targets in 'political', 'ethnic' or other terms. In any case these are merely categories that analysts impose to classify phenomena, not constitutive ideas of the actions that make these up. What we do know is that throughout this period, political and other identity markers were intertwined.

Although many genocidal episodes occurred in conflicts fought for nationalist goals, the Cold War political and ideological context led many insurgent nationalisms to adopt Marxist ideology and counter-insurgency campaigns to be defined as anti-Communist. For this reason alone, the genocide of this period often defies classification as either 'political' or 'ethnic/national', but was usually both at the same time.

It is clear that international relations in several senses – notably Cold War rivalries and ideologies, rivalries between regional powers, and cross-border linkages of peoples – were central to the genocidal conflicts in this period. However the Cold War 'system' of conflict, centred on US–Soviet relations, was not the only driver of genocidal violence as it was of the nuclear arms race. Instead, the Cold War worked variably, interacting with regional and national conflicts. Indeed it was not a simple bipolar system. Maoist China emerged from bitter international and civil war into the new rivalry between the Soviet bloc, with which it was initially aligned, and the USA. Its high-genocidal period, from the late 1950s to the early 1970s, was when Mao perceived enemies on *both* sides of the Cold War. He sought to compensate for China's economic and military inferiority to the USSR and the USA with fantastic development plans, as well as to preserve his own power through social terror. Pol Pot's Kampuchea, likewise, saw itself threatened by pro-Soviet Vietnam as well as by the USA, and supported only by China, as it embarked on its destructive experiment.

Outside East and South East Asia, the Cold War was a world-level framework within which diverse regional and national conflicts operated. Crucially, the Cold War was a system of regional alliances, through which the resources – political, ideological, military, diplomatic and financial – necessary for insurgency and counter-insurgency were obtained. The USA, USSR and their allies provided support for regimes and their opponents across the world, raising the capacities of both states and (especially) rebels, and leading the latter to develop what Stathis Kalyvas and Laia Balcells (2010) call 'robust insurgency'. Marxism-Leninism(-Maoism) and anti-Communism provided universal political vocabularies for local struggles, and Soviet and US backers provided military training and doctrine. To this extent many of these struggles were indeed 'proxy wars' for superpower and bloc rivalries, and, not surprisingly, the end of the Cold War in 1989–91 coincided with a decline in the number of civil wars and especially insurgencies (Kalyvas and Balcells 2010: 423).

A crucial driver of the conflicts that fostered genocide was the emergence of post-colonial nation-states, in competition not only with the superpowers and old European empires, but with each other and subaltern nationalisms within their territories or on their borders. The creation, expansion and consolidation of large and medium-sized quasi-imperial states in Asia and Africa, and the challenges to them, were at the centre of the genocidal processes in this period. In Latin America, on the other hand, where states were more securely established and more closely tied to the USA, genocidal violence was a response to largely class-based challenges to social and political power, linked to US strategies to maintain regional dominance. Here the language of Marxism and anti-Communism was most coherently and meaningfully used to interpret conflicts.

The modalities and organization of genocidal violence varied hugely in the Cold War period – so much so, of course, that the narrow definitions of comparative genocide studies would not admit to the field many of the cases I have discussed. Only in some cases was genocide in this period a matter of a concerted national campaign by a central regime or powerful elements within it against whole population groups, as in Chile, Argentina and Saddam's Iraq. Mostly genocide did not take the form of such campaigns. Often it comprised the loosely coordinated actions of coalitions of state and non-state actors, as in India in 1946–8, Indonesia in 1965 and Bengal in 1971. In some counter-insurgencies, genocidal policies were centrally determined, but perhaps more often they were produced by elements within armies, either in a relatively concerted way across broad areas, or in local 'genocidal massacres' without a clear overall aim to destroy a population even regionally. Sometimes genocide was overwhelmingly a policy or practice of one side in a political or armed conflict; sometimes it was a two- or many-sided, even 'mutual' process. However Gerlach's (2010) idea that 'mass violence' is the product of 'extremely violent societies' may be taken too far in de-emphasizing the role of state actors in this period. 'Non-state' violence still reflected national political fractures, and usually the roles of elements of state machines were pronounced. If there were often 'coalitions' of non-state and state actors, the latter were often crucial in initiating or coordinating violence.

Since genocidal violence was a phenomenon of political conflict and counter-insurgency war, it is often difficult to separate from these processes. The difficulty is exacerbated because many cases discussed here are only now being seriously investigated, decades after the events concerned, or are only now being investigated from a genocide perspective. Often we are still some way from fully establishing the dynamics of genocidal conflict and the relationships between different violent actors and targets of violence. Indeed we are often still fighting our way through the nationalist myths that surround all these events to try to establish credible scholarly narratives.

# 7 | *The end of the Cold War and genocide*

We saw in Chapter 5 that even as the United Nations adopted the Genocide Convention, expectations of a post-genocidal world were undermined by genocide perpetrated by its member-states and others, in some of which the UN itself and Western powers were complicit. Following this, Chapter 6 showed that genocide was part of many political and armed conflicts during the era of the Cold War and decolonization. Moreover the idea of genocide was widely invoked, although the Convention was almost entirely in abeyance: neither the signatory states nor the UN itself took seriously their duties to 'prevent and punish'. This situation appeared to change with the end of the Cold War, which ushered in a new era of genocide awareness and anti-genocidal policy making. However I shall argue in this chapter that the transition of the late 1980s, like that of the late 1940s, involved a change in the pattern of genocide and its relation to the international system, rather than a decisive shift towards suppressing it.

## Genocide prevention as a Western and UN interest

Major changes in the international political significance of genocide certainly developed around the end of the Cold War. The UN Security Council, liberated from the automatic vetoes of the Cold War period, authorized more peacekeeping missions and set up the International Criminal Tribunals for Former Yugoslavia (ICTY) and Rwanda (ICTR), the first international legal bodies since 1946 to indict perpetrators and the first ever to apply the genocide charge (Schabas 2006). Western states, sometimes with UN backing, embarked on what was called 'humanitarian intervention' to halt violence against civilian populations (Wheeler 2000). After a chequered history of intervention across the world during the first post-Cold War decade, this development was formalized in 2006 with the UN's adoption of the Responsibility to Protect (R2P) principles (Bellamy 2009).

The role of the genocide idea in this change was complex. Political and legal authorities were often reluctant to acknowledge genocide, preferring to use euphemisms such as 'ethnic cleansing' and 'humanitarian crisis' and to apply charges of crimes against humanity and war crimes. As Samantha Power (2002) shows, US policy makers had long consistently avoided recognizing or acting on genocide. Yet the USA finally ratified the Genocide Convention in November 1988 – after President Ronald Reagan's embarrassing visit to an SS war cemetery in Germany in 1986 – and this cleared the way for campaigners to press US policy makers for anti-genocidal policies. The changing understanding of the Holocaust in Western society and the related emergence of academic genocide studies, which really took off around 1990, influenced public discourse and policy making especially in the USA. After the UN's and the USA's failures to recognize the Rwandan genocide as it happened (Barnett 2002), leaders of both apologized in Kigali, and 'never again' once more became a widespread mantra. When the Darfur crisis developed, a US administration finally recognized 'genocide' as it was happening, even if it continued to avoid meaningful preventative action.

In the light of these transformations, a dominant Western perception developed that sees genocide in the post-Cold War period as a residual problem of authoritarian regimes, state failure and armed conflict in the non-Western world. In this perspective, the relation of Western states and the UN to genocide is seen exclusively in terms of prevention, intervention and punishment, none of which Western and UN leaders carry out consistently or effectively. Much of the literature follows Power in seeing this problem in terms of failures of imagination, will, determination, and resourcing by policy makers. This view, which Dirk Moses (2006) calls the 'liberal' approach, generally informs the comparative genocide paradigm.

This approach is not simply wrong. For the most part, Western states and the UN are not directly responsible for genocide; they do possess the political, financial and military resources to halt genocide in many parts of the world; and their politics are increasingly influenced by genocide prevention ideas. Why they often or usually fail to prevent or halt genocidal violence when they could do so is a real question, and the failures of will, etc., are part of the answer. However the recurrences of both genocide and Western–UN failures are so endemic that these explanations are insufficient. Deeper explanations must investigate fundamental lacks of *interest* and *capacity* as well as will. Political and armed conflicts in small states and peripheral regions of large ones often simply fail to engage perceived Western strategic, economic and diplomatic interests – or are offset by larger interests in collaboration with perpetrators and their allies. Moreover Western states, even the USA, are not all-powerful: while they have considerable influence and capacity for intervention in some non-Western regions and in smaller states, their capacity is much weaker in relation to other regions and the larger, more powerful non-Western states. The UN, of course, notoriously lacks strong, independent capacity and is dependent even for its decision making on major states, including Russia and China as well as the Western members of the Security Council.

If interests must be taken into account, these do not exist objectively, as functions of an objective structure in the international system, but are socially constructed and changing. In the post-Cold War world, genocide prevention has become an interest of Western states and the UN, especially as it has been institutionally embedded. However it would be difficult to claim that it is a very strong interest, or one normally likely to prevail over others. In 1997, the British Labour government of Tony Blair proclaimed a foreign policy 'with an ethical dimension'. This was simplistically hailed as an 'ethical foreign policy', but the *dimension* idea accurately captured both the policy's potential and its limitations. The ethical dimension signified an enhanced interest in ethical concerns, but it sat alongside other, more traditional, dimensions of interest (strategic, commercial, etc.). Ethical policy existed in tension with these deeper and more powerful interests, and was hardly guaranteed to prevail over them.

This limitation also applies to the specific genocide prevention policies and institutions of the USA and the UN. Therefore we need to question the simple assumption that Western–UN intervention can solve genocidal crises. We need to investigate the structural relations in which genocide is produced, and how Western as well as non-Western states are involved. In the following discussion, I shall argue that the idea of a post-Cold War movement to a post-genocidal world is as illusory as was the idea of a post-Second World War transition; but the end of the Cold War did involve a further transition in genocide history. The conditions for anti-population violence, as well as the possibilities for preventing it, underwent significant changes, some related very directly to this geopolitical change and the linked expansion of democratization, others less so. Alongside an increase in anti-genocidal consciousness and policy making came new mutations in the forms and incidence of genocide itself. The very Western states and UN that the 'liberal' mainstream sees as preventers of genocide were implicated in these mutations.

## The end of the Cold War and the international system

To understand the significance of the end of the Cold War for genocide, we need to grasp the character of the transformation in the international system that it represented. This change was often seen as the shift from a 'bipolar' to a 'unipolar' world. To the extent that the Western–Soviet conflict defined world politics, obviously the removal of the USSR left one dominant global power centre, the West, and at its centre the 'sole superpower', the USA. However we saw that the Cold War, while the dominant conflict between the late 1940s and late 1980s, was only one element of a larger, more complex pattern of political and armed conflict. The emergence of power centres independent of both blocs was also a crucial development in the international system.

Thus the end of the Cold War, like the earlier endings of the world wars, set off processes of international political change, but many features of the Cold War world continued. Indeed the Cold War did not simply 'end' in 1989 in the same way that hostilities had ceased in 1918 and 1945. The Cold War was not a 'war' in the straightforward sense, but a system of political, ideological, economic and military conflict in the global North, linked to 'hot' wars and genocides in the South. One dimension of its ending was the political–military accommodation between the superpowers, precipitated by the USSR's recognition (after Mikhail Gorbachev's rise to power) that it could no longer sustain the costs of military competition. In this sense, as many Americans believed, the USA won the Cold War. However another dimension was political transformation in Europe, brought about partly through the East–West Helsinki accords on human rights, but principally through the demands of Eastern European citizens for change and Communist leaders' recognition of its inevitability. The 1980s began with millions on the streets of Western European capitals, protesting against the renewal of the Cold War nuclear arms race; they ended with millions on the streets of Eastern European capitals, demanding democracy and the end of Soviet domination. In countries such as Hungary, Communist leaders pre-empted popular movements with democratic reforms; in others like East Germany, Czechoslavakia and Romania, rulers were removed by the revolutions of 1989. These movements turned the accommodation between US and Soviet leaders into a far-reaching political change, centring on democratization and the reassertion of national sovereignty, far more radical than was envisaged by Gorbachev and Reagan.

Globally, however, '1989' was associated with far more than democratization (Lawson 2010). Among other changes, I argue in this chapter that this upheaval in the international system was more or less directly associated with three major genocidal developments:

1 Mass expulsions, killing, rape and other harm in political conflicts and wars resulting from the break-up of the Soviet Union
2 Similar genocidal violence in the parallel conflicts resulting from the break-up of Yugoslavia
3 Destructive international sanctions and low-level genocidal civil war in Iraq, resulting from the crisis of the Saddam Hussein dictatorship and the interventions of the USA, UK and UN.

The first of these has not been extensively discussed in the genocide literature, because although Western states and international bodies developed considerable involvements, the conflicts remained largely regional in scope, directly concerning mainly the rump Russian Federation. The second, the first genocide in four decades close to the West's rich and pacified heartland, shocked Western public opinion in a way that atrocities elsewhere rarely did. The wars of Yugoslav succession were the primary context of Western intervention in the 1990s and stimulated international institutional development and policy making on a global scale. Here the West and the UN were extensively involved over a decade, in numerous and changing situations, in attempting to manage a complex regional system of genocidal wars. The third development has been even less examined within a genocide framework. Certainly, the genocidal violence of the Saddam Hussein regime in the 1980s (Chapter 6) has begun to be addressed (Travis 2010). However the end of the Cold War coincided with a drastic alteration in the situation of Iraq, and the 1991 Gulf War began a new phase of conflict. Not only the Saddam regime, but also the USA, UK and UN were responsible for extensive mass harm to civilians, first through economic sanctions and second through invasion and occupation that led to genocidal civil war. Through sanctions, as Joy Gordon (2010: 240) remarks, 'the humanitarian disaster was brought about through the demands and devices of a superpower, using the vehicle of international governance'. After the invasion, the very military power sometimes justified by the overthrow of a genocidal regime led instead to extensive harm to civilians.

In this chapter, I examine in turn each of these areas of genocide connected to the end-of-Cold War transition, and draw some general conclusions which inform the wider discussion of contemporary genocide in chapters 8 and 9.

## Genocide in the disintegration of the Soviet state

Because the popular movements of 1988–91 cut with the grain of Soviet retreat and superpower accommodation, they led to largely peaceful revolutions in east-central Europe: the Czechoslovak uprising was called the 'Velvet Revolution'. However their wider spread was often far from peaceful: even close to Czechoslovakia, in Romania, the overthrow of Nicolai Ceauşescu involved significant violence. When demands for democracy and national sovereignty developed inside the USSR itself, force was used at first to put them down, but by 1991 Gorbachev was forced to concede the break-up of the Union. The Soviet Union was an empire in all but name: it had managed the 'nationality question' through a complex system of republican and sub-republican institutions that nominally recognized the range of ethnicities, but in reality privileged particular nationalities within what were often arbitrary borders. The pattern was complicated by internal migration policies, which had created large Russian populations inside many non-Russian republics. Thus the disintegration of the Soviet empire brought about problems familiar from the Ottoman as well as Romanov experiences three-quarters of a century before.

Yet post-Soviet conflicts were also products of the space that new forces of liberalization and democratization opened to competing nationalisms. These conflicts were exacerbated by the capture of power by authoritarian rulers in many successor states, which involved rigged elections and imprisonment and torture of political opponents. Even in the relatively democratic Baltic states (Lithuania, Latvia and Estonia), which soon joined the European Union, the recovery of national sovereignty led to repression of Russian minorities whose loyalty to the new nation-states was suspected by nationalists. In the post-Soviet Caucasus and central Asia, repression of ethnic minorities (not only Russians) as well as political opposition was a common feature of authoritarian post-Soviet states like Kazakhstan, Kyrgyzstan and Turkmenistan.

In several cases, the creation of new independent states involved more radical conflicts in which genocidal violence emerged. The first developed between Armenia and Azerbaijan (T. de Waal 2003). Gorbachev's openings to political freedom inside the USSR allowed Armenian leaders to demand the union of Nagorno-Karabakh, an Armenian-majority enclave inside Azerbaijan, with the republic of Armenia. (The anomalous borders in the region had been imposed by Soviet officials in the early 1920s after two years' war between the independent Armenia and Azerbaijan resulting from the collapse of the old Russian empire.) The resulting tensions between Armenian and Azerbaijani governments and populations led to forced displacements of Azeris and a pogrom of Armenians in Sumgait in 1988, resulting in the flight of almost all the Armenian population from the Azerbaijani city. In the subsequent 1990–4 war between Armenian and Azerbaijani armies, hundreds of thousands of civilians were forced from their homes as victors obliged members of the opposite population to leave, with several massacres, most notoriously of Azeris in the Nagorno-Karabakh town of Khojaly in 1992.

In Georgia, independence from the USSR led to conflicts between South Ossetian and Abkhaz nationalists and the Georgian state, with wars in 1991–2 and 1992–3 respectively, in which all sides forced members of the other populations from their homes. This resulted in large numbers of refugees, especially of Georgians forced from Abkhazia, most of whom are still unable to return twenty years later. In Tajikistan, a flawed 1991 election led to a civil war in 1992, in which hundreds of thousands from ethnic groups on both sides of the conflict were forced to flee their homes, many of whom were also unable to return (HRW 1995). In Uzbekistan, an exceptionally brutal regime repressed 'independent' (non-state-regulated) Muslims (HRW 1995, 1998a) and massacred protestors in Andijan in 2005 (HRW 2005a). Although some of the early 1990s conflicts and their genocidal violence died down, none of them were resolved, and several countries still have large displaced populations two decades later.

Moreover conflicts continue to cause violence involving forced removals of populations. In 2008, the Georgian government attacked South Ossetia in a bid to reincorporate it, resulting in further removals of Georgian villagers by Ossetian militia, under the protection of Russian troops, who repelled the Georgian force. In 2010 in Kyrgyzstan, the overthrow of an authoritarian regime led to widespread violence in which government forces facilitated attacks on ethnic Uzbek neighbourhoods in the south of the country (HRW 2010a).

The Caucasus and central Asia have remained largely in the Russian sphere of influence, and the Russian Federation was implicated in all of these conflicts, especially in protecting the secessionist regimes of South Ossetia and Abkhazia. In Chechnya, the Russian army itself was responsible for widespread extrajudicial executions and disappearances of those suspected of affiliation with insurgents, together with burnings of villages (HRW 2002a). However, continuing post-Cold War rivalries between Russia and the West also affected these situations. After the 2001 terror attacks, the USA used a base in Uzbekistan, which like other states in the region took advantage of the 'war on terror' to justify internal repression. The Georgian government was also emboldened to launch its disastrous 2008 campaign by its increasingly close relationship with the USA and NATO.

## Yugoslavia: a regional system of genocidal conflict

Like the USSR, Communist Yugoslavia was a multinational state. The territory had been a site of widespread genocidal violence in the Balkan Wars of 1912–13 and both world wars, and Tito's own victory involved what Paul Mojzes (2011: 109–24) calls 'retaliatory genocides' of Germans, Hungarians, Italians and Croats. Consolidating his power, however, Tito redesigned the Yugoslav state as a complex system of republics and nationalities to prevent a dominant nationalism emerging. Yet after his death in 1980, republican Communist parties pursued increasingly competitive nationalist agendas. Democratization at the end of the 1980s led to the rise of demagogic nationalists both within the Communist parties (notably Slobodan Milošević in Serbia) and outside (particularly Franjo Tudjman in Croatia). The federal Yugoslav structure fell apart as Serbian leaders were determined to retain control of Albanian-majority Kosovo (a Serbian province and historic Serb heartland) and to include the

Serb population of Croatia (threatened by Croatian discrimination) within Serbian political space. Croatian and Slovenian leaders responded to the Serbianization of Yugoslavia by moving towards independence.

The results were the wars of Yugoslav succession, principally in Slovenia in 1991, Croatia in 1991–2, Bosnia-Herzegovina in 1992–5 and Kosovo in 1998–9, although there were other conflicts. Except in Slovenia, these wars saw large-scale forced removals of populations accompanied by extensive targeted violence against civilians. In Croatia, Bosnia and Kosovo, Serbian forces systematically forced the vast majority of the non-Serbs from areas they controlled, through a combination of deportations with killings, widespread rape and concentration camps which created terror and encouraged flight. Croatian forces, while protecting Croats against Serbian violence, also pursued similar policies at times, notoriously against Muslims in Bosnia-Herzegovina in 1993–4 and against Serbs during the conquest of the Serbian-controlled Krajina in Croatia in 1995. The forces of the Bosniak (Muslim)-dominated Bosnian government mainly defended against Serbian and Croatian aggression, but were also responsible for ethnic removals. Likewise the insurgent Kosovo Liberation Army (KLA), while attacking Serbian forces and defending Kosovo Albanians from Serbian assaults, was implicated in attacks on Serb civilians. After Albanian nationalists' accession to political power under NATO rule, most of the remaining Serb population left.

These wars introduced the idea of 'ethnic cleansing', used by nationalists to describe their population removals (and with a long history in Balkan discourse), to international politics (Shaw 2007: 48–9). For political discourses conditioned by the equation of genocide with Holocaust-style extermination, 'ethnic cleansing' seemed a useful term to describe anti-population policies centred on the apparently more limited goal of forced removal. It avoided the legal and political implications of intervention to prevent and punish genocide, and partly for this reason was widely adopted in subsequent conflicts. The idea also gained general academic currency as a term to describe anti-population violence that fell short of mass murder (Bell-Fialkoff 1996, Naimark 2003, Mann 2005). Yet 'cleansing' was an inherently euphemistic idea: forced removal always involved violence or its threat and usually significant levels of killing. It was already covered by the idea of genocide as targeted 'destruction' of societies or social groups, even if it had been deliberately excluded from specific mention in the Genocide Convention (Chapter 5).

The extensive anti-civilian violence of the Yugoslav wars therefore posed major interpretative challenges for both international law and scholarship, which have greatly influenced the interpretation of both subsequent and earlier conflicts. ICTY prosecutors mostly charged perpetrators with war crimes and crimes against humanity, but the 1998 conviction of Serbian general Radislav Krstić established that the massacre at Srebrenica in 1995 should be regarded as genocide. Milošević (who died during his trial) was charged with genocide in relation to acts committed by Serbian forces in Kosovo as well as Bosnia. Paul Behrens (2007: 133) argues that the ICTY has 'struggled long to evaluate the phenomenon of ethnic cleansing in the context of genocide' with inconclusive results, sometimes but not always regarding 'forced removal' as a means of genocide. The international legal and political consensus was summed up by the 2007 verdict of the International Court of Justice in the case of Bosnia and Herzegovina vs Serbia and Montenegro. The Srebrenica massacre was ruled to have been genocide, but not the larger pattern of the destruction of Bosniak, Croat and plural communities in Bosnia by Serbian forces beginning in 1992 – although it was in relation to the early stages of this process that the Bosnian government had brought the case, originally against Yugoslavia, in 1993. The judgment was justified by the argument that only at Srebrenica could the 'special intent' to destroy the targeted groups, required by genocide law, be established. Yet since the same destructive intentions of Serbian leaders towards Bosniaks were manifest in the whole pattern of violence, this was a perverse decision, which illustrates the way in which the legal understanding of 'intent' has become distorted. The decision can be explained on the one hand by an implicit assumption that only mass murder constitutes genocide, and on the other by the political context of the late 2000s, in which a comprehensive finding would have upset the delicate process of integrating Serbia, under a new democratic leadership, into Western institutions.

Academic authorities have also been divided in their treatment of the Bosnian and other Yugoslav wars. While according to numerous authors (including Cushman and Meštrović 1996, Allen 1996, Sells 1996, MacDonald 2009 and Mojzes 2011) genocide occurred in Bosnia, influential interpretations largely or wholly avoid the concept.

Principally this is because war and genocide have been treated as distinct phenomena, and the events have been treated primarily as war. In addition, 'ethnic cleansing' was a new term in Western discourse; despite the long history of forced removals in the twentieth century, it seemed a 'new' phenomenon after its absence in Europe for four decades. The Yugoslav wars appeared different from recent wars in other important ways, so that 'ethnic cleansing' was sometimes treated as a feature of a distinctive type of war. For James Gow (2003), anti-civilian violence was the product of a Serbian 'strategy of war crimes'. For Mary Kaldor (1999), 'ethnic cleansing' based on identity politics was combined with a mixed interstate and civil conflict and a parasitic, globalized war economy (running down existing capital and exploiting diaspora subventions and international aid), making Bosnia the archetype of 'new wars'.

For Stathis Kalyvas and his collaborators, on the other hand, the novelty of the wars was overstated: although these were wars of 'conventional' civil war rather than the 'insurgent' type that had prevailed in the Cold War era (Kalyvas and Balcells 2010), 'ethnic cleansing' was basically a strategic answer to the classic problem of population control in conquered territory, rather than a form of targeted destruction. Kalyvas and Nicholas Sambanis (2007) argue that the *process* through which Serbian forced removal policies developed followed the logic of control, with the level and type of resistance to Serbian power influencing the variable local *extent* of the removal of non-Serbs and of violence in the process. However the Serbian political rationale for expelling much of the Bosniak and Croat population was already determined before violence began. Gerard Toal and Carl Dahlman (2011) show that the 1990 elections in Bosnia had involved a process of 'ethnopoliticization' leading to 'ethnocratic rule' at the local as well as national level, which paved the way for 'ethnoterritorialization' once conflict broke out. Serbian nationalists in the republic (backed by the regime in Serbia) launched a violent territorial drive because of their rejection of an independent, plural, democratic state, in which Serbs would live alongside Muslims, Croats and others. Instead, they aimed to gain control of as large a part of Bosnia as possible, including the main areas in which significant Serb populations lived, linking their area of control to Serbia, and to ensure a clear Serb majority not only in their area of control as a whole, but in each local area. Since the pre-war population of the area controlled and conquered by Serbian forces contained as many non-Serbs as Serbs, with many districts largely or overwhelmingly non-Serb, the logic of removing much of the non-Serb population was already clear.

Nevertheless war was essential in magnifying the genocidal dimensions of the Yugoslav conflicts. While Serbian and Croatian political leaders envisaged forced population movements before the onset of war – Milošević and Tudjman had even discussed carving up Bosnia between them – the courses of the conflicts decisively influenced the spread of population removal. The success of Slovenia and Croatia in defying the Yugoslav National Army and securing independence (although the Croatian regions of Krajina and East Slavonia remained under Serbian control from 1991 to 1996) ensured the break-up of Yugoslavia. In this situation, Bosniak leaders had little choice but to try to secure Bosnia-Herzegovina's own independence. Serbian success in militarily securing parts of Croatia and expelling Croats encouraged Bosnian Serbian nationalists to secure much of Bosnia and set the scene for genocide there. Croatian forces in Bosnia-Herzegovina copied Serbian successes, and when they had the opportunity to end Serbian control in parts of Croatia, expelled Serbs in turn. Bosnian forces, although fighting for a unified, multi-ethnic state, were likewise tempted in places into their own 'cleansing' of non-Muslims. Kosovo's crisis, a decade old by the time serious warfare developed in 1998, was unmistakably affected by the experience and outcomes of the earlier wars. Many Albanian nationalists came to believe that mere civil resistance would not produce international intervention: only armed struggle would provoke Serbia enough to force the West to intervene (Kuperman 2008). On the other side, Milošević clearly believed, after Serbia's relative success in Bosnia, that the West would not prevent it from holding on to Kosovo. Even after NATO's air campaign began, he felt confident enough to escalate terror-massacres, killing around ten thousand people, and forcing over a million to flee Kosovo or hide in its mountains (Independent International Commission on Kosovo 2000).

The location of Yugoslavia meant that war and genocide there was of great significance to Western Europe and hence to the USA. Tito's Yugoslavia had escaped the Soviet bloc in 1948 and was de facto within the Western sphere of influence throughout the Cold War. Therefore unlike conflicts in the former USSR, the Yugoslav wars were globalized from their onset. Although the West was distracted in 1991 by crises in the USSR and the Persian Gulf, the Yugoslav conflicts were the objects of Western diplomatic interventions, of UN peacekeeping from the Croatian war onwards, of deeper UN and NATO military involvement as the Bosnian war deepened, of legal intervention (the ICTY), and of serious military action (bombing of Serbian positions) in the final stages. These wars were the key laboratory of 'humanitarian intervention' – largely failed, it is argued, because Western interest remained limited (Rieff 1996, Simms 2001, Power 2002, Gow 2003). Indeed they involved, in Kosovo, the first 'humanitarian war': initially this was not only unsuccessful, but led Serbia to escalate genocidal violence. However after NATO escalated its bombing and the ICTY indicted Milošević (Gow 2003: 292–301), the war became a success in removing Serbian power and restoring most of the expelled to their homes.

Thus unlike the post-Soviet conflicts, the post-Yugoslav conflicts had a more general character within the region of the former federal state, involving all the republics (including also Macedonia and Montenegro) to a greater or lesser extent. The wars showed some of the features of a regional *system* of genocidal conflict, in which one genocidal war led to another and there were episodes of 'counter-genocide' when Croatian, Bosnian and KLA forces expelled Serbs. This system was reminiscent of 'the great game of genocide' in the first quarter of the twentieth century and especially (despite its much more limited scale and lower levels of murderousness) of the system that developed during the Second World War in east-central Europe as a whole. Yet whereas the Second World War system involved some great powers directly as perpetrators, and was conditioned by the general conflict of great powers, in Yugoslavia the West and the UN were secondary and – partly because of the limited engagement of their interests – often ineffectual actors.

The centrality of global surveillance and Western–UN intervention indicated, however, the importance of this regional system's integration in larger international structures. Western and UN involvements were at all times central reference points for local actors. The prospect of Western–UN recognition stimulated the republics' demands for independence; Western-global political, media, civil society and legal surveillance constantly conditioned, enabled and constrained genocidal actions; the prospect of Western support was crucial for

Bosnian and Kosovo Albanian resistance to Serbian power; and Western intervention helped prevent a complete victory for Serbia and the Serbian nationalists, as well as sometimes (as at Srebrenica) enabling genocide. Moreover Western power was ultimately crucial to the ending of both the Bosnian and Croatian conflicts, with the Dayton settlement of 1995, and the whole series of genocidal wars, with the Serbian withdrawal from Kosovo in 1999. This in turn helped precipitate the overthrow of Milošević, the prime mover of the 1990s conflicts, by a popular movement following his attempt to rig further elections in 2000.

Western–UN institutions also oversaw post-conflict development, directly through international administrations of Bosnia and Kosovo, and indirectly through NATO and EU accession processes affecting the entire post-Yugoslav region. The West also presided over the patchwork consolidation of many of the results of the Serbian and Croatian genocide in Bosnia-Herzegovina. US President Bill Clinton insisted on early elections after Dayton, in the belief that democratization was a way out of the country's impasse. But like the 1990 elections that had laid the basis for territorial division, the post-Dayton elections were manipulated by local powerholders to boost their own population group's electoral registration and absentee voting, while blocking the participation of the expelled, so confirming territorial division. As Toal and Dahlman (2011: 234) comment, 'rapid elections ... mostly served to entrench nationalist parties and collective rights', at the expense of the individual rights of expelled people. They enabled local ethnonationalist elites to solidify their power in municipalities, using patronage networks built up during the genocidal war. Moreover, Dayton recognized Republika Srpska, the principal state apparatus involved in wartime genocide, as an 'entity' within the 'unitary' Bosnian state, able to reinforce municipalities within Serbian-controlled areas.

Toal and Dahlman show how, despite the Dayton commitment (in Annex 7 of the General Framework Agreement) to facilitate the return of displaced peoples, these processes resulted largely in the failure of 'minority' returns (the return of people to areas not controlled by 'their' ethnic nationalists). When, belatedly, 'the international community' tried to counter local powerholders' obstructionism, it 'soon realised that it was insufficiently equipped to monitor and enforce Dayton's provisions across two entities, ten cantons and 148 local governments, each with its own tactics for discouraging returns and repossession' (Toal and Dahlman 2011: 237). A parallel process could be observed in Kosovo, where after NATO's victory Serbs were driven from, left and were unable to return to Albanian-controlled areas, while Albanians continued to be driven from, left and were unable to return to Serbian-controlled enclaves. Thus the forms of the Western–UN interventions have helped ensure that many of the political conflicts of former Yugoslavia remain intractable at the time of writing. The most that can be said is that Western power, manifested in the protectorates in Bosnia and Kosovo and the movement towards NATO and EU membership for Balkan states, also ensured that the genocidal wars of the 1990s, unlike some of those in the former Soviet region, did not recur in the 2000s.

## Iraq: Saddam's campaigns, Western intervention and civil war genocide

We saw in Chapter 6 that, radicalizing Ba'athist policies of ethnic expulsion, Saddam Hussein conducted a murderous campaign against Kurds in northern Iraq in the late 1980s. During the war with Iran, Iraq had the direct or indirect support of the West, the USSR and many Arab states, and the atrocities attracted little attention. However, international support for Saddam ended abruptly when the regime overreached itself by occupying and attempting to annex neighbouring oil-rich Kuwait in 1990. This began a new cycle of mixed international and civil conflicts that pitted Saddam against his former allies, opening up several phases of genocidal violence by different actors over two decades.

The UN-authorized attack on Iraq by a US-led international coalition in early 1991 quickly overcame Saddam's million-strong army, mainly through intensive bombing. This produced only limited direct civilian casualties, but larger indirect harm to civilians through precision targeting of infrastructure that disrupted water and sewage systems. Moreover, Saddam's defeat triggered uprisings by Shia in the south and Kurds in the north of Iraq, which the victorious coalition allowed the regime to brutally suppress, in turn generating a huge refugee exodus, especially of Kurds. Partly because of the media coverage of the refugee crisis (Shaw 1996), the USA, UK and France were forced to intervene to create a 'safe haven' for the Kurds in northern Iraq – a key precedent for later 'humanitarian interventions'. South of Kurdistan, however, the regime remained in power and continued policies of 'Arabization', expelling over 100,000 people from Kirkuk and other areas up to 2003. It continued to carry out genocidal violence, especially in the south, including the destruction of the Marsh Arabs' society by draining their habitat and massacres of Shia in Basra after the 1999 al-Sadr intifada (HRW 2005b).

The failure of the coalition to overthrow Saddam Hussein also left unresolved conflict with the USA and the UK, which suspected him of developing nuclear weapons. They mobilized the UN Security Council to authorize both aerial control over and wide-ranging economic sanctions against Iraq throughout the 1990s. Air strikes to enforce the 'no-fly' zone caused intermittent civilian casualties (Global Policy Forum 2002), but greater harm was caused by sanctions. These systematically damaged the Iraqi economy (already weakened by eight years of war with Iran), including food and medical supplies, and amounted to a form of 'collective punishment' of the Iraqi population (Gordon 2010: 239). The sanctions are estimated to have produced a minimum of 100,000 excess child deaths (Garfield 1999: many estimates are higher). Although US policy was not calculated to destroy the Iraqi population, and publicly policy makers expressed concern about the children of Iraq, 'Internally, in the process of policy-making, it was quite a different matter: there is absolutely no evidence of concern about Iraqi children or any other aspect of the suffering in Iraq' (Gordon 2010: 224). Structural failures and corruption in the Iraqi government also contributed to the toll, but the destructive consequences of the sanctions policies were known, understood and willingly accepted by Western leaders and officials. Thus Gordon argues that they could be held liable for genocide: 'dozens of US officials had the necessary intent and knowledge to be found criminally responsible under the Rome statute' which established the International Criminal Court (Gordon 2010: 227).

By 2001, controversy over these effects led Western leaders towards the idea of 'smart' sanctions targeted against the Iraqi elite. However this development was overtaken by al-Qaeda's attacks on the USA on 11 September 2001. President George W. Bush declared a 'war on terror' and intervened in Afghanistan, where the Taliban regime (responsible for massacres of Tajiks and Hazaras in the 1990s) had sheltered al-Qaeda. Although there was no connection between al-Qaeda and Saddam Hussein, Bush mobilized patriotic outrage in the

USA to prepare a war of 'regime change' against Iraq. Under the pretext of stopping Iraq from developing weapons of mass destruction, a US–UK invasion overthrew Saddam in 2003, but without the legally required support of the Security Council (Sands 2005). In controversy about the subsequent civilian death toll (in which estimates range upwards from a minimum 105,000 calculated by Iraq Body Count 2012), the point is often missed that the vast majority of deaths have resulted not directly from the US invasion and insurgency against the occupation, but from its indirect consequences. The USA, notoriously failing to make careful preparations for the aftermath of the invasion, allowed parties based in Iraq's Shia majority to take power and so contributed to a sectarianization of Iraqi politics (Dodge 2005b) with violent consequences.

In the resulting low-level civil war (Fearon 2007, Cordesman and Davies 2008), genocidal violence was initiated by Sunni-based militia, especially by the organization al-Qaeda in Iraq (whose creation ironically was facilitated by the US invasion), and reciprocated by Shia-based militia. The International Crisis Group (2006: i) described 'a dirty war being fought between a small group of insurgents bent on fomenting sectarian strife by killing Shiites and certain government commando units carrying out reprisals against the Sunni Arab community in whose midst the insurgency continues to thrive'. The ICG emphasized the role of elections in 2005 in underscoring 'the newly acquired prominence of religion' that produced these attacks. Roberta Cohen and Francis Deng summarize the situation:

following the bombing of the al-Askari Shia shrine in Samarra in 2006, radical Shia and Sunni militias, frequently tied to political parties, police or army units, began to systematically and purposefully persecute, kill and expel Sunnis and Shias, respectively, from their home areas in order to gain control over those areas. More than 1.5 million people became uprooted within the country in 2006 and 2007 as a result of the sectarian violence while 2 million fled abroad. The brutality used in uprooting people on ethnic and religious grounds was intended to ensure that they would not return to their home areas, and to date it has largely succeeded. According to the International Organization for Migration, at least 40 per cent of those who fled the sectarian violence within the country do not expect to return to their original homes. Of those who fled abroad, who are largely Sunni and Christian, only small numbers have indicated a desire to return to Iraq.

(Cohen and Deng 2009: 21)

Although the epicentre of this violence was conflict between Sunni- and Shia-based militia in Baghdad, Kurds were also targeted together with minorities such as Yezidis, Mandeans, Shabaks and Assyrians (Travis 2010: 532–44), partly because of conflicts between Sunni insurgents and northern Kurdish authorities. Indeed possibly the largest single massacre was a 2007 attack which killed more than 300 Yezidis and wounded more than 700, destroying nearly 400 homes, in the Sinjar district (HRW 2009).

The treatment of these Iraq conflicts in the genocide literature is often very one-sided. As Mahmoud Mamdani (2007: 5) points out,

The similarities between Iraq and Darfur are remarkable. The estimate of the number of civilians killed ... is roughly similar. The killers are mostly paramilitaries, closely linked to the official military, which is said to be their main source of arms. The victims too are by and large identified as members of groups, rather than targeted as individuals. But the violence in the two places is named differently. In Iraq, it is said to be a cycle of insurgency and counter-insurgency; in Darfur, it is called genocide. Why the difference? Who does the naming? Who is being named? What difference does it make?

Mamdani raises these questions in order to question the 'genocide' appropriation of Darfur, but the refusal of a genocide frame for the Iraqi wars is equally striking. Clearly, linkage with the US invasion that provoked the violence after 2003 has proved an obstacle to recognition by scholars and activists who take for granted the essentially anti-genocidal character of the US world role.

Remarkably, even the key role of al-Qaeda in Iraq has not stimulated widespread reflection on the genocidal character of these events. Although the activities of al-Qaeda in Iraq constitute the major example of actual genocidal violence by an al-Qaeda organization, they tend not to play a major role in the tendentious literature on 'genocidal Islamism'. This is perhaps not only because of the US involvement, but also because the victims have been mainly other Muslims rather than Christians or Jews. Instead, a typical polemic argues that 'Political Islam is many things: totalitarian, aggressive, conquering, cocksure about its superiority and destiny to rule, intolerant, bristling with resentment, only tenuously in touch with aspects of reality.' These are the 'hallmark features of past and present eliminationist regimes', and political Islamists make 'persistent threats to practice eliminationist politics' (Goldhagen 2009: 492). Daniel

Goldhagen makes no real distinctions between al-Qaeda, Hamas and the Iranian regime, all of which (in his view) show explicit 'exterminationist and eliminationist discourse' toward Israel and Jews, matched only by the Nazis (2009: 503–5).

Instead, anti-Islamist argument about genocide has increasingly concentrated on the perceived threat to Israel of the Iranian nuclear programme. An activist organization, Genocide Prevention Now, run by genocide writers such as Israel W. Charny, has focused continuously on this issue for a number of years. A resolution adopted by a large majority of members of the International Association of Genocide Scholars (IAGS 2006) saw the prospect that the civil Iranian nuclear programme might lead to the production of nuclear weapons as a 'genocidal risk' to Jews because of the anti-Israeli rhetoric of Iranian President Mahmoud Ahmadinejad. (The IAGS passed no resolution, however, about the actual civilian harm caused by Israeli bombing of Lebanon in the same year, or of Gaza in 2009.) This capture of a major international organization of genocide scholars by Israeli nationalism played a small part in the campaign that led in 2011–12 to demands for US and Israeli military strikes on Iran. The case dramatically illustrates the problem of Western bias in the genocide field, and worse the abuse of 'genocide' discourse to incite military action that would, in all probability, include attacks on civilian groups.

# PART III

# New patterns of genocide

# 8 | *Genocide in political and armed conflict: theoretical issues*

I have criticized the dominant approach of comparative genocide studies for its concentration on a few mega-genocides, compared transhistorically with little attention to their international historical contexts. In the study of contemporary genocide, this approach is represented by concentration on the Rwandan genocide of 1994. The only other widely considered conflict is the crisis in the Darfur region of Sudan since 2002, the main focus of the new genocide activism in the USA and elsewhere in the 2000s. Other cases are considered from time to time, but comparative genocide studies has produced no overall account of the pattern of or trends in genocide in the post-Cold War world. Indeed the key question – have changed conditions of world politics been associated with changes in genocide in the decades since 1989? – has hardly been asked, let alone answered.

Michael Mann (2005: 506–18) is a rare author who has considered current trends in 'ethnic cleansing' and genocide. He argues that there had been a decline in the global North, largely as a result of the success of earlier waves of genocide in creating mono-ethnic states. In the remaining Northern multi-ethnic states, he argues, politics is largely defined by class, region and gender, while continuing ethnic politics, both historic and new, is largely non-violent. This seems broadly valid, although I have argued that the production of mono-ethnic states and ending of genocidal conflicts in Europe was the outcome of the Second World War, and especially of the victory of the Soviet programme to reorder European borders and national patterns. This settlement survived because the Cold War system (reinforced by the post-Cold War embedding of nation-states in the European Union) blocked the revival of conflict. We might add that, where genocidal violence has emerged in the North, especially in former Yugoslavia, it has been more strongly internationally managed than in most other world regions. The Balkan genocidal violence of the 1990s appears to have subsided, and Western regulation combined with the expansion of Western international institutions appear to be key mechanisms of containment.

Mann argues that in the South, in contrast, the diffusion of the 'ideal of the nation-state' and the accompanying conflation of 'demos' and 'ethnos' create new threats of 'cleansing', reinforced by the decline of class politics, the weakening of liberalism and socialism and the rise of fundamentalism (including 'theo-democracy', which Mann suggests could represent a third variant of his perversion-of-democracy thesis, alongside ethnic and class versions). Settler 'cleansing' continues against indigenous peoples, especially in Latin America; 'middlemen ethnicities' like the Chinese in South East Asia remain vulnerable. However Mann (2005: 517) argues that there are few cases in which rival bi-ethnic claims are capable of fuelling the large-scale genocidal developments that occurred in Rwanda and Burundi: 'I can think of no other closely analogous case to Rwanda/Burundi elsewhere in the world. Perhaps this was the last of the world's genocides.' In line with his belief in the possibility of more or less peaceful cleansing, Mann (2005: 525) recommends that 'In some cases it may be better to deflect hatreds onto milder stages of cleansing achieved by mutual negotiation through agreed-upon population and property exchanges, border alterations and so on than to risk further cleansing by force.' Perhaps, he implies, we are entering an era in which 'cleansing' can be managed so as to avoid the most murderous genocide. Morever, genocidal violence may be less globally important: 'Most [ethnopolitical] conflicts occur in some of the poorest, most isolated parts of the world, and so they become only local black holes' (Mann 2005: 518). Similarly Gurr (2000) argues that 'ethnic wars' as such are on the wane.

This discussion provides some pointers to the changed historical situation of genocidal violence in the twenty-first century: the idea that it is chiefly low-level, localized and geopolitically marginal has considerable descriptive validity. However four problems can be identified. First, while Mann is correct to suggest that localized violence is unlikely in most cases to escalate to large-scale, nationally coordinated genocide, serious escalation is difficult to predict: no one foresaw the scale of the Rwandan genocide. Second, genocide is not only the result of 'isolated' conflicts in 'marginal' areas: it may sometimes be a consequence of geopolitically important conflicts, as in Iraq (Chapter 7). Third, even crises in isolated areas can still be on a relatively large scale and can become regionally and globally significant, through political campaigning, media coverage, and UN or regional interventions, as the Darfur and Congolese crises have showed. Fourth, while some crises, like Darfur, remain mainly confined to a particular region of a single state, many if not most conflicts are extensively internationally linked. Even Darfur is a very large area of a large state, and the crisis affects neighbouring Chad. Genocidal violence is often part of complex regional patterns of political conflict and combined civil–international war, as we shall see in the case of the African Great Lakes (Chapter 9).

## Phenomenology, perceptions and terminology

Some problems in identifying contemporary trends reflect mutations in the phenomenology and perceptions of violence. Genocide does not usually appear apart from other types of social conflict: it is often a phenomenon of political and military conflict. There is a widespread consensus that war has changed its appearances: classical interstate war has declined and the majority of contemporary wars are civil wars, albeit usually internationalized. According to Kaldor (1999) we are in an era of 'new wars' combining civil and interstate dimensions, para-militarism, identity politics and ethnic targeting with parasitic, global-ized war economies. Her account emphasizes 'ethnic cleansing' as a novel feature, although this begs questions about historical patterns of 'cleansing' and genocide in what she calls 'old' war. While this novelty is disputed (Kalyvas 2001, Newman 2004), the idea that the appear-ance of conflict has changed is widely shared. Indeed contemporary organized violence is not always straightforwardly recognizable as war: analysts frequently prefer the term 'armed conflict'.

The recognition of genocide has naturally been affected by changing perceptions of war. Even the best-recognized 'genocides' took place in contexts of general war and were often seen at the time as excesses of war. Their analytical recognition depended on simultaneously distin-guishing genocide from and understanding its linkages to war, as well as overcoming denialist ideas representing genocidal violence as 'only' war. The recognition of genocide in earlier periods is facilitated by the fact that the main perpetrators were centralized regimes in major states, even if paramilitaries and social constituencies were also typic-ally involved. These regimes' genocidal policies were identifiable through formal ideological positions and policies of discrimination, and seemed relatively coherent over time, even if 'intentions' evolved in response to changing circumstances. However it has long been recognized that genocidal violence also occurs in localized forms such as 'genocidal massacres' and with non-state as well as state perpetrators, and so its distinction from the wars and political conflicts of which it is a part may be less obvious. In considering these conflicts as wholes, moreover, it may be appropriate to use 'war', 'armed conflict' or 'political conflict' as the dominant frame, and to conceptualize genocidal violence as a component of such conflicts.

The problem of recognizing such genocidal elements is exacerbated by the fact that genocide is often perceived as linked to the 'totalitarian/ radical party' type of regime, the prevalence of which has declined together with twentieth-century types of extreme ideology. Actors' commitments to clear ideological frames, through which relatively coherent anti-group policies are formulated, have become less common. At the same time, the 'sacred evil' quality of the Holocaust has increasingly been extended to genocide in general. Together with the beginnings of international enforcement of anti-genocide law and policy, this has increased the stakes in using the term. The term 'genocide' has become an even more crucial ideological prize, claimed by representatives of victim-groups to elevate their victim experience to the highest level, and used in the new activism. For the opposite reason, states, interstate organizations and NGOs mostly avoid the terminology because of its political and legal baggage. Academic analysts of anti-population violence, armed conflict and war have often followed suit, inventing new terminologies to describe violence that could be considered within the genocide frame. I have already commented (Shaw 2007) on the adoption of the euphemism 'ethnic cleansing' and the proliferation of '-cide' concepts. Another widely used euphemism is 'humanitarian crisis', a term as applicable to natural disasters as to the results of targeted violence against civilians, which serves to create vagueness about the latter.

There have also been more focused attempts to conceptualize violence against civilians in twenty-first-century conflict. The Uppsala Conflict Data Program (UCDP 2009), for example, proposes the concept of 'one-sided violence', defined as '[t]he use of armed force by the government of a state or by a formally organized group against civilians which results in at least 25 deaths in a year'. The low quantitative criterion (like the similar Uppsala criterion for 'armed conflict') usefully recognizes that such force can be used on a much smaller scale than that recognized by the widely used older 1,000-battle-death criterion for a 'war'. Ekaterina Stepanova (2009: 39–40) explains the idea: 'One-sided violence is not armed conflict as such, as it directly and intentionally targets civilians who cannot defend themselves with arms. It is also distinct from battle-related violence that incidentally harms civilians, for example when civilians are caught in crossfire between combatants.' In 'contrast to indiscriminate violence, one-sided violence is a matter of conscious political and strategic choice and not a technologically inseparable part of modern warfare' (Stepanova 2009: 40).

By implication, 'one-sided violence' is selective and political; but since it includes 'massacres, arbitrary killings and terrorist attacks', it covers violence with a range of objectives. Yet this Uppsala idea echoes influential definitions of genocide: the widely cited sociological authorities Frank Chalk and Kurt Jonassohn (1990: 23) actually use the term 'one-sided mass killing' in their definition. Like genocide, 'one-sided violence' captures the crucial distinction of combatant–noncombatant from combatant–combatant violence. Indeed Cohen and Deng (2009: 20) confirm that the Uppsala terminology was adopted as much for reasons of political context as of intellectual coherence, describing 'one-sided violence' as 'a UCDP term that moves away from the highly emotive words "terrorism" and "genocide"'. However the genocide theorists who emphasize one-sidedness are also those who narrow the modalities of genocide to mass murder, and similarly Uppsala *defines* violence in terms of killings, even if it recognizes mass population displacement, for example, as increasingly 'a central and direct goal of armed violence, rather than a side effect' (Stepanova 2009: 42), and a 'devastating transformation' of peoples' lives (Walter Kälin, quoted by Cohen and Deng 2009: 16).

## Extermination and control

More theoretically conceived work in social science also tends to write genocide out of armed conflict, often by simply not referring to it. Even where genocide is recognized conceptually, it tends to be marginalized analytically. For example in Kalyvas' influential *The Logic of Violence in Civil War*, whose 'focus is on violence committed intentionally against noncombatants' (Kalyvas 2006: 5), genocide is mentioned only briefly. Kalyvas recognizes, as I do, that actual civil wars comprise different types of violence, and in distinguishing between different types, he argues that violence 'can be used to *exterminate* a group or to *control* it' (2006: 29, emphasis added), and focuses on the latter type, 'also known as coercive violence'. In particular, Kalyvas concentrates on a particular type of violence, 'civil war violence', which he explains as a strategically rational form based on the need of parties in civil wars to control populations. Although he too restricts his attention to homicidal violence, he claims that his theory also does well for 'violence that stops short of homicide (e.g. arrest, torture, displacement)' (Kalyvas 2006: 7), and recognizes that 'Analytically akin to physical destruction is mass deportation, sometimes referred to as "ethnic cleansing"' (Kalyvas 2006: 26). This analytical kinship lies, presumably, in the fact that forced population removal (of which direct deportation is only one method) is also a means of 'exterminating' a group, in the sense of destroying its physical, social and cultural presence within its historic territory.

More formally, Kalyvas (2006: 30, Table 1.1) also presents a typology of mass political violence, differentiated by whether or not a political actor 'intends to govern the population targeted'. He sees 'state terror' and 'civil war violence' as forms of violence reflecting the intention to govern, and 'genocide and mass deportation' and 'reciprocal extermination' as forms that reflect the lack of this intention. Genocide is also defined as 'unilateral': this captures the defining one-sidedness of the relationship between perpetrator centre and target group, but this seems an insufficient characterization since genocide may be practised by both sides in a conflict. (Presumably this is what Kalyvas intends by 'reciprocal extermination', but this indicates, in my view, a different type of conflict rather than of violence.)

The two ways of distinguishing violence that Kalyvas uses, 'control/ extermination' and 'intention to govern/not' seem similar (he apparently uses them interchangeably) but they should be separated. The intention to govern or not is a more precise formulation of the criterion for genocide: at the point when a collective actor enters into the realm of removing, exterminating or destroying a given population under its control, it abandons any intention of governing it. Control, on the other hand, is a more overriding concern that may be a rationale for either governance or extermination, and is a feature of both governing and exterminating processes. Thus 'intention to govern' helps *define* the difference between non-destructive coercion and genocide; the logic of 'control' helps *explain* the choice between the two.

Kalyvas regards 'civil war violence' as a specific type of coercive rather than exterminatory violence, explicable by the logic of control. What he fails to explain is why violence goes beyond coercion towards extermination: the escalation of violence from one type to another. As Laia Balcells (2010) suggests, discussing Franco's killing of Spanish Republicans after the end of the Spanish Civil War, exterminatory violence may be explained by the same logic of control that is seen in war violence. Yet Kalyvas, while distinguishing 'civil war violence' as a particular type from civil war as such, tends to assimilate most actual violence in civil wars to this type, so occluding the question of exterminatory or genocidal violence. As we saw in Chapter 7, Kalyvas and Sambanis' analysis of Bosnia (2007) examines Serbian 'ethnic cleansing' without reference to its exterminatory meaning for Bosniak, Croat and plural communities, apparently because they explain it as a function of population control in conquered territory. But this is to confuse the question of 'government/not' with the question of dynamics of control.

The overriding reason why we cannot satisfactorily distinguish 'control' from 'extermination' is that *control is an essential aspect of extermination*. Questions of control are apparent at every stage in the movement to and practice of genocidal violence. Movement towards deportation may be, as Kalyvas and Sambanis suggest it was in Bosnia, a function of the failure of more limited coercion to control a population. But deportation does not necessarily end dilemmas of control: a population needs to be controlled during deportation, and a deported population usually still needs to be controlled where it is deported to. If the deport-to location is within the direct control of the deporters, deportation simply gives them new dilemmas of direct control, as for example for the Nazis with Jews in Polish ghettos and the Stalinist regime with the remnants of deported minorities in their regions of exile. If the deport-to location is outside the deporters' control, different issues of control may still arise: Israel managed to remove most Palestinian Arabs from its territory in 1948, but has since spent over six decades attempting to control the responses of the resulting refugee populations. Moreover, since deportation is rarely total, removal of the majority of a population will usually be combined with issues of the control of the remaining minority, as Israel has also found.

Fully murderous policies certainly involve additional issues, but still include questions of control. To starve or kill on any scale requires prior control over the target population, and control during destruction processes. Moreover it is important to *represent* murderous policies as policies of control. For example, deportation may be presented as relocation for work, even where it is taking people to death, since target populations and third parties acquiesce more willingly in policies that they perceive as for control rather than for destruction. Indeed mass murder is usually combined with less destructive measures of control, because the killing of some is often designed as a means of controlling larger populations. For example, Feierstein (2010) argues that the Argentinian dictatorship's 'disappearance' of leftists in the 1980s was a means of reordering the whole national society.

Moreover, as Kalyvas (2006: 26) notes, 'the methods used to achieve compliance and physical destruction may be similar', even if the objectives differ. To operationalize the distinction (govern or destroy) we therefore need to infer perpetrators' objectives from the context in which violence occurs. In the case of victims who have surrendered – whether originally combatants or not – it should be relatively simple to determine genocide. The same should be true of civilians murdered or expelled *after* armed conflict has concluded, and of course *outside* the context of armed conflict. In the case of those killed or expelled *during* civil war, however, the distinction will be less straightforward, requiring detailed knowledge of the relationships between the targets of violence and the armed conflict. Like the distinction made between victims of 'civil war violence' and of 'collateral damage' and victims of intercombatant violence, it is easier to outline in principle than to apply conclusively in practice. Actors may *combine* these types of objective: by having partially destructive and partially governing objectives towards the same population; by using destructive methods against one section of a population in order to reinforce government of a larger population; and of course by having governing objectives at one point in time and destructive objectives at another. Mann (2005: 6–7) notes that escalation towards more destructive ends is a normal feature of genocide: but *de-escalation* is also normal, in the sense that governance may be reasserted once a certain level of destruction has been accomplished. And of course, among the 'members' of a collective actor which has a governing policy, elements or individuals may pursue destructive policies – or vice versa.

All these elements of indeterminacy, arising from common issues of control in both governance and destruction, may complicate the ascription of *either* destructive *or* governing objectives to a given actor in a given situation. When control is to be achieved through selective violence, any perception of a distinct section of the population as an 'enemy' in a fundamental sense (whether 'ethnic', 'political' or other) will offer a rationale to extend civil war violence to genocidal violence. These questions arise, moreover, on the interfaces between all three levels of civil war that Kalyvas (2006) specifies: macro, meso and micro. Introducing the genocide question means re-problematizing the macro level, because genocidal drives often crystallize mainly at that level. However it does not necessarily mean a macro-down approach. Research on the Holocaust has emphasized the interconnections between levels in both directions, for example how Nazi officials managing conquered populations in different jurisdictions 'worked to' Hitler and the central leadership, evolving 'solutions' to racial 'problems' which influenced the regime's overall policies. Gerlach's (2010) work on 'extremely violent societies' shows how central militaries and local movements have interacted to produce mass killing, for example in Indonesia in 1965 and in Bangladesh in 1971. Toal and Dahlman (2011) show how local political elites, controlling municipalities, were central to mass deportation and the consolidation of its results in Bosnia. Historical work, for example on 'genocidal moments' in settler colonization in Australia (Moses 2000) and on the local genocide of Jews by Polish civilians in Jedwabne (Gross 2001), suggests that genocide may arise at the micro level. This perception is very pertinent to the patterns of violence that I discuss later.

## Generalizations about civil war and their relevance to genocide

The larger political science literature on civil wars also skirts the question of genocide. Nevertheless, to the extent that genocide widely arises from armed conflict, the study of the latter may offer useful insights. Political science often suffers from an excessively abstract quantitative approach, which subsumes regional and national peculiarities in conclusions about global trends, which turn out to be misleading. For example, James D. Fearon and David Laitin's much-cited study of civil war onset concluded that 'the prevalence of civil war in the 1990s was *not* due to the end of the Cold War and associated changes in the international system' (2003: 77–8, emphasis in the original). However Kalyvas and Balcells (2010: 418) have shown that this conclusion neglected statistically cancelling regional changes: 'With the end of the Cold War, civil wars shifted away from Asia and Latin America and towards Eurasia, sub-Saharan Africa, and to a lesser degree, the Middle East and North Africa.' Kalyvas and Balcells conclude that 'an exclusive and highly aggregated focus on civil war onset has prevented us from realizing how the end of the Cold War affected civil wars'.

Most of this literature also agrees with Kalyvas (2006) in treating civil wars as categorically distinct from international conflicts. However even he uses examples from the wars following US-led interventions in Afghanistan and Iraq to illustrate civil war violence, which suggests that international and civil wars cannot always be clearly distinguished. Meanwhile, statistical work has emphasized the extent of internationalization of civil wars: Lotta Harbom and Peter Wallensteen (2005) found that one-fifth of civil conflicts between 1946 and 2004 involved external troops, while three-quarters involved other, for example financial and logistical, international (mostly governmental) support. It is not surprising therefore that the literature has seen more challenges to the 'closed polity' approach to civil war, in terms which parallel criticisms of domestic explanations of genocide. So when Kalyvas (2010: xi) argues that recently 'a previously residual type of war turned into the main, if not the only, war actually fought: civil war', he overstates the shift from international conflict.

Moreover much work points towards *transnational* as well as interstate linkages. Myron Weiner (1996) introduced the idea of 'bad neighbourhoods' in which violence and refugee flows both spread across borders. David Carment and Patrick James (1997) argued that the overwhelming majority of recorded episodes of political violence since the Second World War had taken place in regional clusters. David Lake and Donald Rothchild (1998) likewise pointed to the transnationalization of ethnic conflict. In more recent work, Halvard Buhaug and Kristian Gleditsch (2008) show that 'geographic contagion' is an important factor for the risk of violent conflict. In a statistical analysis, they find two dimensions positively correlated with civil war onset: the existence of ethnic groups spanning borders, and the existence of conflict in neighbouring states. Regional democracy and economic integration, in contrast, are associated with less conflict. (To the extent that genocide is located within armed conflict, this disaggregated examination of transnational factors should lead us to question Harff's (2003: 65) conclusion that 'The greater degree to which a country is interdependent with others, the less likely its leaders are to attempt geno-/politicides.') However Buhaug and Gleditsch (2008) dispute the idea that the risk of contagion depends on the degree of exposure to proximate conflicts. They find that contagion is primarily a feature of separatist conflicts, working through transnational ethnic linkages. They find that 'the increase in risk from proximate insurgencies will be the largest among those states that are the most likely to experience civil war in general, as these will have a higher baseline risk at the outset' (2008: 230). Likewise it is probable that the risk of *genocidal* contagion will be greatest where transnational ethnic groups have prior genocidal experiences, as in the African Great Lakes region (Chapter 9). Moreover as Kalyvas and Balcells emphasize, we need to disaggregate regional experiences, since the regional pattern of civil wars has changed. A historical narrative should capture similar differences in regional experiences of genocide.

As I noted in Chapter 2, IR has assumed that global institutions respond to violence, neglecting the role of international relations in producing violence. Too little systematic attention is given to the impacts of the extensive global surveillance – by international organizations, states, NGOs, media, courts, markets and activists – that now routinely affects all practice of war (Shaw 1996, 2005). In particular, little attention has been paid to the role of global international organizations and powers in exacerbating as well as managing conflict and violence.

## Electoral democracy, democratic upheaval and genocidal violence

A key issue that recent sociology and political science highlights is that violent conflicts do not always develop from a pre-existing civil war, but often from political – especially electoral – conflict that has *not* developed into civil war. The comparative genocide paradigm assumes that genocide develops in the domestic politics of authoritarian non-Western states, that democracy is a major part of the local answer to genocide, and that Western democracies provide the basis for a larger global response to localized genocidal violence. Goldhagen promotes a naive version of this case, arguing that promoting democracy will overcome genocide: where it has been tried in Europe, he says, '*it has worked brilliantly*' (2009: 596, Goldhagen's emphasis). Harff offers a more measured version, linking elites with 'exclusionary ideologies' to state failures, and 'failures in states with autocratic regimes' to the incidence of geno-/politicide. But she too is clear that 'partial or full democracies' are much less likely to have genocidal violence. She identifies 'political upheaval', defined as 'an abrupt change in the political community caused by the formation of a state or regime through violent conflict, redrawing of state boundaries, or defeat in international war', as 'the necessary condition for genocide and politicide' (Harff 2003: 62). She does not, however, investigate the possibility that in political upheavals, democratization may enlarge the potential for ethnopolitical mobilization and hence for genocide. These authors have clearly failed to notice the role that democratization played, in creating the conditions for and possibility of consolidating genocide, in the wars in the former Yugoslavia and the low-level civil war in Iraq (Chapter 7), and in Rwanda (Chapter 9).

Mann (2005) offers the fullest general account of linkages of democracy and genocide. He argues that 'cleansing is a hazard of the age of democracy since amid multi-ethnicity the ideal of rule by the people began to intertwine the *demos* with the dominant *ethnos*, generating organic conceptions of the nation and the state that encouraged the cleansing of minorities'. His argument is complex, involving a wide-ranging historical survey that takes in authoritarian as well as democratic regimes, and he suggests that the relationships are often indirect, since 'cleansing' results less from democracy itself than from its perversion. 'Regimes that are actually perpetrating murderous cleansing are never democratic, since that would be a contradiction in terms,' he contends. 'Indeed as escalation proceeds, all perpetrating regimes become less and less democratic.' Yet some relationships are more direct: while 'stabilized institutionalized democracies' are the least likely to commit 'cleansing', he points out that they often have it in their pasts, the more violently where 'settler democracy' took hold. 'The more settlers controlled colonial institutions, the more murderous the cleansing ... It is the most direct relationship I have found between democratic regimes and mass murder' (Mann 2005: 2–9).

The key appears to lie with the stabilization of democracy: Mann (2005: 4) generalizes that 'regimes newly embarked upon democratization are more likely to commit murderous ethnic cleansing than are stable authoritarian regimes'. The political science literature allows little doubt about the acute relevance of this generalization to the post-Cold War world. The period since the 1980s has been a period of unprecedented expansion in the number of states holding free or partially free elections and allowing some democratic freedoms. According to Freedom House (2012), the number of 'electoral democracies' – states combining electoral processes with minimum freedoms – rose from 41 to 60 per cent of states between 1989 and 1995, and has remained around or above that level since. Yet Freedom House classifies only 45 per cent of 192 states as fully 'free'. The Economist Intelligence Unit (2011) breaks this down further, classifying only 15 per cent of 167 states surveyed as 'full democracies' but over 30 per cent as 'flawed democracies'. For Freedom House, over 30 per cent of states are 'partly free'; the EIU classifies over 20 per cent as 'hybrid' (semi-authoritarian) regimes. Freedom House reports around a quarter of states as 'unfree', while the EIU regards over 30 per cent as 'authoritarian'. Despite differences of criteria and classifications, the mixed picture (half or more of all states are *in between* stable democracy and authoritarianism) is clear, as well as the battle-ground between authoritarian rule and democratic change that it defines. Indeed, unaccountable rule is increasingly contested in authoritarian as well as semi-authoritarian states. Since the 1980s, states in all world-regions have seen extensive political upheavals in which popular demands for democracy have been to the fore, and many of these have raised ethnic and national issues. Some democratic transitions have been relatively peaceful, as in most of central Europe, Latin America and South Korea. But many others, not only in the former Soviet and Yugoslav areas but also in Asia, Africa and the Middle East, have involved extensive violence.

This has sometimes resulted from the repression of democratic movements by authoritarian rulers. However it has also centred on electoral processes in states undergoing reform. The discrediting of Cold War authoritarianism (anti-Communist as well as Communist), the example of democratic change in many countries and increasing Western–UN democracy-promotion have all pushed states towards elections, even where substantial democracy remains lacking. Many semi-authoritarian and even authoritarian states now hold them, because electoral environments offer elites controlled citizen participation and enhanced international legitimacy. They also offer opportunities for many types of manipulation, including intimidation, vote-rigging and outright theft. Elections are therefore often flash-points both for elite rivalries and for conflicts between population groups supporting rival parties. Since most societies are plural in terms of ethnicity, nationality, religion, etc., and most parties mobilize along these lines (class divisions often remain, as Mann suggests, politically latent), electoral processes open up possibilities of violent conflict, often turned against ethnopolitically or religiopolitically defined sections of the population. Where elections are not accompanied by entrenched citizen rights and institutional accountability, they can be as dangerous as no elections. Paul Collier (2009: 45) notes 'the dysfunctional results of partial democracy' for reform: 'if democracy means little more than elections, it is damaging to the reform process'. Ursula Daxecker (2012), using original data on electoral manipulation and reputable international election observation missions, shows that not only the presence of election fraud, but also that of international observers, increases the likelihood of post-election violence.

Indeed an increasing body of literature points towards electoral conflicts as prime contexts of political upheaval, civil war and genocidal violence. The complacency about the pacific benefits of democracy for the elimination of genocide shown by writers like Goldhagen and Harff has its counterpart, of course, in the 'democratic peace' theory that democratic states do not go to war with each other. This theory, popular in the 1990s, always begged important questions that are raised by the international-historical perspective advocated in this book. (Rather than 'democracy' explaining 'peace', the democratic and pacific qualities of many states after 1945 were simultaneous products of the particular international configuration that made the states of North America, Western Europe, Japan and Australasia part of a single military-political-economic bloc, within which members did not fight each other and democracy was increasingly normalized: Shaw 2000.) The theory also had the same blind spot that we have already noted: the failure to distinguish between stable democracies and democratizing states undergoing political change. As Edward Mansfield and Jack Snyder (1995: 94) argue, 'promoting democracy may not promote peace because states are especially warprone during the transition to democracy'. In many cases, electoral democracy also sharpens ethnic and national differences: 'Democratization produces nationalism when powerful groups within the nation not only need to harness popular energies to the tasks of war, but they also want to avoid surrendering real political authority to the average citizen' (Snyder 2000: 32). As Snyder (2000: 15–16) summarizes, 'Rocky transitions to democracy often give rise to warlike nationalism and violent ethnic conflict.'

However it is not only in the context of democratization that electoral democracy can be linked to violence. Even elections in established democracies can be dangerous, as Steven Wilkinson's (2006) work on electoral competition and ethnic riots in India, the non-Western world's oldest democracy, shows. 'Since 1950,' he points out, 'the number and gravity of Hindu–Muslim riots in India has grown to alarming proportions, reaching a dangerous peak in 1992–93, when nationwide riots broke out after the destruction of the Babri mosque by Hindu militants in the northern Indian town of Ayodhya. Since 1992 there has been one further major outbreak of rioting, in the western state of Gujerat in 2002, in which an estimated 850 to 2,000 people were murdered' (2006: 12). Altogether there have been approximately 10,000 deaths and 30,000 injuries since 1950: much smaller numbers than in the Partition or the Bengali crisis, but still very substantial. Wilkinson suggests that local electoral incentives lead to violence: 'polarizing events occur disproportionately before elections because politicians use inflammatory issues to consolidate their own community's support or intimidate their ethnic opponents' (2006: 25). On the other hand, state governments halt – and sometimes fail to halt – violence in line with their own electoral interests: 'intra-Hindhu competition for the Muslim vote led to governments ... that were serious about stopping Hindhu-Muslim riots' (2006: 17). In 2002, there were attempts to create riots across India, but only in Gujerat did large-scale deaths occur, because other state governments prevented them (2006: 60). In Gujerat there were extensive 'intercommunal' riots, but elsewhere more limited violence resulted mainly from police breaking up riots (2006: 60n).

Although Donald Horowitz (2001) sees the 'deadly ethnic riot' as a specific form of violence, it can be regarded as a limited and localized form of genocide, often driven by electoral rivalry. While often responses to events, riots are organized by local parties and activist groups linked to them and are often tolerated or promoted by state, regional or even national political leaders. Within relatively stable state structures, this kind of violence remains temporarily and geographic-ally limited. Nevertheless, the same destructive animus towards 'other' groups is mobilized, and the same kinds of violence are shown, as in larger-scale, longer and more extensively murderous episodes in less stable conditions. For example, when violence broke out after the stolen presidential election in Kenya in December 2007, the most publicized single act saw 31 people (from a section of the population presumed to support the 'victorious' president) burnt alive in a church by opposition supporters. The act rightly reminded observers of many similarly horrific episodes during the 1994 Rwandan genocide, even though the structural conditions for a large-scale, nationally coordin-ated campaign of mass murder did not exist. The linkage may have been hyped, but was nevertheless suggestive of the connections that exist between limited, localized violence and large-scale, extremely murderous campaigns.

An important issue in this literature is 'the constructivist insight that individuals have many ethnic and nonethnic identities with which they might identify politically. The challenge for politicians is to ensure that the one that most favours their party is the one that is most salient in the minds of the majority of voters ... in the run-up to an election' (Wilkinson 2006: 4). By the same token, the challenge for activists mobilizing riots and other electoral violence is to stigmatize the 'enemy' through the most lethal combination of identities that can be ascribed to it. In electoral contexts, party and more fundamental social (ethnic, religious, etc.) identities act as proxies for each other, and so both are likely to be utilized in varying combinations according to situations. The challenge for analysis is, as I noted in previous chapters, to avoid essentializing differences between 'ethnic', 'religious' and 'political' groups where identity markers and their functions are often highly fluid.

# 9 | Genocide in twenty-first-century regional and global relations

Genocide at the beginning of the twenty-first century takes a wide range of forms. Much consists of small episodes of genocidal violence (terror, expulsion, killing and rape) that are either relatively contained events, or relatively isolated events of this type within larger political conflicts and wars. Some constitutes large-scale regional or national episodes of violence and mass murder. The discussion in Chapter 8 suggests that the danger of genocide is most acute in situations of state crisis, upheaval and civil war, but it may also erupt through national and sub-national political and socio-economic competition, especially electoral processes. The connection with national political competition means that national context is an important reference point; in the most contained cases, international elements may be limited. However, since most civil wars and even political crises are internationalized, and 'neighbourhood' effects are often strong, contemporary genocide needs to be analysed in world-regional contexts. This chapter therefore presents an overview of genocide since the end of the Cold War, organized primarily in regional terms.

Genocide today also has, almost invariably, an explicit global dimension. Global human rights norms spur victim-groups to seek international redress. Globally promoted democratization means that national and local power needs to be obtained or legitimated by electoral means, which often spur violence. Multi-dimensional global surveillance (political, legal, media and internet, etc.) means that all but the most contained conflicts are played out, to greater and lesser extents, with an eye to political and military interventions by the UN, the West and regional powers. Unlike in the Cold War period, today genocidal crises almost invariably gain attention in, if not always effective responses from, the Security Council. Global interventions are best conceptualized as normal components of contemporary genocidal processes, which may, even if unintentionally, provoke or facilitate as well as halt genocide. As Danny Hoffman (2004: 211–12) generalizes of African conflicts, 'humanitarian' interventions 'are now an integral component ... it is hard to imagine an inter- or intra-state conflict anywhere that is not shaped in part by the presence of peace-keepers, emergency relief or development operations, or by the possibility of such a presence'. Africa is the main field of intervention for the UN and the West, but this is not only an African phenomenon. In this chapter I look at regional patterns of genocide in the context of emerging global relations, starting with Africa.

## Africa: a continental context of genocide?

As the end-of-Cold War violence in the former Yugoslav and Soviet regions has died down, 'Rwanda' and 'Darfur' have overwhelmingly named the problem of contemporary genocide in scholarly as well as public discourse. But these episodes have only been the most visible nadirs of much wider regional patterns of conflict in which genocide has been a recurrent problem. Since the crises in Rwanda and Sudan were themselves connected – Uganda was involved in both, and both Rwanda and Sudan were involved in the second Congo war – it would be possible to talk about a larger central and north-east African region of genocide. Going further, since the second Congo war (dubbed 'Africa's Great War') directly involved states in an arc from Sudan to Namibia, and indirectly involved states in a line from Libya to South Africa, we might be tempted to see almost the whole of Africa as a region of genocidal conflicts.

The involvement of so many states certainly showed the existence of linkages between 'regional' contexts. It reflected a continent-wide deepening of international rivalries between states and ethnicized rivalries between powerholders, subsidized by global economic flows. Violent rivalries were widely exacerbated by the 'movement to multi-party politics' that dates (in Africa as elsewhere) to the end of the 1980s (Bayart 2009). Moreover democracy, according to Jean-François Bayart (2009: xxiv), 'is no more than yet another source of economic rents' for elites, and so exacerbates their conflicts. But armed conflicts, too, are sources of rent: Bayart gives as an example the 'direct financial aid by friendly governments and multilateral institutions, such as the World Bank, the IMF and the European Development Fund, which have all made contributions to the Ugandan war-effort in Rwanda and

Congo-Kinshasa since 1990, in the guise of structural-adjustment aid' (Bayart 2009: xxv). Indeed as he goes on to point out, humanitarian aid, export of primary products and diaspora flows all often fulfil the same functions. It is easy to follow Bayart in seeing both democracy and war as 'strategies of extraversion', through which powerholders take advantage of how Africa is inserted in the global economy and political relations. And to take the argument one step further, genocide might be seen in the intersections of globalization, democracy and war.

However the idea of Africa as a 'continent of genocide' is misleading. A loose continental context does not mean that a truly continental international *system* is generating war and genocide. As Gérard Prunier (2009) shows, 'Africa's Great War' hardly lived up to its name. Except for Rwanda, the states involved lacked either the deep interests or the mobilizing capacities to sustain, let alone deepen, the conflict. The 'continental war' and the nationwide DR Congo civil war fizzled out as most states no longer saw their interests engaged, leaving messy local conflicts in eastern Congo. In general, then, it makes most sense to think of loose, shifting regional-cum-national clusters of conflict, with more or less dense internal connections, inserted in global power relations, which sometimes become interregionally connected.

We should be cautious, moreover, about drawing longer-term conclusions from a single decade. Students of African wars have noted that while in the 1990s, wars in sub-Saharan Africa increased and those in other world regions declined, during the 2000s African wars declined in number, lethality and as a proportion of the world total. Scott Straus (2012: 179) summarizes:

Contemporary wars are typically small-scale, fought on state peripheries and sometimes across multiple states, and involve factionalized insurgents who typically cannot hold significant territory or capture state capitals. Episodes of large-scale mass killing of civilians are also on the decline. That said, other forms of political violence that receive less attention in the academic literature are increasing or persistent. These include electoral violence and violence over access to livelihood resources, such as land and water.

Indeed quantitative measures show that overall levels of 'non-state' war and 'one-sided violence' (in the UCDP sense, which includes genocidal violence) have *not* fallen as war in general has declined (Williams 2011: 4).

## The Great Lakes regional context

In a regional approach to African genocide, the Great Lakes and the Sudan stand out as sites of repeated conflicts over several decades, traceable to decolonization and its aftermath. There is a growing acknowledgement in the literature of the Rwandan genocide of the international-regional context from which it came, and to which it contributed new dynamics. International 'regions' are not geographically given but socially and politically constructed. Sometimes regional contexts are recognized through the formation of regional interstate organizations, as in West and Southern Africa, but in other cases they can only be recognized through informal patterns.

The African Great Lakes have increasingly been identified as a region precisely through political, armed and genocidal conflict over several decades. René Lemarchand (2009: 12, 4) sees Rwanda, Burundi, eastern Congo and southwestern Uganda as the region's core, arguing that 'The theme of exclusion runs like a red skein through the history of the Great Lakes in a multiplicity of crises which, while historically distinct and occurring in distinct national contexts, have set off violent chain reactions.' In these 'interlocking' crises, 'murderous, cross-border tit-for-tat' can be traced back to post-independence conflicts. As we saw in Chapter 5, the 1959–62 so-called Hutu Revolution in Rwanda and the consequential massacres of tens of thousands of Tutsis contributed to a powerful ethnic backlash in Burundi, leading to the 1972 genocide in which over a hundred thousand Hutus were killed. In Congo-Kinshasa, the Kanyarwanda war had seen large-scale massacres of Hutu and Tutsi. In Rwanda, 'the blowback of the Burundi carnage took the form of violent anti-Tutsi pogroms, which paved the way for the rise to power of Juvénal Habyarimana in 1973' (Lemarchand 2009: 16–17), and the consolidation of an exclusivist Hutu regime.

New genocidal crises in Rwanda and Burundi in the early 1990s can be traced fairly directly to this earlier history. Nearly thirty years after the original expulsion and flight of Tutsis from Rwanda, this 'served as the propelling force behind the 1990 invasion of Rwanda by the Rwandan Patriotic Front' (Lemarchand 2009: 12), which was in turn the catalyst for the civil war culminating in the 1994 genocide. In Burundi, 20,000 had been killed in 1988, and 3,000 in 1991 (Lemarchand 1996: xxv). The post-Cold War democratizing trend had major impacts. In Burundi, great hopes were placed on elections in 1993: one Western embassy described them as 'one of the most remarkable transitions to democracy yet seen in Africa'. However 'two years and tens of thousands of dead later, not to mention hundreds of thousands forced into exile' (Lemarchand 1996: xi), 'democracy' had proved the catalyst for violence. Army elements assassinated the country's first Hutu president, Hutus rose in revolt, and the army retaliated by massacring Hutu civilians. These events also contributed to Rwandan Hutus' fears of the RPF. Violence against Banyarwanda, a section of the population closely linked to Tutsis, also broke out in eastern Zaire in 1993.

Thus the 1994 murder of up to 800,000 Rwandan Tutsis and anti-regime Hutus can be seen as the culmination of serial, interlocking crises over four decades in Burundi, Uganda and Zaire as well as Rwanda. Yet it also reflected the new post-Cold War international context. Although Western states and the UN had been involved in earlier phases – Belgium, the departing colonial power, had helped set the disastrous courses of Rwanda, Burundi and Congo-Kinshasa in the early 1960s – the early 1990s saw different international involvement. This included heightened international media and NGO surveillance, highlighting human rights abuses, but it also saw wider state engagement. On the one hand, France (which prized Rwanda as a member of the *Francophonie*) gave military aid to the Rwandan government, which bought arms from Egypt, South Africa and China in preparation for a showdown with the RPF and the Tutsis. On the other, the USA and the Organization of African Unity (OAU, forerunner of the African Union) increasingly recognized the RPF.

In 1992, 'to appease his western backers', Habyarimana formed a power-sharing government with internal opposition parties, and agreed to peace talks with the RPF in Tanzania under US sponsorship. The 1993 Arusha Accords were 'a truly international effort', also involving the OAU, Burundi, Zaire, Senegal, Uganda and Tanzania (Melvern 2000: 52), envisaging a transitional government until free elections within twenty-two months. The Rwandan army was to be divided 60:40 between regime and RPF soldiers, with a 50:50 joint command. Not surprisingly this could be seen as a victory for the RPF, so that regime hardliners felt marginalized and resented the accords, while the RPF did not believe in Habyarimana's sincerity or trust that they would be implemented. However as Linda Melvern (2000: 47) puts it, 'International pressure continued for Rwanda to democratize . . . [but t]he objective of installing a multi-party coalition government, under the trusteeship of Rwanda's external creditors, was considered by some to be impossible.' According to US under-secretary of state Herman Cohen, 'the international community's obsession with getting a peace agreement led to a lack of analysis and a failure to consider whether the Accords could be implemented' (Melvern 2000: 101–2).

As the northern-based ruling circle centred on Agathe Habyarimana was reported to be preparing to exterminate Tutsi, with death squads and militia mobilized, organized killing had already become more evident in 1992 (Melvern 2000: 43–5). A new RPF invasion, breaching the ceasefire agreement, left 1 million people (one-seventh of the population) homeless. Hutu fears of the RPF, fed by real atrocities, were tellingly mobilized by Hutu Power leaders before, during and after the genocide (Straus 2006: 17–40). The extreme Hutu Power station, Radio-Télévision Libre Les Milles Collines, openly called for violence against Tutsis. The UN recognized that there was a serious crisis, but 'American soldiers who died in Somalia were killed two days before the [Security] Council was due to vote on whether or not the UN would provide peacekeepers for Rwanda: it was a grave accident of timing' (Melvern 2000: 79). Melvern (2000: 85) comments on the minimal mission, UNAMIR, that was sent: 'How half-hearted was the UN's effort for Rwanda was plain to see. [Its commander, Canadian General Roméo] Dallaire lacked the barest essentials.'

The crisis reached its head with the assassination of President Habyarimana in early April 1994. Regime forces captured and killed the prime minister, opposition politicians and some Belgian peacekeepers. Amidst the first large massacres of Tutsi civilians, UNAMIR withdrew because of the risk to its soldiers. Belgian, French and Italian troops were sent only to rescue Western expatriates: 'To the extent that states exhibited any sense of duty, it was for their citizens and not for the Rwandans' (Barnett 2002: 173). The UN and its permanent members, notably the USA, regarded the killings as excesses of civil war; it was 25 May before Secretary-General Boutros Boutros-Ghali (who as Egyptian foreign minister had been involved in arms sales to the regime) recognized that 'genocide' had occurred (Barnett 2002: 196). Although on 17 May the UN authorized 5,500 additional troops for UNAMIR, by then over half a million people had been killed; in any case, the troops did not arrive. On 22 June the Security Council finally approved a French invasion of south-west Rwanda: although this saved some Tutsis, it also protected many *génocidaires* from the advancing RPF, whose victory eventually ended the genocide.

However this was not the conclusion of this series of genocidal crises, but the beginning of a major new phase, centred on eastern Zaire. The flight of many Rwandan Hutus, including *génocidaires*, into Zaire after the RPF victory led the new government to invade Zaire to defeat the Hutu Power militia, which had regrouped in internationally run camps. Rwanda's 'destruction of the refugee camps in October 1996, followed by the killings of tens of thousands of civilian refugees by the forces of the Rwandan Patriotic Front' (Lemarchand 2009: 17) has now been confirmed in a detailed UN mapping exercise which concluded that they could have amounted to genocide (UN Office of the High Commissioner for Human Rights 2010: paragraphs 512–18). This invasion provoked the series of Congolese civil wars which continue to the time of writing. In the first (1996–8), Congolese insurgents with Rwandan and Ugandan support overthrew the corrupt long-time president, Sese Seko Mobutu, replacing him with Laurent-Désiré Kabila. Then Kabila rapidly lost support and was faced with a new insurgency, also backed by Rwanda and Uganda, which rapidly turned into the second, 'continental' war (1998–2003), in which many states intervened on both sides in pursuit of their and their elites' security and commercial interests (Prunier 2009). This war was eventually halted due to Western-led political intervention as well as the diminishing interests and capabilities of the parties. It left civil war in the eastern provinces closest to Rwanda, which continued to intervene into the 2010s, when Western governments finally began to distance themselves from the RPF regime.

These wars had a very high overall death toll. The International Rescue Committee (2007) estimated 5.4 million, and although this figure has been questioned, it is not disputed that this was one of the most destructive recent wars. Many deaths were from hunger and disease, but the UN Office of the High Commissioner for Human Rights (2010) showed extensive targeted violence by numerous actors against different population groups. This included sexual violence and slavery, violence against children, and widespread population displacement as well as killing. Genocide had been committed on many sides, resulting from the political aims of Rwanda (to destroy the Hutu population that supported the militias), from the partly economic goals of some Congolese actors (to drive out Congolese 'Tutsi' or Banyuma-lenge, long discriminated against under Mobutu), and from local dynamics such as the emergence of the often-predatory Mai-Mai armed groups. International intervention, involving both the largest UN peacekeeping force in the 2000s and democracy promotion, at best helped to contain violence and at worst exacerbated it, due to failures of peacekeeping (Tull 2009). New conflicts were provoked by electoral competition in a society that had not escaped from civil war at the time of the first relatively free polls in 2006.

Genocide studies has not come to terms with these complex, shifting patterns of violence in the Great Lakes. They do not fit into the conventional idea of neatly demarcated domestic genocides, because they are so clearly internationally and transnationally framed: even the 1994 genocide began with international invasion. Here genocide cannot be defined by mass murder (even Straus 2006 falls into this trap), because forced displacement and sexual violence are such central processes. As Lemarchand (1996: 60–1) argues, Tutsi refugees' experience, 'brutally uprooted from their traditional habitat, haunted by memories of homes destroyed and relatives killed', was a crucial precondition for the 1994 events, but this was hardly unique. From Burundi, Uganda and the Congo, as well as Rwanda, large populations (Hutu and other as well as Tutsi) were displaced in successive rounds of political violence and war. Moreover the social isolation of exile was often the context in which ethnic 'purity' was refined: as Liisa Malkki showed in her seminal study of 1980s refugees, 'the camp had become the most central place in which to imagine a pure Hutu national identity' (Malkki 1989: 3). In turn, the genocidal massacre became the *means* of achieving the categorical purity of the nation (Malkki 1989: 258).

Ethnic identities were socially reconstructed through experiences of violence. Lemarchand (2009: 8) warns against reducing group relations to a conflict between Hutus and Tutsis:

Length of residence, ecology and history have shaped identities in ways that defy simple categorizations such as Hutu and Tutsi ... New coalitions are built for short-term advantage, only to dissolve into warring factions when new options suddenly emerge. In this highly fluid political field, conflict is not reducible to any single identity marker. It is better conceptualized as involving different social boundaries, activated at different points in time, in response to changing political stakes.

Ethnic violences themselves become 'a mode of discourse and a mode of political action' (Lemarchand 1996: xxvi). 'To the extent that [ethnicity] does provide a meaningful point of reference', Lemarchand (2009: 7) writes, its 'contours are constantly shifting, as are the human targets against which it is directed'. Communities seen as allies one day are seen as enemies the next: 'Otherness has less to do with objective identity markers than with the perceived threat posed by one community to another' (Lemarchand 2009: 11). Christopher Taylor (2002: 139) argues that methods of violence too are culturally acquired: 'Much of the violence ... followed a cultural patterning, a structured and structuring logic.' Representations concerning bodily integrity developed through earlier violence, and observed in fieldwork before 1994, 'emerged in the techniques of physical cruelty employed by Hutu extremists during the genocide'.

The multiple, many-sided processes of genocide in the Great Lakes contained, therefore, many moments 'when victims become killers', in the phrase of Mamdani (2002). As studies of 'subaltern' genocide have highlighted (Moses 2008, Robins and Jones 2010), the sense of victim-hood is often a source of new violence. This does not mean, of course, that all genocide has the same dynamic or type of murderousness. In particular, the 1994 Rwandan genocide of Tutsis and anti-regime Hutus and the RPF killings of Hutus during their invasion and subsequent repression followed different logics and were *not* equal parts of a 'double genocide'. Philip Verwimp (2003) tested this thesis in a survey in the Rwandan prefectures of Gitarama, Gikongoro and Kibuye, in which there was evidence of killings of both Hutu and Tutsi by the Hutu Power Interahamwe militia, the Rwandan army (FAR) and the RPF. He reported that one out of three Tutsi households in the pre-genocide sample had all its members exterminated in 1994, very often on the same day and in the same place by the same people; only two of twenty-seven Tutsi households (8.3 per cent) reported no members lost during the genocide. This pattern was not found in the killings of Hutus, 91 per cent of whose households reported not having had members who died violently. Thus the patterns of killing of Tutsi and Hutu were clearly different. Verwimp (2003: 441) concludes that 'the term genocide should be reserved for the killings committed by the Interahamwe and the FAR, and another word should be used for the killings committed by the RPF. That word could be massacre or terror or another word, depending on the event.' This is wrong, since *some* Hutu were certainly targeted for killing – especially after 1994 and in Zaire/DRC – but his research underlines the need to discriminate between different genocidal events.

In understanding this pattern of genocidal crisis, then, we need to grasp a complex set of regional and global political dynamics in which ethnic polarization has been shaped and has led, widely but variably, to genocide. Despite the conflicts' internationalization, exclusion rather than international aggression is the root cause: 'the central pattern which recurs time and time again is one in which ethnic polarization paves the way for political exclusion, exclusion eventually leading to insurrection, insurrection to repression, and repression to massive flows of refugees and internally displaced persons, which in turn become the vectors of further instability' (Lemarchand 2009: 31). Or more simply, 'refugee flows were the crucial factor behind ethnic polarization. Everywhere, refugee-generating violence has produced violence-generating refugee flows' (Lemarchand 2009: 34).

Therefore the fundamental dynamics, through the last half-century, have been largely *transnational*: cross-border as well as internal circulations of displaced people, ethnic resentments, ideologies, activists, and political and military organization. However these have been reinforced in the post-Cold War era by two more largely *international* developments. The first is the increased tendency of regional African states to make military interventions: RPF-run Rwanda is the most dramatic example, but the second Congo war drew in an impressive array of states. This added a new layer of internationalization to the Great Lakes conflicts, dramatically widening their region of impact and spreading genocide. The second is the global intervention of the UN, Western powers, international courts, NGOs and media, attempting to manage and resolve crises and promote political settlements, elections and justice. At its best, this has contained conflict, helped some victims and brought perpetrators to account. However global intervention has also reinforced and deepened conflict, contributing to genocidal outcomes. The failed Arusha Accords and democratization of Rwanda in 1993–4 helped provoke the renewed Rwanda war; the internationally run camps' role as militia bases helped provoke the new Congo war. Moreover Barnett (2002: 166, 167) asks: 'how precisely might the UN be responsible for the genocide?' and answers that 'The failure to prevent harm can be tantamount to causing that harm.' He sees the keys in the UN's bureaucratic culture, the totemic importance of rules, wilful indifference and institutional self-regard. 'While there were risks' of intervention, Barnett argues, 'these risks were always defined in terms of what threatened the UN and not the Rwandans' (2002: 168).

## Darfur and Sudan

The other African location synonymous with genocide in the first decade of the twenty-first century was Darfur in western Sudan. The Rwandan genocide and the global failure to prevent it precipitated a new wave of genocide awareness among Western elites and in civil society. President Clinton's and UN Secretary-General Kofi Annan's apologies in Kigali signified a new 'never again' mantra, whose policy consequence was the Responsibility to Protect agenda which gathered pace in the late 1990s and early 2000s. This emergent new global politics of genocide crystallized with the Darfur crisis of 2003–4 (the Rwanda connection is analysed by Brunk, 2008), when the Sudanese government responded to regional rebellions by the Sudan Liberation Army and the Justice and Equality Movement by backing Arab-based Janjaweed militia to attack Darfur's 'African' populations, principally the Fur, Masalit and Zaghawa. Widespread massacres, summary executions, burnings of towns and villages, rapes and expulsions quickly led to the displacement of hundreds of thousands into improvised camps in Darfur and Chad. As Alex de Waal (2007) summarizes, 'The period of intense conflict in Darfur was from about April 2003 to January 2005. The great majority of massacres were committed between July 2003 and April 2004. Mortality from hunger and disease peaked at the end of 2004 and fell away rapidly after that.' By early 2005, the lowest estimate of civilian deaths from all causes was approaching 200,000.

'Genocide' was an important element in international responses. Although the UN, most Western governments and even NGOs eschewed the term, an anti-genocide coalition in the USA, bridging the Christian right and the liberal left, forced the idea onto the US political agenda (Straus 2005). The State Department commissioned a documentation survey from the Coalition for International Justice (ICJ) that enabled the latter 'to cut through the Gordian knot' of proving genocidal intent, by arguing that a genocide determination was possible on the basis of the provision of the UN Convention that 'deliberately inflicting on the group conditions of life calculated to bring about its physical destruction' constitutes genocide (Hagan and Wright 2011). So in late 2004, US Secretary of State Colin Powell famously reversed his position and declared that genocide was ongoing. The report of the UN Security Council's International Commission of Inquiry on Darfur (2005) avoided this conclusion – it seemed for political reasons – but provided much of the evidence and reasoning to support it (Shaw 2007: 167–70). Thus when the report was referred to the new International Criminal Court, the chief prosecutor surprised many by indicting Sudanese president Omar al-Bashir for genocide.

Practical international responses, in contrast, treated the situation as a civil-war-cum-humanitarian-crisis. Forces sent under UN auspices by the newly founded African Union gave some protection to aid agencies working with the displaced; there was international pressure on the government and rebels to negotiate. This succeeded in diminishing but not in halting the violence, let alone returning the population to its homes. Darfur remained a site of continuing displacement, the result of 'generalized insecurity, much of it banditry and extortion rackets, some of it fighting between militias, as the government-armed tribal militias turn[ed] on one another' (de Waal 2007), but even those who argued that genocide had been committed now argued that it was no longer ongoing (Prendergast 2007). By the late 2000s, international attention had moved elsewhere.

As in the Great Lakes, there was a regional context to the Darfur violence. As explained above (Chapter 6), Sudan in the second half of the twentieth century was a huge, loose state of very late colonial formation, quasi-imperial since northern Arab elites ruled over non-Arab populations in the south and west. Long before the Darfur crisis, the fracture between north and south had produced a protracted civil war in which the state pursued genocidal counter-insurgency strategies. As de Waal (2007: 27–9) recounts, 'Since 1985 if not before, the Sudan government's strategy for pursuing its counter-insurgency has set every major campaign down a particular path. In that year, the then-government ... decided on what was subsequently called the "militia strategy", using militia as "proxies" to attack insurgents and the populations that supported them.' Darfur represented a continuation of this pattern; the main difference was that the changed global, and especially US, politics of genocide led to greater international attention and intervention.

The debate on 'genocide' in Darfur was predictably confused by the counter-insurgency context, as it had been initially in Rwanda. The International Commission of Inquiry on Darfur (2005) rather disingenuously concluded that because the regime was carrying out counter-insurgency, it could not be committing genocide – as though they were mutually exclusive! The sociologist John Hagan and his collaborators, in contrast, argue that racial stereotyping by the Sudanese regime as well as the Janjaweed militia establishes genocidal intent (Hagan and Rymond-Richmond 2009). In an analysis of the ICJ documentation survey, they show that attacks on civilians do not correlate with clashes with insurgents (Hagan and Wright 2011). Alex de Waal, meanwhile, who as we have seen acknowledges repeated genocide in Sudan according to the UN definition, began in 2003–4 by developing an 'alternative genocide' narrative of Darfur. However, believing that genocide recognition advocacy blocked awareness of the civil war roots of violence, and hence of the need for negotiation to end the conflict (de Waal 2009), he moved to 'a narrower interpretation of the genocide convention to apply to projects of racial or ethnic annihilation – which Darfur is not. Racist insults by militiamen simply aren't proof of genocidal intent' (de Waal 2007).

In the present perspective, these arguments about 'race' and 'annihilation' are both misplaced. The campaigns of the Sudanese regime and the militia were genocidal because they aimed at the destruction of large parts of Fur, Masalit and Zaghawa society. Whether these groups were 'racially' categorized, and how far this was the motivation for the attacks, were secondary questions (Shaw 2011). But so is the extent to which social destruction developed into the physical annihilation of these groups. De Waal was correct, however, to point to the civil war context, and to suggest that political solutions could de-escalate violence. Despite Powell's labelling and the efforts of the genocide lobby, there was little likelihood of an international military intervention that would have defeated the genocidal regime. Moreover, unlike in Rwanda, there was no prospect of military victory by the insurgents. Global policy was caught between humanitarian and political interventions that required relationships with the Sudanese government, and legal intervention that charged its leader with genocide. These contradictions were heightened when the wider Sudanese context returned to the global agenda, as deep tensions between north and south reignited in the late 2000s. This led to the UN managing a more or less peaceful break-up of Sudan, with independence for South Sudan in 2011, in turn swiftly followed by renewed insurgency and genocidal repression in the Nuba mountains that remained in Sudan.

## Wider genocidal violence in north-east and East Africa

International debate about north-east Africa has focused on Sudan, whose government has been condemned by the USA and which allies with China, while gaining considerable protection from other OAU states. However civil war has also produced extensive patterns of violence against civilians elsewhere in north-east Africa, including by Western-backed governments. In Ethiopia, the downfall of the Dergue (Chapter 6), in 1991, led to the rise to power of the pro-Western Meles Zenawi in 1995 under a 'democratic' regime, while Eritrea became independent. However, the 1998–2000 border war between Ethiopia and Eritrea, which caused an estimated hundred thousand dead and a million refugees, was also accompanied by mass deportations of Eritreans by Ethiopia and of Ethiopians by Eritrea. In Ethiopia, opponents were massacred in protests after disputed elections in 2005, while Eritrea had become notorious for its repressive rule. Following a new insurgency in 2007, Somalis in the Ogaden region of Ethiopia were subjected to a 'brutal counter-insurgency campaign': the military 'deliberately and repeatedly attacked civilian populations', forcibly displacing entire communities, ordering villagers to leave or witness their houses being burnt down (HRW 2008b). Extensive killings, torture and rape are reported, targeting the Ogadeeni clan perceived to support the insurgents. The Ethiopian government is also pursuing highly coercive 'development' policies in Gambella, the Lower Omo Valley and other regions (HRW 2012a, 2012b), involving extensive forced displacement of people, 'villagization' reminiscent of the Dergue, and disruption of livelihoods and food supply which threaten the existence of indigenous peoples.

Further south, Kenya is the other main pro-Western state in the region, long regarded as a regional bulwark, and indeed a major base for international organizations operating in both the Great Lakes and north-east Africa. However, as Human Rights Watch (HRW 2011b: 5) points out, 'Post-independence Kenya's reputation across the globe as relatively stable and peaceful is not supported by the country's political history.' Ethnic Somalis and Somali refugees have long been targets of repression and violence, including genocidal massacres in the 1980s. Competition between Kenyan elites for political power has been entwined with competition between ethnic groups for land, becoming increasingly deadly with democratization: analysts have noted the links of vigilantism to politics (Anderson 2002). Violence has had a long history in post- as well as pre-independence Kenyan politics and built up as the 30 December 2007 presidential election loomed. The subsequent escalation, in which over a thousand people died and 600,000 were displaced, was more than a response to a stolen vote. At the beginning of 2008, militia linked to the thwarted opposition parties and their ethnic bases targeted Kikuyu and other presumed supporters of the 'victorious' president in the Rift Valley, driving them from their homes. In response, police and pro-government militia carried out extensive violence against opposition supporters, especially in Nairobi's slums. As noted in Chapter 8, the burning of 31 people in a church recalled the methodology of the Rwandan genocide, drawing attention to the essentially genocidal nature of the violence. Militia closely linked to regional and national politicians took the opportunity to partially destroy particular politico-ethnic sections of the population within significant parts of the country. It is important to note the malleability of political and ethnic identities in the Kenyan context as well as in the Great Lakes: Gabrielle Lynch (2011) shows that the key Kalenjin group is a recent construct, which did not exist before the mid twentieth century. It is not possible to say that people were targeted simply for either 'ethnic' or 'political' reasons, when these two types of identification were so intertwined and changeable.

After 2008, Kenya became the focus of a strong international political and legal intervention. A UN team led by the ubiquitous former Secretary-General, Kofi Annan, cajoled the Kenyan parties into a power-sharing agreement and defused the short-term potential for violence. Four major national politicians were indicted by the International Criminal Court in 2012 for their role. Within Kenya, however, impunity has remained intact (Kenya Human Rights Commission 2011), creating an impression that the local leaders will escape punishment. Indeed Uhuru Kenyatta, one of those indicted by the ICC, was elected president in 2013. Most of those displaced in 2008 have not returned to their homes.

Throughout the 2000s the Kenyan and Ethiopian militaries have also been important actors in Somalia, where state failure has led to extensive war over two decades, with huge civilian harm. Accounts emphasize indiscriminate targeting, cruelty and varied 'abuses', rather than strategies of the Sudanese type, by numerous different Somali armed groups as well as by would-be governments and international interveners (HRW 2008a, HRW 2011a). Within this pattern of civil war violence, people suffered what Catherine L. Besteman (2007), describing the Jubba Valley, calls 'genocidal acts', as well as being 'caught in the crossfire' and becoming 'economic refugees'. She argues that

the local expressions of violence make it difficult to disentangle the reasons that caused Jubba Valley villagers to flee and feel unable ever to return. Genocide, political persecution, a civil war that caught civilians in the crossfire, and economic distress all describe what happened in the Jubba Valley after 1991. Militias massacred groups of villagers who defied their efforts to exert control in the valley. Several villages, for example, lost all their men in such acts. Militias forcibly divorced young Somali Bantu women from their husbands in order to abduct them into involuntary marriages, specifically in order to ensure their children (whose identities follow the patrilineage) were members of the militia clans rather than Somali Bantus.

Whereas in Sudan and Ethiopia it is easy to identify the role of the central state alongside paramilitaries, in Somalia, 'no state authority orchestrated the violence, which was carried out by many different militias fighting for their own particular interests'. Besteman concludes that 'it is difficult to ascribe genocidal intent to a specific authority. What happened in the Jubba Valley illustrates the difficulties in clearly distinguishing genocide from other forms of violence.'

## West Africa

In West Africa, where the post-independence period saw the horrors of the Biafra conflict, the Nigerian federal state, fuelled by oil revenues, has more or less held together in subsequent decades. However, localized anti-population violence that prevailed under unstable military rule has accentuated with democratization, while in neighbouring Liberia, Sierra Leone and Côte d'Ivoire, messy civil wars have seen extensive patterns of violence against civilians, followed in Côte d'Ivoire by post-election violence. In all three cases, cross-border movements of fighters, populations and refugees have been highly significant for the development of conflict and violence, in ways similar to the Great Lakes. Regional organizations centred on Nigeria, together with the UN and the West, have played crucial roles in managing conflict (Adebajo 2002a, 2002b).

The recent series of West African civil wars began in Liberia in 1989, after insurgents led by Charles Taylor, partly trained by Libya, invaded from Côte d'Ivoire. Taylor's forces targeted civilians of the Krahn tribe to which President Samuel Doe belonged, and were responsible for mass rape during their assault on the capital, Monrovia, while a brutal counter-insurgency targeted peoples believed to support Taylor. The war, leading to the involvement of the Economic Community of West African States (ECOWAS) (Harris 2011), ended in 1996, and Taylor took power after an election in 1997. A second civil war broke out in 1999 when opponents attacked from neighbouring Guinea; Taylor's forces attacked both Guinea and Sierra Leone, leading to a complex war in the latter country. In 2003, under UN auspices, ECOWAS sent Nigerian troops into Liberia, and Taylor was indicted for war crimes.

In Sierra Leone, the Taylor-supported Revolutionary United Front (RUF) insurgency began in 1991, quickly taking over large parts of the east and south, where alluvial diamonds were extracted. However the army together with Executive Outcomes, a South Africa-based private military company, restored some governmental control, leading to a peace accord in 1996. Yet in 1997 a military coup brought to power officers who collaborated with the RUF to capture the capital, Freetown, with a wave of looting, rape and murder. After this, ECOMOG (Economic Community of West African States Monitoring Group) forces intervened, and under global pressure the 1999 Lomé Peace Accord gave Foday Sankoh, the RUF leader, the vice-presidency and control of Sierra Leone's diamond mines in return for a UN-supervised disarmament process. However the RUF failed to comply and in 2000 was advancing on Freetown; intervention by the former colonial power, Britain, finally defeated the RUF. The Special Court for Sierra Leone has convicted both RUF leaders (although Sankoh died awaiting trial) and (in 2012) Taylor himself.

The Liberian and Sierra Leone civil wars became bywords for brutality against civilians: in Liberia, 'Taylor's bid precipitated a descent into a seven-year civil war characterized by total state collapse and a relentless campaign of sadistic, wanton violence' (Cain 1999).

Atrocities became part of daily life, with both sides kidnapping, conscripting, robbing and raping on a wide scale: as in the DR Congo, there was a 'prevalence of war-related sexual violence' (Amowitz et al. 2002).

Men, women and children, probably numbering in the thousands [were abducted] for use as combatants, forced laborers, or sexual slaves. Women have been actively targeted through sexual violence, including rape and sexual slavery. Children have been targets of killings and violence and are forcibly recruited as soldiers. In addition to various forms of physical abuse, innumerable Sierra Leoneans suffer from psychological trauma due to intentionally cruel methods of inflicting harm against these individuals and their communities. (HRW 1998)

The RUF had an 'essentially mercenary character': it was 'organized mass delinquency ... mainly aimed at criminal expropriation' (Gberie 2005: 8). Despite this, Paul Richards (1998) argues that the RUF was not simply 'barbaric'. Its brutal tactics reflected strategic goals: chopping off hands prevented fighters from returning home to help with the harvest or from participating in elections. Similarly, Hoffman (2004: 211) argues, based on ethnographic research with the *kamajor* militia in the Mano River region, that humanitarian interventions have altered militia behaviour, leading 'combatants to employ atrocities against civilians increasingly as a military tactic, making the bodies and futures of non-combatants a crucial terrain of the frontline'. This meant that 'a campaign that targeted civilians rather than the opposing military, which included the displacement of the civilian populace and if necessary the mutilation of non-combatants – could be the only strategy guaranteed to produce the necessary international aid to secure combatants a post-conflict future. In an age of dramatic violence, only more dramatic violence would do.' (2004: 219)

In Côte d'Ivoire, too, civil war broke out in 2002, between the government of Laurent Gbagbo and an opposition centred in the north, involving Liberian and Sierra Leonean fighters. Its first phase saw 'limited direct fighting between the nominal warring parties, but serious and sometimes systematic abuses against civilians' (HRW 2003b). Later, 'The various rebel factions targeted some women for abuse because of their ethnicity or perceived pro-government affiliation, often because their husband, father or another male relative worked for the state. Many others have been targeted for sexual assault for no apparent reason' (HRW 2007). Straus (2011) argues that there were two central dynamics of violence: urban repressive violence on the part of pro-Gbagbo state and non-state forces in order to intimidate any real or potential political opposition, and rural violence, primarily between 'native' and 'non-native' communities in the west of the country. In addition to targeting demonstrators, the first often had an identity component: northern Muslim Ivoirians and other West African nationals were targeted. In the second, less well-documented case, violence appeared to follow a spiral pattern of reprisal killing, sometimes on a large scale, as civilians of one group were collectively punished for the violence of their co-ethnics. Both pro-Gbagbo and opposition groups were implicated. (The mobilization of restrictive notions of citizenship to designate sections of the population non-national, evident in Côte d'Ivoire, has been noted as a widespread tactic of African regimes to block electoral opposition: Whittaker 2005.) The continuing political stalemate culminated in the election of 2010, when Gbagbo was finally defeated by Alassane Ouattara but refused to concede power despite pressure from ECOWAS, the UN and the West. He was ousted only after a revival of the civil war and military intervention by France, the former colonial power. In this situation, widespread violence against civilians developed:

The post-election crisis then evolved from a targeted campaign of violence by Gbagbo forces to an armed conflict in which armed forces from both sides committed grave crimes. Six months later, at least 3,000 civilians were killed and more than 150 women were raped in a conflict that was often waged along political, ethnic, and religious lines. (HRW 2011c)

These analyses suggest that, in the words of Sierra Leone scholar Yusuf Bangura (cited in Hoffman 2004: 211), 'violence does not have only one logic, but several'. Civilian violations of many kinds were elements of all three West African civil wars, following distinct but entwined strategic and ethno-political rationales. These were often implemented in apparently erratic ways according to the whims of local commanders and groups of armed men, even of individual 'fighters', adding to the 'wanton' and 'barbaric' appearances of violence. None of these wars were 'genocides' with coherent central campaigns, but all of them were genocidal in the sense that various segments of the population – defined in shifting ethnic and political terms – were regarded at times as enemies and targeted strategically or tactically with destructive violence, using many different methods.

Nigeria's role in these wars was that of regional power, dominating ECOWAS and ECOMOG. However, deep political divisions along shifting ethnic and religious lines have continued to mark Nigeria's own society. Partly because of memories of destructive secessionist war, elites have mostly preferred to compete less violently for the proceeds of power, and there has been no nationwide armed conflict. Nevertheless, violent intersections of ethnicity and religion with politics, which marked Nigeria even before the territory's unification by the British in the early twentieth century (Falola 1998) and have continuously erupted since independence, have been accentuated since the return of 'democracy' in 1999. Fourchard (2007) notes the widespread association of the civil regime with the development of private armed organizations and an upsurge of violent religious, interethnic and communal conflicts. Posing the question 'Are these violences marginal or central to the functioning of the political game in Nigeria?', he answers that political interests are increasingly harnessing violence in pressing their demands. As Toyin Falola (2009: 5) puts it, 'the 1980s and 1990s were known for riots and outright political violence'.

One expression of this is the increasing violence of election cycles. Ebere Onwudiwe and Chloe Berwind-Dart (2011: 4) describe how, in 2003, 'intraparty clashes, political assassinations, and community unrest in already volatile areas such as Nigeria's oil-producing Niger Delta, characterized [the] elections. This cycle also marked the unchecked proliferation of another worrisome development: the hiring and arming of militias to serve narrow political ends. One concerned nongovernmental organization (NGO) monitoring the elections characterized them as "a low intensity armed struggle".' Onwudiwe and Berwind-Dart (2011: 7) identify four types of electoral violence: intraparty feuding, interparty clashes, electoral events violence, and communal unrest – 'election tensions tend to exacerbate preexisting community conflicts'. Politicians ally with armed groups: as Human Rights Watch (HRW 2008d) notes of oil-rich Rivers state, 'gangs have grown powerful and violent through ties to influential politicians and because of the impunity long accorded them by political leaders and law enforcement agencies ... Rivers' wealth has not just been squandered; it has also been put to work sponsoring violence and insecurity on behalf of ruling party politicians.' In electoral crises, gangs often go to work attacking population groups seen as supporting political enemies.

Since ethnic and political divisions are partly calibrated in religious terms, Falola (2009: 5) claims that since 1980, 'The scale of religious violence is greater, with many outbreaks ending in hundreds of deaths and massive destruction.' In the late 2000s, the Islamist group Boko Haram launched a campaign of terror massacres against Christians, which provoked retaliatory violence. Often described as more or less spontaneous 'communal violence', the repeated massacres of recent years, targeted according to entwined political, religious and ethnic logics, always contain significant elements of organization by armed groups, often linked to larger political interests. They are best seen as serial genocidal moments in the larger patterns of often violent conflict that affect Nigeria.

## Southern Africa

This survey risks becoming repetitive, because similar elements are to be found in the patterns of violence in different African regions. However what the discussion so far has shown is that the overall character of the pattern is distinct in each regional context, because of the different characters of the international relations as well as of the societies involved. These differences are partly to do with differences in the state units: in the Great Lakes, the giant Congolese state has decayed and fractured while small Rwanda has been relatively strong and centralized; in north-east Africa, Sudan is much stronger than the DR Congo but subject to enormous centrifugal pressures, as is Ethiopia, while Somalia has collapsed; in West Africa, Nigeria projects considerable international power while subject to huge internal tensions, while several smaller states have fractured. Partly the differences are to do with how states and other political and armed actors relate in complex national and regional contexts. All relate across borders, while populations – not only when victims of violence – move in ways which feed distinct regional patterns. Finally, differences are to do with how regional and global international relations intersect: varied linkages (in the case of Sudan, conflict) of states with the West, and varied scopes for and UN–Western interest in interventions. These relations affect, of course, the character of the state units and the scope for genocidal violence: major regional bulwarks of Western interests, such as Nigeria, have held together better than other states; and genocidal violence in them has been contained, including by UN and Western interventions, as in Kenya.

In this light, we can also note contrasting experiences of genocidal violence in southern Africa. In South Africa, the 1990–4 transition saw violence reflecting rivalries fostered during the apartheid era, particularly between supporters of the Zulu-based Inkatha Freedom Party and the African National Congress. A potent mix of political and ethnic targeting produced considerable harm, before being contained in the political settlement which has held, despite tensions, since 1994. In Zimbabwe, the independence war stimulated conflict between the dominant ZANU-PF party of Robert Mugabe and opposing parties, culminating in the Matabeleland campaign of 1985–6 in which Mugabe's forces are believed to have caused many thousands of deaths among the Ndbele. The renewed democratic opposition of the 2000s provoked Mugabe's government to new violence, through a combination of party militia and state forces, against many sections of the population presumed to support the Movement for Democratic Change. In 2005, Operation Murambatsvina cleared 700,000 poor people from their homes in Zimbabwe's urban areas, probably in order to break up the potential for revolt (HRW 2005d). Yet Mugabe's government, ostracized by the West, received considerable cover from South Africa and the Southern African Development Community (SADC).

In Angola, following the independence war of the 1960s and 1970s, a long civil war lasted until 1992, with Cold War alliances sustaining the MPLA government and UNITA rebels. Despite the removal of this support, war resumed in the late 1990s, after UNITA lost elections, with new massacres and other atrocities. Both sides displaced large numbers of civilians, UNITA allegedly to increase the pressure on the government arising from supporting displaced people (another instance of Hoffman's point that humanitarianism can affect strategies), the government in order to deprive UNITA of populations from which they could derive material support (Norwegian Refugee Council/Global IDP Project 2002).

## North Africa and the Middle East

North Africa and the Middle East remained for the most part, even after the Cold War, regions of relatively stable authoritarian regimes, many of which were allied to the USA, while Iran, Syria and (between 1990 and 2003) Iraq were in conflict with the West. Monarchical and republican dynasties alike rested on ethnically and religiously defined segments of their populations, routinely using violence to reinforce rule. Yet while minorities and even majorities were repressed, they were rarely targeted for destruction. Iraq was the main exception to this picture, where extensive genocidal violence was committed under Saddam Hussein (Chapter 6) and in the aftermath of the US invasion (Chapter 7). Another was Algeria, where the army aborted electoral democracy in 1991, as the Front Islamique du Salut looked likely to win elections. In response to this suppression, the insurgency of the Groupe Islamique Armé used widespread violence against civilians to demoralize, intimidate and subjugate its opponents, against women who refused to wear veils, and as retaliation upon communities for having withdrawn support. In a murky war (Martínez 2000), state forces were also implicated in atrocities. In Chad, too, substantial atrocities against civilians have been regularly committed, principally by government forces during counter-insurgency. In the 2000s, the Islamist network al-Qaeda was responsible for sporadically targeting Shia Muslims, Christians and Westerners in a number of countries, notoriously playing a key role in stimulating the genocidal civil violence in Iraq (Chapter 7).

Israel, established through the wholesale expulsion of Palestinian Arabs in 1948, plays a key role in the Middle Eastern international system and the global system of US power. Opposition to it helps legitimate authoritarian regimes across the Arab and Muslim world, and is sometimes expressed (for example by the Iranian president, Mahmoud Ahmadinejad) in Holocaust-denying terms. Israel itself has gradually extended the exclusion of Arabs from parts of the West Bank territories that it occupies illegally as a result of the 1967 war, slowly pushing out Palestinian residents in a process that continues to the present day. Palestinian armed resistance, especially indiscriminate suicide-bomb and rocket attacks by Hizbollah (from Lebanon), Hamas (from Gaza) and others on Israeli civilians, has provided a 'security' rationale for Israeli measures against Palestinians. Some of these measures, for example towards the population of Gaza after it elected Hamas, have included an element of collective punishment, and the Israeli wars on Hizbollah in Lebanon in 2006 and on Hamas in Gaza in 2009 have accentuated this element. In Gaza, the targeting of the civilian police suggested a genocidal element (some might call it 'politicide') in the Israeli campaign.

The situation in the Middle East and North Africa changed rapidly after 2009. Popular movements for political change and democracy (similar to those in other regions around 1990) emerged across countries with all types of regimes and international affiliations. These began with the challenge of the Green movement to the clerical dictatorship in Iran, after the stolen presidential election of 2009. Brutal repression finally succeeded in suppressing the opposition by late 2010. Around the same time, the first of the Arab revolts began to develop in Tunisia, quickly leading to the overthrow of the dictatorship, followed by the overthrow of the thirty-year-old Mubarak regime in Egypt. Movements in many other countries, notably pro-Western monarchies such as Saudi Arabia, Morocco, Jordan and Bahrain, were met with a mixture of repression and limited reforms (although in Bahrain, Saudi troops aided the regime in harshly suppressing the protest movement). Even where democracy movements initially succeeded, subsequent polarization produced or threatened violence: in Egypt, for example, in military repression and radical Islamists' hostility to Coptic Christians.

In three countries, however, extensive violence followed initially peaceful anti-regime, pro-democracy protests in early 2011. In Yemen, where violence already characterized political life, a new escalation accompanied the complex fallout from the campaign to force a long-standing US-allied dictator to resign. In Libya, where Muammar Gaddafi had long ruled through brutal repression (including a massacre of over a thousand prisoners at Abu Salim in 1996), protestors were almost immediately fired on. With the suppression of protest, many oppositionists moved to armed struggle, quickly liberating eastern parts of the country. During an eight-month civil war, the regime targeted rebel-held towns with indiscriminate bombardments, and in several cases mass murders of rebel supporters occurred. The success of the uprising was secured only with the aid of NATO bombardment authorized by the UN, with the support of the Arab League (Gaddafi was isolated among Arab regimes). It led, in turn, to allegations of new violence by victorious militias against minorities, migrant workers and religious opponents. An international effect of this war was the return to neighbouring Mali of Tuareg fighters who had fought on Gaddafi's side, contributing to a new crisis there in 2012; in response, mobs in the capital, Bamako, attacked Tuaregs and their homes.

In Syria, the long-lived Assad regime responded to peaceful protests with similar repression to Gaddafi's, bombarding the populations of opposition-supporting towns and killing some opposition supporters. However civil war was slower to develop, and international military intervention was blocked by Syria's long-time alliance with Russia, as well as by Western reluctance. The Red Cross finally designated the conflict a civil war in mid 2012 after fifteen months of protest, regime violence, and the gradual mobilization of armed opposition with regional support from Saudi Arabia and Qatar. Three reported elements of the conflict raise genocide issues: indiscriminate assaults, massacres and executions by pro-regime militias in urban areas (these began before armed opposition had significantly developed); general rounding-up of the entire male population in some regime-conquered opposition towns; and violence against opposition-supporting, Sunni-majority villages surrounded by pro-regime Alawite villages. There have also been allegations of war crimes against some opposition fighters, and the outcome is uncertain at the time of writing.

## Indonesia and East Timor

Indonesia was also a major arena of genocidal violence in the 1990s and early 2000s. This populous, far-flung quasi-imperial state was the site of anti-Communist genocide in 1965 and it crushed East Timor after its annexation in 1975 (Chapter 6). Timothy Lindsey (2011) sees the New Order rule of General Suharto (president from 1967 to 1998) as a lawless, mafia state, which created the conditions for violence; Kai Thaler (2012) sees it as a 'genocidal regime', emphasizing the links between the two episodes. With the end of the Cold War, strains on Suharto's rule increased and US support began to be withdrawn. As in the Soviet and Yugoslav crises (Chapter 7), democratic movements in the Javanese core (which included violence against ethnic Chinese) combined with centrifugal tendencies in peripheral provinces which produced widespread political violence, some of it genocidal. The crisis in East Timor became an international issue because Indonesian rule was illegitimate; however there were also crises in Aceh, Maluku, West Kalimantan, West Papua and elsewhere.

Despite the often-genocidal counter-insurgency after 1975, East Timor remained largely unsubordinated to Indonesia. In 1991 protestors in the territory's capital, Dili, were massacred by the military (HRW 1991b), leading to new international support for East Timorese independence. The fall of Suharto in 1998 led to Indonesian agreement to a UN-sponsored referendum in East Timor, but the military organized militias to prevent the Timorese from voting for secession (Tanter et al. 2006). These militias were responsible for extensive violence in 1998–9: two-thirds of the population were displaced, with hundreds of thousands fleeing or forced into Indonesian West Timor, and there were many killings, often under the gaze of helpless UN civilian staff (HRW 2000, CAVR (Commission for Reception, Truth and Reconciliation in East Timor) 2005). However after an Australian-led peace-keeeping force was sent, a large majority of Timorese voted for independence; this unleashed a further wave of attacks, but in the end Indonesia withdrew.

Elsewhere, Indonesia faced secessionist conflicts which failed to attract serious global attention. In Aceh, a region of Sumatra with a history of rebellion under Dutch rule and in the early independence period, by the 1980s a new armed secessionist movement, Gerakan Aceh Merdeka (GAM, the Free Aceh Movement), posed a serious challenge. The Indonesian military responded with summary executions, disappearances, torture and arbitrary arrest (HRW 1991a). Throughout the 1990s, opposition in Aceh was met with 'ferocious and indiscriminate force, killing more than a thousand civilians' (HRW 1999a). Following the fall of Suharto, protest grew, but the army responded by massacring protestors in May 1999 (HRW 1999b). GAM believed it could emulate the Timorese in seceding from Indonesia, but despite the transition to 'democracy', the Indonesian security forces continued to carry out 'extrajudicial executions, "disappearances", torture, and collective punishment' against the population (HRW 2002b).

Elsewhere much violence of the post-1998 transition had a many-sided, 'communal' character, and has often been seen as 'horizontal conflict' (Farid 2011). The largest-scale case occurred in Malaku province and North Malaku on Halmahera island in 1999–2000, when thousands were killed and hundreds of thousands were displaced in conflict between Makians and Kaos. Chris Wilson (2011) argues that this was initially about control of territory and government partiality, but escalated to religiously defined violence, exploited by political actors. Militia carried out violence against women and children, burnt down large numbers of houses and aimed at 'ethnic cleansing'. Similar violence occurred in West Kalimantan even before the fall of Suharto, in 1996–7 (HRW 1997); in Poso, Central Sulawesi, over four years from 1998 (HRW 2002c); and between Dayaks and Madurese in Central Kalimantan in 2001 (HRW 2001).

As we have seen, Gerlach (2010: 17–92) regards Indonesia as an example of an 'extremely violent society' and analyses the roles of sections of society in 'coalition' with military elements in generating the 1965 violence. Although sometimes seen as 'spontaneous communal riots', the recent episodes of violence lasted many months and involved significant elements of organization. Often initially using existing communal or tribal structures, they generally produced local militias that committed much of the violence. Although not simply movements for political power, they were influenced by local politicians, and affected by the larger crisis of the Suharto state and the transition to a democratic regime. As in all cases of localized non-state violence, the question of why central state institutions largely failed to control violence is relevant. The abatement of violence in the later 2000s suggests that the macro-context of Indonesian political change was a major factor in these conflicts.

## South and West Asia

We have seen that South Asia was an arena of major genocidal violence during the independence period (1946–8) and the war of Bengali secession (1971). In recent decades – although India and Sri Lanka have maintained democratic institutions, Pakistan has seen a fragile consolidation of electoral democracy, and even Burma (Myanmar) has begun moves towards democratization – political violence has remained a constant in all countries and has frequently had locally or regionally genocidal dimensions.

India has not seen nationwide violence since the 1940s, but anti-population violence remains endemic in 'communal' and 'electoral' contexts (Chapter 8) and in secessionist conflicts in Kashmir and

Nagaland. It frequently recurs too against Dalits or 'untouchables', who are extensively discriminated against, with 'caste atrocities' and massacres committed by local militias organized by upper-class landlords in Bihar (HRW 2008e). In Pakistan, violence is even more endemic in the society and political system, which has seen frequent coups, brutal suppression of opposition and insurgency, a high level of violence in electoral politics, and extensive violence against women. In Karachi in the 1990s, for example, the Muttahida Quami Movement (MQM) based on Mojahirs (the descendants of those who fled India in 1947) mobilized young men to carry out systematic violence over many years: 'virtually all ethnic and political groups were the targets of political murders, kidnappings and high levels of criminality involving Mojahirs', and 'during the burning and looting of shops during riots, members of rival ethnic groups were shot indiscriminately' (Khan 2010: 6, 70). As with much localized violence, MQM's was not directed at wholesale destruction of 'enemy' communities, but was opportunistically and episodically genocidal, a part of 'normal' political competition and even group economic advancement. It indicates how low-level destructive violence can be institutionalized in the politics of a large city or region.

Burma and Sri Lanka, in contrast, have seen more extensive, if intermittent, genocidal violence linked to counter-insurgencies. In Burma, under military dictatorship until the junta civilized rule with limited reforms in 2011, the army has waged a series of brutal campaigns, in the context of civil wars against armed organizations, against minorities that constitute more than one-third of the population. Patterns of extrajudicial killings, sexual violence, forced labour, razing homes and mass forced displacement have been documented against the Mon (HRW 1994a) and Karens (HRW 2005e) over long periods, and continued (after the liberation of the opposition leader, Aung San Suu Kyi) with attacks on Kachins (HRW 2012b) and Rohingya Muslims (HRW 2012c).

In Sri Lanka, the civil war described in Chapter 6 continued until 2009, when after several failed ceasefires and negotiations, the government finally defeated the secessionist LTTE. In the war's brutal conclusion, the LTTE committed atrocities against the civilians in its zone of control, while the Sri Lankan army bombarded them and after victory concentrated Tamils in huge camps in the north of the island. Despite widespread international condemnation of the atrocities, documented by a UN panel of experts (UN 2011), the Sri Lankan government was mostly able to mobilize international allies to deflect criticism (at one point obtaining a supportive resolution from no less than the UN Human Rights Council). By a combination of discrimination, counter-insurgency and intermittent genocidal violence, the Tamil proportion had been reduced from one-quarter of the population of Sri Lanka in 1948 to no more than one-tenth (Sivanandan 2009: 95). Not surprisingly, the Tamil diaspora is one of the most active in organizing international opposition to violence.

## East Asia: a lasting reduction in genocidal violence?

The case for partly distinguishing Cold War from decolonizing and post-colonial genocide (Chapter 5) is supported by the diminution of genocidal violence in East Asia and Latin America – two regions where it was especially closely connected to Cold War international polarization – after the Cold War. The reduction in East Asia is especially striking, and bears loose comparison with genocide's elimination in Europe from 1949 to 1989, although the processes of international change and genocidal reduction were both very different. The transformation can be linked to the simultaneous weakening of international tensions between Communist China and the West, increasing global economic interdependence, and the internal transformations of China from the 1980s. China remains quasi-imperial and continues to suppress political and cultural autonomy in the regions where non-Han Chinese prevail, particularly Tibet and the Uyghur-populated Xingjiang region. The genocidal violence of the Maoist period has gone, but tensions continue to produce conflict and repressive violence. In Cambodia, despite continuing Khmer Rouge violence in the 1980s, the post-genocide regime has consolidated its rule and an uneasy collaboration with the UN has produced a hybrid national–international court to try surviving Khmer Rouge leaders. However North Korea, where an unreformed Communist regime is the centre of international tensions with South Korea, Japan and the USA, saw a state-made famine in the 1990s similar to China's thirty years earlier if on a smaller scale (Howard-Hassmann 2012). This resulted largely from the state priority given to military rivalry with the South over domestic and especially rural consumption, and callous indifference to the resulting suffering: an estimated 600,000 people died (Cumings 2011).

Despite drastic reductions in violence compared to the Cold War period, there must be a big question mark over East Asia's ability to avoid genocide in the future. A combustible mixture of unresolved international conflicts among regional states and with the USA, rapid economic growth, stalled democratization in most states, and extensive minority and diaspora problems, mean that the sorts of conflicts seen elsewhere could occur in the future.

## Latin America: accounting for violence?

Latin America, likewise, has seen a big change. Although many under-lying social problems have changed little and endemic violence – much of it from state agencies such as the police – still affects sections of the urban and rural poor, targeted violence against population groups has diminished. Some indigenous communities remain vulnerable to attacks by ranchers, often backed by police, which threaten to destroy their societies: for example in Brazil's northern Roraima state in the early 1990s, indigenous people suffered violent evictions, beatings, destruc-tion of homes and property, illegal arrests, torture, rape and homicide (HRW 1994b). In many places, however, the post-Cold War period has involved accounting for the genocidal violence of the early 1980s. This has been far from a smooth process: large-scale anti-population violence has often given way to smaller-scale targeted attacks, especially on campaigners for justice themselves. In Guatemala, for example, where a UN-sponsored Historical Clarification Commission reported in 1999, there were significant attacks on returning refugees and human rights activists (HRW 2002d). In Argentina and Chile, the 'disappearances' and atrocities of the 1970s and 1980s remain crucial political and legal issues decades later. The larger international context – principally the involvement of the USA in Cold War genocide – remains the focus of genocide activism and scholarship (Feierstein 2007 and 2012, Esparza, Huttenbach and Feierstein 2010).

The biggest exception to the pattern of diminishing violence has been Colombia, where the many-sided violence of the Cold War period has continued, although its political and organizational contours have partially changed. The FARC's long insurgency gained ground in the 1990s, and the government promoted right-wing paramilitary groups, reorganized into legal CONVIVIRs. According to Human Rights Watch (HRW 1998c) at the time, both sides to the conflict 'overtly and aggressively target civilians, yet claim that civilian casualties are in fact combatants in disguise. All sides also seek to draw civilians into direct participation in the war.' HRW noted that in 1997, the Banco de Datos de Violencia Política recorded no fewer than 185 massacres in Colombia, often serving 'the closely weighed and measured purpose of promoting terror. In one blow, massacres eliminate those close or perceived to be close to an opposing side, punishing a family or population for the perceived action of one or a few of its members. The threat to those who survive or witness or hear of the massacre afterwards is clear. If you have had or may be seen to have had contact with the enemy, it is best to flee.' In fact, army operations 'prompted widespread and credible reports that soldiers coordinated openly with paramilitary groups and attacked civilian dwellings indiscriminately, provoking mass displacement ... While in some places paramilitary threats were enough to convince people to flee, in others the paramilitaries executed village leaders or other residents to show that they meant business.'

Violence by the paramilitary coalition Autodefensas Unidas de Colombia (AUC) continued into the 2000s. Despite a government-sponsored 'demobilization process' for paramilitaries, HRW (2010b) reports that 'successor groups regularly commit massacres, killings, forced displacement, rape, and extortion, and create a threatening atmosphere in the communities they control. Often, they target human rights defenders, trade unionists, victims of the paramilitaries who are seeking justice, and community members who do not follow their orders.' Gómez-Suárez (2010) notes that violence against former members of the Unión Patriótica, the left-wing group targeted for destruction by a 'bloc' of army officers, paramilitaries and criminal networks in the 1980s and 1990s, continued in the 2000s after the UP disbanded. Gómez-Suárez's discussion of the role of criminals emphasizes the blurred boundaries of crime and politics, also evident in Mexico's drugs wars at the end of the first decade of the twenty-first century, with civilian killings by security forces as well as by drug gangs.

## Conclusions

This survey, although wide-ranging, makes no claims to completeness. It has shown complex patterns of genocidal violence in the context of contemporary political and armed conflict, in many world-regional, national and sub-national contexts. Read together with the account of genocidal violence in the post-Cold War transition (Chapter 7) and the critique of the literature on political violence (Chapter 8), it suggests that targeted anti-population violence remains a recurring feature of many conflicts, deeply embedded in regional international as well as domestic power relations, often reinforced by the global power net-works in which the UN and Western states are dominant actors. The survey shows that although genocide remains a significant feature of global-era international relations, its pattern and its international roots have changed significantly since the Cold War/decolonization period. I elaborate these conclusions further in the final chapter.

# 10 | *Conclusions: history and future of genocide*

This study has ranged widely over late modern genocide. It has shown that the phenomenon, in the original sense of targeted, destructive anti-population violence, has been an accompaniment of very varied political and armed conflicts throughout the twentieth and into the twenty-first century. Contrary to the assumptions of the comparative genocide paradigm, such destructive violence mostly does not take place in discrete national, domestic circumstances, between regimes and their 'own' civilians. Rather, genocide is commonly directed against civilians across borders, and not always by regimes; and even when it takes place within borders, it is almost invariably conditioned by international relations, in the twin senses of relations between states and between nations.

## Shifting patterns of genocide, changing international contexts

I have recognized the relationship between genocide and the modern international system pointed out by other scholars. However I have argued distinctively that patterns of genocide have changed rapidly together with the changing world political and military conditions of modernity, even during the relatively short period under discussion. I have given substance to the proposal, already made by others, that 'international context' is the key to understanding genocide. By focusing on the synchronizations of major changes in the history of genocide with major changes in the international system, I have tried to show what kinds of transformations are most important.

This book has relied on the growing historical studies of colonial genocide and of European genocide in the first half of the twentieth century, but has reinterpreted these stories as two sides of the inter-imperial, Europe-centred international system over several centuries. Colonial genocide, I have argued, was not restricted to the settler variant that has mostly been the centre of academic attention. It was a general accompaniment of European empires in the rest of the world, widely manifested in periods of conquest, resistance and repression, even where settlement was not the main form of European intervention. However genocide also became, increasingly, a feature of the crisis of the inter-imperial system in Europe itself, from the end of the nineteenth century to its climax in the Second World War in the middle of the twentieth. Again drawing on recent studies, I have argued that genocide became generalized in European international relations in this period. The Ottoman destruction of the Armenians in the First World War and the Nazi mass murder of the Jews in the Second, commonly seen as the major European genocides, need to be understood rather as nadirs of larger patterns of anti-population violence. These can be seen as expressions of an increasingly generalized exclusive nationalism, but that nationalism itself was powerfully conditioned by international conflict. I have argued that the militarized international system that climaxed in world war in the early 1940s was the structural context that generalized genocide, drawing in Allied as well as Axis states.

Key tests of my thesis that international change conditions genocide are periods of transition themselves. I argued that the late 1940s was a key period of transition from the multi-centred imperial system of previous centuries to the bipolar bloc-system of the Cold War, the most fundamental change in the international system in late modern times. This was also the period, of course, of the birth of the United Nations and the adoption of many key international instruments including the Genocide Convention. My reinterpretation of this period therefore provides some of the key arguments of this book: this was a transition *in* genocide, not *from* a genocidal to a post-genocidal world; the ending of genocide in Europe for a generation resulted from the victory of one genocidal project, the Soviet, over another, the Nazi; and the counterpoints of the process of drafting the Genocide Convention were the completion of genocidal expulsions in Europe and new patterns of decolonizing genocide and post-colonial genocide of which the Indian Partition was the prime example. That neither of these greatly troubled the drafters of the Genocide Convention, even Raphael Lemkin, is a profound comment on the limitations of the new instrument.

In relation to the Cold War period, I argued that while some genocide was closely related to the Cold War itself – understood for most of the period as a three-way contest involving China as well as the Soviet and Western blocs – much, while indirectly linked to the Cold War, was more directly rooted in the conflicted emergence of a multiplicity of new states out of the declining European empires. The argument here was designed as a corrective to North-centric accounts of this period in international relations as well as of genocide. I also argued that while some genocide resulted from the central policies of authoritarian regimes, much developed more haphazardly in wars of decolonization and secession and other political conflicts in post-colonial states.

My discussion of the end of the Cold War focused on the significance for the history of genocide of another major transition in international relations, although I evaluated it as less fundamental than the changes of the 1940s. Here I proposed that the break-ups of the Soviet Union and Yugoslavia at the end of the Cold War could be seen as comparable to the dissolution of other European empires after the two world wars earlier in the twentieth century, and resulted in the return of genocide to Europe. Likewise, the effect of the USA's new belligerence, once it was left as the 'sole superpower', was not only to harness military power for anti-genocidal ends (as its protagonists believe), but also to provoke new wars which stimulated genocidal violence, as happened in Iraq after the 2003 invasion.

In moving to the analysis of post-Cold War genocidal violence, I also moved from intellectual territory that mostly belongs to historical research into that often-ahistorical present where social scientists prevail. To mark this shift, I devoted a chapter to engaging with some of the work on political conflict, civil war, armed conflict and violence that has been produced, mainly by political scientists, in recent years. Although I found major problems with this work – it tends not to distinguish genocidal violence clearly as an aspect of conflict, if at all; and it tends towards the comparative treatment of discrete national cases rather than the understanding of international and regional patterns – it has produced some important analyses of trends, which are helpful in approaching the phenomena in which I am interested.

Having critically examined this literature, I moved in the last chapter into a regional survey of genocidal violence in the first two post-Cold War decades. Here I showed how various types of genocidal conflict had developed through international and transnational relations in different regional contexts, and how these regional contexts were linked to global power networks and relations. I tried to keep to the fore the tensions between local, national, regional and global contexts, recognizing that many conflicts are linked to local and national (often electoral) power contests, but that these conflicts are almost always deeply embedded in, and involve, regional relations, and tend to become globalized. My goal was to show at the same time the international-regional contexts of most genocide and the different ways in which global power (the UN, the West and other major world powers) is involved.

## The nature of 'international contexts', regional and global

'International context' was the emergent idea that I appropriated from the existing genocide literature. I have interpreted it historically in the various chapters of this book. I rejected a rigid idea of the 'international system', but I have continued to use this notion in a historicized way, arguing that we should understand the system as one that undergoes constant change, not only of an evolutionary but also, through periods of major upheaval, of a more radical kind. In a broad sense, the phases of the modern international system that I have distinguished – inter-imperial, Cold War bloc, and global – have constituted the macro-contexts that have framed this account. However I have also been concerned with different international contexts *within* each of these broad periods. These have mostly been specified, within all three periods, in primarily regional rather than world senses. This is partly because world-level international dynamics – the competition of European and other major empires; Cold War rivalry and nation-state formation in the South; and post-Cold War globalization – have always worked through regional conflict. And although these dynamics can all be seen as contexts of genocide, the latter is never a ubiquitous consequence of world-level relations. On the contrary, international-regional (as well as national and local) dynamics are those to which we must chiefly pay attention.

Moreover genocide, in contrast to some other aspects of inter-national relations, involves direct power-projection against populations, and so must necessarily be conceptualized as taking place in spaces. Genocide has not generally been thought of as territorially based, but I argued in my last book that one of the things we should learn from the 'ethnic cleansing' literature and the attention it has drawn to forced displacement is the importance of territorial context. Genocidal power generally aims to destroy groups, whether by terror and expulsion or by outright murder, *within particular spaces*. The corollary is that with genocide we are always looking at where people are – and where they are going. Sometimes, it is true, they are going far: perpetrators are often imperial agents or colonists who travel from one side of the world to another; and sometimes victims are forced into exile in distant continents. However most victims, in most cases, go shorter distances, often into camps in neighbouring states; and indeed many perpetrators, even when recruited internationally, operate not far from home. 'Neighbourhood' effects are notorious in the study of genocide.

I have suggested that both the nature of regional patterns of genocide, and the linkages between these and world-level relations are very historically and spatially variable. Over the half-millennium that concluded with the Second World War, European empires competed among each other, and latterly with the USA and Japan too, on a world scale. Yet colonial genocide was mostly the product of their local and at most regional interactions (and especially those of their colonists) with indigenous polities and peoples. Although I have not explored this issue in this book, it would appear that the connections of genocide with inter-imperial conflict were more often indirect than direct.

From the end of the nineteenth to the middle of the twentieth century, south-eastern and increasingly eastern Europe as a whole constituted regions of genocide. Bloxham's metaphor 'the great game of genocide' suggests how nationalist conflicts that repeatedly produced anti-population violence were entwined with the larger rivalries of the western European and US world empires as well as the decline of the historic empires in these regions. The pan-European First World War, following other regional wars, provoked the most extensive and murderous violence, primarily but not only by the Turkified Ottoman state against Armenians and other Christians, and placed the consequential issues of national and minority rights at the centre of the wider European international settlement at Paris. Following this, a truly unique feature of the Second World War was the regional system of genocidal war that developed. The pattern of genocide was driven by war between great powers, other states and armed movements.

Since Nazi Germany and the Soviet Union were not just regional but world powers, their regional conflict was part of their gigantic world conflict with the USA, Britain and Japan, so regional and national contexts of genocide were conditioned by these larger conflicts. Moreover genocide was actually part of the 'war system', the specific form that the world and regional international system took during the Second World War period.

None of the other regional patterns of genocide have taken this particular form. The genocidal violence of the Korean war was part of a world struggle of the Soviet bloc with the West – although China rather than the USSR itself was the direct international protagonist – but here genocide was limited to Korea. The larger regional pattern in East Asia during the Cold War was one of sequential rather than systemically integrated genocide. The conflicts in former Yugoslavia in the 1990s constituted a regional system, in which genocidal war between different republican (and in Kosovo, provincial) proto-states spread from one republic/province to another. After 'ethnic cleansing' in one republic, refugees poured into others, stimulating conflict there. The genocidal war system was simultaneously interstate and civil, international and domestic, within the ever-important Yugoslav regional context. Although there was extensive and influential 'global' involvement by the UN, EU, USA, NATO, ICTY, etc., the conflict was defined by the Yugoslav parties.

Something similar might be said of the regional patterns of genocide in the post-Cold War period discussed in Chapter 9. Although variable combinations of global and regional organizations and powers have been significantly involved – the UN, the USA, former European colonial powers such as Britain and France, China, the African Union, ECOWAS, SADC, not to mention the ICTR, the ICC, etc. – the primary drivers of conflict have lain in different complexes of regional, national and local power relations. However, mostly these have not been inter-state conflicts to the same extent as in Yugoslavia. In the African Great Lakes, for example, regional, cross-border flows of refugees, fighters and weapons have fuelled genocidal conflicts within several states over decades; although these led to interstate war in the DR Congo at the end of the 1990s, this has not generally been the case.

While *in general* the international system at a world level cannot be seen as genocide-producing in any simple sense, each of its main late-modern manifestations has been structurally implicated in genocide. The inter-imperial system systematically produced geno-cidal relations in local and regional conflicts with indigenous pol-ities, while culminating in world wars which generalized genocidal tendencies. The Cold War bloc system militarized social, political and ethnonational relations in many regions, while linked processes of decolonization and contested post-colonial power led to geno-cidal insurgency and counter-insurgency. Global-era international relations, while institutionalizing norms of genocide prevention to which only lip service was paid during the Cold War, have also helped produce violence. Western–UN military interventions (whether 'humanitarian' or not), conflict management and democracy promotion, for example, have all been implicated in producing as well as containing genocide.

I have also emphasized how changes in international relations can play key roles in generally eliminating or reducing genocide in entire world-regions. The post-Second World War changes in international relations involved the ending of genocide in Europe, while stimulating it elsewhere; post-Cold War changes were linked to the closing of the genocidal period in East Asia, while stimulating genocide else-where. These negative correlations of international change are quite as impressive as positive cases in demonstrating the importance of international context for genocide.

## Continuity and change

As I have indicated at numerous points, any attempt to historicize genocide must confront evident continuities in its history across the 'periods' within which we divide the story. Historical periodization itself is not a given, but a product of the perceptions of historians as well as of the actors themselves. My account has emphasized two particular historical turning points, the ends of the Second World War and of the Cold War, which have divided three periods within which I have considered late-modern genocide. Undoubtedly one could propose other transitional moments for consideration. One might be the First World War, which escalated the previously episodic pattern of genocide in south-eastern Europe and produced the first modern mega-genocide, of the Armenians, which antici-pated the even greater horrors of the Second World War. However I have followed Bloxham in treating the three-quarters of a century culminating in 1949 as a single period, on the grounds not only of his coherent story of unfolding European genocide, but also of the inter-imperial structure that the largely Eurocentric international system exhibited throughout.

At the other end of my timescale, readers might think more should be made of the 2001 terror attacks. These certainly seemed for much of the 2000s to have defined a new period in international relations, and there has been no shortage of writers hailing radical Islamism as the source of a new wave of genocide. Here I feel on even stronger ground in rejecting any temptation to recognize a major world-historical transition. There is no denying the huge provocation that 9/11 represented to US and Western society, or the overreach to which it tempted George W. Bush's USA, represented in this book by the genocidal aftermath of the 2003 invasion of Iraq. Yet it is difficult to see it as having produced anything like the structural changes in world politics following 1989, let alone the even bigger ones after 1945. Likewise while I acknowledge the genocidal tendencies of al-Qaeda (ironically, these have been expressed nowhere more than in Iraq after Bush opened up that country to the Islamist network), the record of Islamist genocide is too thin to see it as a major strand of contemporary anti-population violence.

More serious objections to my framework could arise from arguments about continuities across the periods. These could be posed in several ways. Empirically, there is (as I have noted) considerable evidence that genocide recurs in the same locales at different historical moments. This is usually because no lasting political solution has been found to the local contradictions that helped produce genocide in the first place. It is also because experiences of genocide feed new genocidal movements: imaginaries of victimization are grist to the mill of violent movements. It is, too, as anthropologists have shown, because cultures of genocide, embedding understandings of violent practices, become established and are learnt in imagined regional contexts.

All these elements of continuity are important. However it is also evident that genocide can end. In many territories that were zones of genocide during the 1940s and before, it never returned in the 1990s even when it did in the Balkans and the Caucasus. And even in the latter, we need to explain why four decades of peace finally unravelled. Clearly earlier histories of genocide are part of the story, but those histories were there during the decades without violence, for example in Yugoslavia under Tito. While we might explain the post-Yugoslav conflicts primarily in terms of Yugoslav conditions after the fall of Tito, I have given reasons why it is more cogent to regard it as an extreme case of the general conditions of the end of the Cold War, collapse of Communism and onset of democratization, which elsewhere did not always or generally produce genocide. Without recognizing these world-historical processes of change, we would be at a loss to fully explain events in former Yugoslavia.

Continuity can be specified, too, in sociological terms: similar social processes, actors and methods utilized across the historical periods of modernity. General processes such as othering, dehumanization and enemy formation, and specific methods such as expulsion, rape and murder, can be identified in different times and places. So one should not deny that what I have called 'transhistorical' comparisons of these processes can pinpoint useful connections. Nothing in my critique of the narrow comparative approach is meant to deny this. However I hope to have demonstrated that while such analyses may be helpful, they are not sufficient. Others, 'sub-humans' and enemies are seen in widely different ways, not just in different historical cases, but generally in each historical period. For example, nationalist and racist othering inherited from the nineteenth century was politicized in a specific sense by eugenic and scientific-racist ideas in the early twentieth, and in a very different sense by the later anti-imperialist and anti-Communist ideologies of the Cold War.

Likewise, while typical social actors of genocide can be generalized across the modern period – in terms such as Mann's 'radical elites', 'paramilitaries' and 'core constituencies' – the meaning of each type and general patterns of their relationships vary significantly over time. During the high period of European genocide, typical elites were exclusive nationalists, fascists and Stalinists ('totalitarians'). During the Cold War, insurgent national liberation movements and counter-insurgent militaries became more important. Since the end of the Cold War, as civil wars have become more disorderly and elections ever more significant foci of violence, warlords and democratic politicians have both grown in importance. Older types of genocide actors may remain significant – there is no suggestion that historical change means a blank slate – but new characters appear in the roll call of perpetration.

As important as changes in the types of perpetrator are changes in the typical *combination* of perpetrator social forces. If Mann's trinity applies throughout the modern period, it is necessary to historicize its application. Likewise, if Gerlach is right to point to coalitions for violence in which non-state actors are often powerful, even dominant, we need to recognize that this is not true to the same extent for all periods. In settler and other colonial genocide, central imperial elites often figured only at a distance from the decisions for and practices of expulsion and killing, while paramilitaries were often barely distinct from the general settler population. In contrast, European nationalist genocide of the twentieth century often mobilized highly specialized killing forces and armed auxiliaries, involved its core constituencies less directly in genocide, and was overall a much more centralized, state-centric phenomenon than settler genocide. One could even talk about a 'statization' of genocide in this period, in which great empires and small nation-states both planned and coordinated huge movements of populations that did not fit, and authorized extensive terror, violence and mass murder against them.

The post-colonial transformations of genocide after 1945, in contrast, involved new shifts towards greater roles for paramilitaries, lesser roles for and looser linkages to national political and military elites, and more extensive popular participation. These tendencies have only been accentuated since 1989. Indeed to the extent that genocidal violence has become more localized, linked to messy civil wars and electoral contests, the organizing centres of genocide are often multiple, loosely coordinated, and situated in local as well as national militia–party–community networks. It is important to restate, of course, that these tendencies have been uneven. My narrative has emphasized time and again that while the initiators of local genocide may lie outside the central state machine and national politics, these generally remain core reference points. Therefore genocide is less statist in the twenty-first than it was in the mid twentieth century, but it is not beyond the state. State power, in its most general sense, is a constant of modern genocide, even if its significance varies greatly across periods and locales.

Another constant is empire. While formal empires have faded, many states remain quasi-imperial in their internal relations: so-called nation-states are really nation-state-empires. Thus contradictions between central and subordinate nations remain crucial axes of the political and armed conflicts that generate genocide. However, external dominance remains another key international context of genocide. States like those of the modern West, increasingly post-imperial in their internal make-ups, are major practitioners of external power-projection. So in arguing that the end of the Second World War marked the most decisive shift in the modern history of international relations and genocide, ending the system of multiple inter-imperial rivalries that had developed over several centuries, I did not signify a general end of empire. The USA as superpower took over many of the interests of the weakened British and French as well as the defeated German and Japanese empires, and the Western bloc operated as a kind of super-empire or 'ultra-imperialism', the core of an incipient 'global state'. The USSR, having already reconstituted much of the Tsarist empire, extended it in eastern Europe and briefly strove to compete with the West on a world scale. After the defeat of the USSR in the Cold War, the USA in its short period as 'sole superpower' indulged itself in military adventures, notably in Iraq, which rightly reignited the 'empire' debate in International Relations.

But if empire remains important, the new world rivalries of the USA and China that can be seen in Africa and elsewhere in the early twenty-first century are not a mere revival of the Cold War, still less of the old inter-imperial system. The rise of China and more generally of BRICS underlines the fact that the USA and the West cannot hope to simply dominate in the world. But neither can China, India and other powers – even if they behave imperially within and around their borders – mount a world challenge to the West, at least in the short to medium term. The West remains too powerful, and the global bonds that tie it and its competitors together too tight, for any simple reconstitution of the imperial rivalries that led to two world wars. Empire remains very important but its significance has changed. Genocide is unlikely to be spurred by inter-imperial war, but it will probably continue to recur in the context of rebellions against quasi-imperial power within small and medium-sized states, in which rivalries of great powers (sometimes even, as in Rwanda, among Western states themselves) will remain potent.

## Genocide today, future crises, and genocide prevention

This book has dealt extensively with genocide in the current historical period. In concluding Chapter 9 I briefly summarized the balance of genocide in the early twenty-first century. I showed that while mega-genocides remain rare, genocide remains an all-too-common accompaniment of civil war, counter-insurgency, political and electoral contests in many countries, embedded in regional systems of violence in several cases and closely linked to the workings of the global system. Clearly this picture has profound political implications, notably for the vexed question of genocide prevention. I began this book with a critique of political abuses of the genocide idea, deeply rooted in the way the subject has come to be studied in academia. I argued for clearer distinctions between scholarly analysis, political commentary, and activism, not because I wish to deny scholars the right to comment or act (I do both myself) but because partial and unreflected political commitments prejudice serious scholarship. Here I aim to draw some reflected conclusions from my wide-ranging analysis.

When we consider the literature on genocide prevention, a paradox presents itself. On the one hand it is often argued that genocide is like a disease, a 'scourge' that can be eliminated by proactive international policies. Yet if genocide is considered a 'scourge' of world society and the international system, it can hardly be considered diseaselike: there is no single bacterium to be wiped out or gene to be modified. World society is not an organism that can be medically manipulated, but a highly complex set of networks of social relationships (economic, cultural, political and military, international and national, global and regional, etc.). Genocide, I hope to have shown, does not take a singular form or have a singular cause. To reduce genocidal ideas, for example, to a singular idea such as 'dehumanization', which can be countered through a singular method such as education, is to simplify to the point of meaninglessness. And to consider genocide only as a manifestation of ideas, and not of power relationships, conflicts, institutions, etc., negates the analysis not just of this book but of all credible historical and social-scientific studies. So the elimination of genocide is like the elimination of war or the overthrow of capitalism: an objective which requires a great deal more complex elaboration than is ever attempted by most of its advocates.

On the other hand, genocide prevention is often envisaged (sometimes by the same people as talk about it as a 'scourge') in relatively narrow terms, especially of 'humanitarian' military intervention, and imagined as something that the USA alone could largely solve. What is meant here is, of course, the prevention – or more often the cessation – of particular genocidal violence in given locales. This is an altogether more achievable goal. Since genocide is a form of violent conflict, armed interventions can be among the more effective short-term methods of changing patterns of behaviour. The British military intervention to end the genocidal Sierra Leone civil war is often given as an example, while Rwanda is cited as a negative case where lack of intervention allowed genocide to proceed. Yet while many commentators take a general position for or against intervention, the analysis developed in this book leads to a more cautious and pragmatic approach. Certainly, as critics claim, military interventions are rarely simply 'humanitarian' or devoted to fulfilling the 'responsibility to protect'. States are driven by their calculations of their own interests and hardly leave these at the door when they intervene in other territories. Civilian protection and humanitarianism (not necessarily the same things) are never the sole motives of decision making, but they may nevertheless be real goals, and interventions may still benefit threatened civilian populations, at least in part.

However we judge the politics of stopping genocide when it is imminent or under way, the goal of genocide prevention in general is an altogether more difficult one. If, as I have shown, genocidal tendencies emerge from a wide variety of contemporary conflicts – as they have from different but equally varied historic confrontations – the goal of widespread genocide-prevention appears very challenging. If genocide is repeatedly produced in the international and domestic politics of many regions and countries, and global interventions sometimes accentuate rather than alleviate the danger, then any serious proposal to abolish genocide must pay attention to complex political conditions, and avoid hyperbole in discussing the possibility of general solutions. If it is progressive for the USA, for example, to establish an Atrocities Prevention Board, a serious politics of worldwide atrocity prevention needs to consider not only the atrocities of the USA's enemies but also those of its allies and those produced by US policies themselves.

If hyperbole should be avoided in identifying solutions, it should also be avoided in projecting future dangers. Clearly there are dangers of future genocide from political and military fractures in many regions and countries of the world, and this book has emphasized international conflict as a cause. However, where and when they will occur, or on what scale, is very difficult to predict. When several years ago I began the work that led to this book, some of the outbreaks of genocidal violence that have occurred since, for example around elections in

Kenya and Côte d'Ivoire, might have been foreseen in general terms, since there had been related violence in the recent past and political tensions had not been overcome. Others, however, were less predictable: for example, few expected the atrocities against the protest movement and civilian population in Syria in 2011–12, since few foresaw the Arab Spring and its spread, or (despite the history of murderous repression by Bashir al-Assad's father in 1982) the depths of the regime's response.

Some scholars have avoided the dilemmas of prediction by sketching a future of genocide that works from general destabilizing conditions rather than specific contexts. For example, there has been increasing concern about the effects of climate change on the likelihood of political violence. It is a reasonable hypothesis that, if global warming and its consequences drastically transform human living conditions in many regions, competition for scarce land, food, etc., may increase in places, and contribute to political tensions. It is impossible, however, to draw a straight line between climate change and future political violence. Whether global warming, etc., will have extreme political consequences depends on many other factors affecting human livelihoods and politics in the regions most likely to be affected. If, as I have emphasized, genocide does not have singular causes, then it is unlikely that in the future we shall be able to pinpoint climate change as the sole or main precipitant of violence. It would be as plausible, after the severe economic shocks of recent years, to posit global economic instability as a potential general cause of violence, although it is likely that in any specific genocidal events, economic, climatic and other factors will combine to influence the national and international, political and military contexts from which violence will issue.

What is clear is that in an unstable world, where billions live in or on the edge of great insecurity, in crisis-prone, unstable international and national political environments, genocide is not likely to end soon. And the conclusion that we can draw from this book is that just as genocide often manifests itself today in different forms from those of the past, so it may take still further new forms in the future. The recent aspirations of the UN and some governments to end genocide will not be enough, any more than the commitments of the Genocide Convention proved to be. A world truly without genocide would be a world without war too, and with a global political environment so different from today's that we are far from being able to see it.

# Bibliography

Achkar, G. (2010) *The Arabs and the Holocaust: The Arab–Israeli War of Narratives*. London: Saqi.

Adebajo, A. (2002a) *Liberia's Civil War: Nigeria, ECOMOG, and Regional Security in West Africa*. Boulder: Lynne Rienner.

(2002b) *Building Peace in West Africa: Liberia, Sierra Leone, and Guinea-Bissau*. Boulder: Lynne Rienner.

Adelman, H. and E. Barkan (2011) *No Return, No Refuge: Rites and Rights in Minority Repatriation*. New York: Columbia University Press.

Ahonen, P., G. Corni, J. Kochanowski, R. Schulze, T. Stark and B. Stelzl-Marx (2008) *People on the Move: Forced Population Movements in Europe in the Second World War and Its Aftermath*. Oxford: Berghahn.

Albright, M. and W. Cohen (2008) *Preventing Genocide: A Blueprint for US Policymakers*. United States Institute of Peace/United States Holocaust Memorial Museum.

Albrow, M. (1997) *The Global Age*. Cambridge: Polity.

Alexander, J. C. (2002) 'On the Social Construction of Moral Universals: The "Holocaust" from War Crime to Trauma Drama'. *European Journal of Social Theory*, 5(1), 5–85.

(2009) 'On the Global and Local Representation of the Holocaust Tragedy', in J. C. Alexander, M. Jay, B. Giesen, M. Rotheberg, R. Manne, N. Glazer and E. Katz, *Remembering the Holocaust: A Debate*. New York: Oxford University Press, pp. 173–92.

Allen, B. (1996) *Rape Warfare: The Hidden Genocide in Bosnia-Herzegovina and Croatia*. Minneapolis: University of Minnesota Press.

Alsheh, Y. (2012) 'The Intellectual and Political Origins of the United Nations Conventions on the Prevention and Punishment of the Crime of Genocide 1933–1948'. Ph.D. thesis, Tel Aviv University.

Aly, G., P. Chroust and C. Pross (1994) *Cleansing the Fatherland: Nazi Medicine and Racial Hygiene*. Baltimore: Johns Hopkins University Press.

Amnesty International (1989) *Uganda, the Human Rights Record 1986–1989*. London: Amnesty.

Amowitz, L. L., C. Reis, K. H. Lyons, B. Vann, B. Mansaray, A. M. Akinsulure-Smith, L. Taylor and V. Iacopino (2002) 'Prevalence of

War-Related Sexual Violence and Other Human Rights Abuses among Internally Displaced Persons in Sierra Leone'. *Journal of the American Medical Association*, 287(4), 513–21.

Anderson, D. M. (2002) 'Vigilantes, Violence and the Politics of Public Order in Kenya'. *African Affairs*, 101(405), 531–55.

Anderson, P. (2008) 'The Divisions of Cyprus'. *London Review of Books*, 30(8), 7–16.

Armer, M. J. and R. M. Marsh, eds. (1982) *Comparative Sociological Research in the 1960s and 1970s*. Leiden: Brill.

Balcells, L. (2010) 'Rivalry and Revenge: Violence against Civilians in Conventional Civil Wars'. *International Studies Quarterly*, 54(2), 291–313.

Barnett, M. (2002) *Eye-Witness to a Genocide*. Ithaca, NY: Cornell University Press.

Barta, T. (1987) 'Relations of Genocide: Land and Lives in the Colonization of Australia', in I. Wallimann and M. N. Dobkowski, eds., *Genocide and the Modern Age: Etiology and Case Studies of Mass Death*. New York: Greenwood Press, pp. 237–51.

Bartov, O. (2010) 'Genocide and the Holocaust: What Are We Arguing About?', in U. Jensen, H. Knoch, D. Morat and M. Rürup, eds., *Gewalt und Gesellschaft: Klassiker Modernen Denkens Neu Gelesen*. Göttingen: Wallstein Verlag, pp. 381–93.

Bayart, J.-F. (2009) *The State in Africa: The Politics of the Belly*, 2nd edn. Cambridge: Polity.

Beck, U. (2005) *Power in the Global Age: A New Global Political Economy*. Cambridge: Polity.

Becker, J. (1998) *Hungry Ghosts: Mao's Secret Famine*. New York: Holt.

Behrens, P. (2007) 'A Moment of Kindness: Consistency and Genocidal Intent', in R. J. Henham, ed., *The Criminal Law of Genocide: International, Comparative and Contextual Aspects*. Aldershot: Ashgate, pp. 125–40.

Bell, D. A. (2007) *The First Total War: Napoleon's Europe and the Birth of Warfare as We Know It*. New York: Houghton Mifflin Harcourt.

Bell-Fialkoff, A. (1996) *Ethnic Cleansing*. Basingstoke: Macmillan.

Bellamy, A. J. (2009) *Responsibility to Protect: The Global Effort to End Mass Atrocities*. Cambridge: Polity.

Bertrand, J. (2004) *Nationalism and Ethnic Conflict in Indonesia*. Cambridge University Press.

Bessell, R. and C. Haake, eds. (2009) *Removing Peoples: Forced Removal in the Modern World*. Oxford University Press.

Besteman, C. L. (2007) 'Genocide in Somalia's Jubba Valley and Somali Bantu Refugees in the US', *Crisis in the Horn of Africa* website symposium. New York: Social Science Research Council. hornofafrica.ssrc.org/Besteman.

Betts, A. (2009) *The International Relations of Forced Migration*. Oxford University Press.

Birkeland, N. M. and E. Jennings, eds. (2011) *Internal Displacement: Global Overview of Trends and Developments in 2010*. Oslo: Internal Displacement Monitoring Center and the Norwegian Refugee Council.

Bloxham, D. (2003) 'The Armenian Genocide of 1915–1916: Cumulative Radicalization and the Development of a Destruction Policy'. *Past and Present*, 181, 141–79.

(2007) *The Great Game of Genocide*. Oxford University Press.

(2008) *Genocide, the World Wars and the Unweaving of Europe*. London: Vallentine Mitchell.

(2009a) 'The Great Unweaving: The Removal of Peoples in Europe, 1875–1949', in Bessel and Haake, eds., pp. 167–208.

(2009b) *The Final Solution: A Genocide*. Oxford University Press.

Boix, C. (2008) 'Economic Roots of Civil Wars and Revolutions in the Contemporary World'. *World Politics*, 60(3), 390–437

Bose, S. (2011) 'The Question of Genocide and the Quest for Justice in the 1971 War'. *Journal of Genocide Research*, 13(4), 393–419.

Brandes, D. (2009) 'National and International Planning of the "Transfer" of Germans from Czechoslovakia and Poland', in Bessel and Haake, eds., pp. 281–96.

Brunk, D. (2008) 'Dissecting Darfur: Anatomy of a Genocide Debate'. *International Relations*, 22(1), 25–44.

Buhaug, H. and K. S. Gleditsch (2008) 'Contagion or Confusion? Why Conflicts Cluster in Space'. *International Studies Quarterly*, 52(2), 215–33.

Bull, H. (2002 (1977)) *The Anarchical Society: A Study of Order in World Politics*, 3rd edn. New York: Columbia University Press.

Bulutgil, H. Z. (2010) 'War, Collaboration and Endogenous Ethnic Polarization: The Path to Ethnic Cleansing', in E. Chenoweth and A. Lawrence, eds., *Rethinking Violence: State and Non-State Actors in Conflict*. Cambridge, MA: MIT Press, pp. 57–81.

Buzan, B. (1993) 'From International System to International Society: Structural Realism and Regime Theory Meet the English School'. *International Organization*, 47(3), 327–52.

Cain, K. L. (1999) 'The Rape of Dinah: Human Rights, Civil War in Liberia, and Evil Triumphant'. *Human Rights Quarterly*, 21(2), 265–307.

Campbell, D. (2001) 'Atrocity, Memory, Photography: Imaging the Concentration Camps of Bosnia – the Case of ITN versus Living Marxism', Parts I and II. *Journal of Human Rights*, 1(1), 1–33 and 1(2), 143–72.

Carment, D. and P. James (1997) *Wars in the Midst of Peace: The International Politics of Domestic Conflict*. University of Pittsburgh Press.

CAVR (Commission for Reception, Truth and Reconciliation in East Timor) (2005) *Chega!* Dili: CAVR.

Cederman, L.-E. and L. Girardin (2007) 'Beyond Fractionalization: Mapping Ethnicity onto Nationalist Insurgencies'. *American Political Science Review*, 101(1), 173–85.

Cederman, L.-E., N. B. Weidmann and K. S. Gleditsch (2011) 'Horizontal Inequalities and Ethnonationalist Civil War: A Global Comparison'. *American Political Science Review*, 105(3), 477–95.

Chalk, F. and K. Jonassohn (1990) *The History and Sociology of Genocide: Analyses and Case Studies*. New Haven: Yale University Press.

Chang, I. (1997) *The Rape of Nanking*. Harmondsworth: Penguin.

Charny, I. W. (1988 and 1991) 'The Psychology of Denial of Known Genocides', in Charny, ed., *Genocide: A Critical Bibliographical Review*. 2 vols. London: Mansell, Vol. II, pp. 3–37.

   (1994) 'Toward a Generic Definition of Genocide', in G. J. Andreopoulous, ed., *Genocide: Conceptual and Historical Dimensions*. Philadelphia: University of Pennsylvania Press, pp. 64–94.

Christopher, A. J. (2001) *The Atlas of Changing South Africa*. London: Routledge.

Churchill, W. (2001) *A Little Matter of Genocide: Holocaust and Denial in the Americas 1492 to the Present*. San Francisco: City Lights.

Clausewitz, C. von (1976 (1831)) *On War*, trans. Michael Howard and Peter Paret. Princeton University Press.

Cohen, R. and F. Deng (2009) 'Mass Displacement Caused by Conflicts and One-sided Violence: National and International Responses', *SIPRI Yearbook 2009*. Oxford University Press, pp. 15–38.

Coleman, M. (1998) *A Crime against Humanity: Analysing the Repression of the Apartheid State*. Johannesburg: Human Rights Committee of South Africa.

Colley, L. (2009) *Britons: Forging the Nation*. New Haven: Yale University Press.

Collier, P. (2009) *Wars, Guns and Votes: Democracy in Dangerous Places*. London: Vintage.

Collier, P. and A. Hoeffler (2004) 'Greed and Grievance in Civil War'. *Oxford Economic Papers*, 56(4), 563–95.

Cooper, J. (2008) *Raphael Lemkin and the Struggle for the Genocide Convention*. Basingstoke: Palgrave Macmillan.

Copson, R. W. (1994) *Africa's Wars and Prospects for Peace*. New York: Sharpe.

Cordesman, A. and E. R. Davies (2008) *Iraq's Insurgency and the Road to Civil Conflict*. Washington, DC: Center for Strategic and International Studies.

Cribb, R. (2010) 'Political Genocides in Postcolonial Asia', in D. Bloxham and A. D. Moses, eds., *The Oxford Handbook of Genocide Studies*. Oxford University Press, pp. 445–65.

Cumings, B. (2011) *The Korean War: A History*. New York: Modern Library.

Cushman, T. and S. G. Meštrović, eds. (1996) *This Time We Knew: Western Responses to Genocide in Bosnia*. New York: NYU Press, 1996.

Dadrian, V. N. (2001) 'The Comparative Aspects of the Armenian and Jewish Cases of Genocide: A Sociohistorical Perspective', in A. S. Rosenbaum, ed., *Is the Holocaust Unique? Perspectives on Comparative Genocide*. Boulder: Westview, pp. 133–68.

Dalrymple, W. (2006) *The Last Mughal: The Fall of a Dynasty, Delhi 1857*. London: Bloomsbury.

Darwin, J. (2012) *Unfinished Empire: The Global Expansion of Britain*. London: Allen Lane.

Davenport, C., W. H. Moore and S. C. Poe (2003) 'Sometimes You Just Have to Leave: Domestic Threats and Refugee Movements, 1964–1989'. *International Interactions*, 29(1), 27–55.

Davis, M. (2000) *Late Victorian Holocausts*. London: Verso.

Daxecker, U. E. (2012) 'The Cost of Exposing Cheating: International Election Monitoring, Fraud, and Post-election Violence in Africa'. *Journal of Peace Research*, 49, 503–16.

de Waal, A. (2007) 'Reflections on the Difficulties of Defining Darfur's Crisis as Genocide', *Harvard Human Rights Journal*, 20, 25–33. www.law. harvard.edu/students/orgs/hrj/iss20/dewaal.pdf (accessed 15 September 2011).

(2009) 'Genocide by Force of Habit?' blogs.ssrc.org/sudan/2009/03/23/genocide-by-force-of-habit.

de Waal, T. (2003) *Black Garden: Armenia and Azerbaijan through Peace and War*. New York University Press

Desch, M. C. (2004) 'A "Final Solution" to a Recurrent Tragedy?' *Security Studies*, 13(3), 145–59.

(2006) 'The Myth of Abandonment: The Use and Abuse of the Holocaust Analogy'. *Security Studies*, 15(1), 106–45.

Dikötter, F. (2011) *Mao's Great Famine: The History of China's Most Devastating Catastrophe, 1958–62*. London: Bloomsbury.

Dodge, T. (2005a) 'Iraqi Transitions: From Regime Change to State Collapse'. *Third World Quarterly*, 26 (4–5), 705–21.

(2005b) *Iraq's Future: The Aftermath of Regime Change*. London: International Institute of Strategic Studies.

Drouin, M. (2010) 'Understanding the 1982 Guatemalan Genocide', in Esparza et al., eds., pp. 81–104.

Dubow, S. (1995) *Scientific Racism in Modern South Africa*. Cambridge University Press.

Eck, K. and L. Hultman (2007) 'One-Sided Violence against Civilians in War: Insights from New Fatality Data'. *Journal of Peace Research*, 44(2), 223–46.

Economist Intelligence Unit (2011) *Democracy Index 2011: Democracy under Stress*. London: EIU.

Elkins, C. (2005) *Imperial Reckoning: The Untold Story of Britain's Gulag in Kenya*. New York: Henry Holt.

Esparza, M. (2010) 'Globalizing Latin American Studies of State Violence and Genocide', in Esparza et al., eds., pp. 1–20.

Esparza, M., H. R. Huttenbach and D. Feierstein, eds. (2010) *State Violence and Genocide in Latin America: The Cold War Years*. London: Routledge.

Falola, T. (1998) *Violence in Nigeria: The Crisis of Religious Politics and Secular Ideologies*. Rochester, NY: University of Rochester Press.

(2009) *Colonialism and Violence in Nigeria*. Bloomington: Indiana University Press.

Fanon, F. (2004) *The Wretched of the Earth*. New York: Grove Press.

Farid, H. (2011) 'Political Economy of Violence and Victims in Indonesia', in C. A. Coppel, ed., *Violent Conflicts in Indonesia: Analysis, Representation, Resolution*. London: Taylor & Francis, pp. 269–85.

Fearon, J. D. (2007) 'Iraq's Civil War'. *Foreign Affairs*, 86(2), 2–15.

Fearon, J. D. and D. Laitin (2003) 'Ethnicity, Insurgency, and Civil War'. *American Political Science Review*, 97(1), 75–90.

Feierstein, D. (2007) *El genocidio como practica social: entre el nazismo y la experiencia argentina*. Buenos Aires: Fondo de Cultura Económica.

(2010) 'Political Violence in Argentina and Its Genocidal Characteristics', in Esparza et al., eds., pp. 44–63.

(2012) *Memorias y representaciones. Sobre la elaboración del genocidio*. Buenos Aires: Fondo de Cultura Económica.

Fein, H. (1990) 'Genocide: A Sociological Perspective'. *Current Sociology*, 38(1), 1–126.

Flint, J. and A. de Waal (2005) *Darfur: A Short History of a Long War*. London: Zed.

Fourchard, L. (2007) 'Violence et Ordre Politique au Nigeria'. *Politique Africaine*, 106, 5–28.

Freedom House (2012) *Freedom in the World 2012: The Arab Uprisings and Their Global Repercussions*. Washington, DC: Freedom House.

Furley, O. and R. May (2001) *Africa's Interventionist States*. London: Ashgate.

(eds.) (2006) *Ending Africa's Wars and Progressing to Peace*. London: Ashgate.

Garfield, R. (1999) *Morbidity and Mortality among Iraqi Children from 1990 through 1998: Assessing the Impact of the Gulf War and Economic Sanctions*. London: Campaign Against Sanctions on Iraq.

Gberie, L. (2005) *A Dirty War in West Africa: The RUF and the Destruction of Sierra Leone*. Bloomington: Indiana University Press.

Genocide Prevention Now (2011) special issue, *Co-Victims in the Armenian Genocide: Assyrians, Yezidis, Greeks*. www.genocidepreventionnow. org/1.

Gerlach, C. (2006) 'Extremely Violent Societies: An Alternative to the Concept of Genocide'. *Journal of Genocide Research*, 8(4), 455–71.

(2010) *Extremely Violent Societies: Mass Violence in the Twentieth Century World*. Cambridge University Press.

Gibbs, D. N. (2009) *First Do No Harm: Humanitarian Intervention and the Destruction of Yugoslavia*. Nashville: Vanderbilt University Press.

Girard, R. (2007) 'Caribbean Genocide: Racial War in Haiti, 1802–4', in Moses and Stone, eds., pp. 42–65.

Gleditsch, N. P., P. Wallensteen, M. Eriksson, M. Sollenberg and H. Strand (2002) 'Armed Conflict 1946–2001: A New Dataset'. *Journal of Peace Research*, 39(5), 615–37.

Global Policy Forum (2002) *Iraq Sanctions: Humanitarian Implications and Options for the Future*. New York: GBF.

Goldhagen, D. J. (2009) *Worse than War: Genocide, Eliminationism and the Ongoing Assault on Humanity*. New York: Little Brown.

Gómez-Suárez, A. (2007) 'Perpetrator Blocs, Genocidal Mentalities and Geographies: The Destruction of the Unión Patriótica in Colombia and Its Lessons for Genocide Studies'. *Journal of Genocide Research*, 9(4), 637–60.

(2010) 'US–Colombian Relations in the 1980s: Political Violence and the Onset of the UP Genocide', in Esparza et al., eds., pp. 152–66.

(2011) 'A Genocidal Geopolitical Conjuncture: Con-Textualising the Destruction of the Unión Patriótica in Colombia (1980s–2010)'. D.Phil. thesis, University of Sussex.

Gordon, J. (2010) *Invisible War: The United States and the Iraq Sanctions*. Cambridge, MA: Harvard University Press.

Gow, J. (2003) *The Serbian Project and Its Adversaries: A Strategy of War Crimes*. London: Hurst.

Grayling, A. C. (2006) *Among the Dead Cities: The History and Moral Legacy of the WWII Bombing of Civilians in Germany and Japan*. New York: Walker & Co.

Gross, J. T. (2001) *Neighbors: The Destruction of the Jewish Community in Jedwabne, Poland*. Princeton University Press, 2001.

Gurr, T. R. (2000) 'Ethnic Warfare on the Wane'. *Foreign Affairs*, 79(3), 52–64.

Hagan, J. and W. Rymond-Richmond (2009) *Darfur and the Crime of Genocide*. Cambridge University Press.

Hagan, J. and R. Wright (2011) 'The Displaced and Dispossessed of Darfur'. *British Journal of Sociology*, 62(1), 1–25.

Harbom, L. and P. Wallensteen (2005) 'Armed Conflict and Its International Dimensions, 1946–2004'. *Journal of Peace Research*, 42(5), 623–63.

(2007) 'Armed Conflict, 1989–2006'. *Journal of Peace Studies*, 44(5), 623–34.

Harff, B. (1986) 'Genocide as State Terrorism', in G. Lopez and M. Stohl, eds., *Government Violence and Repression: An Agenda for Research*. Westport, CT: Greenwood Press, pp. 165–97.

(2003) 'No Lessons Learned from the Holocaust? Assessing Risks of Genocide and Political Mass Murder since 1955'. *American Political Science Review*, 97(1), 57–73.

Harff, B. and T. R. Gurr (1988) 'Toward Empirical Theory of Genocides and Politicides: Identification and Measurement of Cases since 1945'. *International Studies Quarterly*, 32(3), 359–71.

(1989) 'Victims of the State: Genocides, Politicides, and Group Repression since 1945'. *International Review of Victimology*, 1(1), 23–41.

(2004) *Ethnic Conflict in World Politics*. Boulder: Westview.

Harris, D. (2011) *Civil War and Democracy in West Africa: Conflict Resolution, Elections and Justice in Sierra Leone and Liberia*. London: I. B. Tauris.

Hartman, G. (2009) 'Preface', in Jeffrey C. Alexander, M. Jay, B. Giesen, M. Rotheberg, R. Manne, N. Glazer and E. Katz, *Remembering the Holocaust: A Debate*. Oxford University Press, pp. i–vii.

Hechter, M. (1999) *Internal Colonialism: The Celtic Fringe in British National Development*. New Brunswick, NJ: Transaction.

Herman, E. S. and D. Peterson (2010) *The Politics of Genocide*. With a foreword by N. Chomsky. New York: Monthly Review Press.

Hiebert, M. S. and P. Policzer (2010) 'Genocide in Chile: An Assessment', in Esparza et al., eds., pp. 64–80.

Hiltermann, J. R. (2007) *A Poisonous Affair: America, Iraq, and the Gassing of Halabja*. Cambridge University Press.

Hobden, S. (1994) *International Relations and Historical Sociology: Breaking down Boundaries*. London: Routledge.

Hobden, S. and J. Hobson, eds. (2002) *Historical Sociology of International Relations*. Cambridge University Press.

Hoffman, D. (2004) 'The Civilian Target in Sierra Leone and Liberia: Political Power, Military Strategy, and Humanitarian Intervention'. *African Affairs*, 103(411), 211–26.

(2011) *The War Machines: Young Men and Violence in Sierra Leone and Liberia*. Durham, NC: Duke University Press.

Hofmann, T., M. Bjørnlund and V. Meichanetsidis, eds. (2011) *Studies on the State-Sponsored Campaign of Extermination of the Christians of Asia Minor (1912–1922) and Its Aftermath: History, Law, Memory*. Scarsdale, NY: Caratzas.

Horowitz, D. L. (1991) *A Democratic South Africa? Constitutional Engineering in a Divided Society*. Berkeley: University of California Press.

(2001) *The Deadly Ethnic Riot*. Berkeley: University of California Press.

Horowitz, I. L. (1979) *Taking Lives*. New Brunswick, NJ: Transaction.

Hovanissian, R., ed. (1987) *The Armenian Genocide in Historical Perspective*. New Brunswick, NJ: Transaction.

Howard-Hassmann, R. E. (2012) 'State-Induced Famine and Penal Starvation in North Korea'. *Genocide Studies and Prevention*, 7(2–3), 147–65.

HRW (Human Rights Watch) (1990a) *Conflict in the Soviet Union: The Untold Story of the Clashes in Kazakhstan*. New York: HRW.

(1990b) *Indonesia: Human Rights Abuses in Aceh*. New York: HRW.

(1991a) *Indonesia: Continuing Human Rights Abuses in Aceh*. New York: HRW.

(1991b) *East Timor: The November 12 Massacre and Its Aftermath*. New York: HRW.

(1992) *Overview of Areas of Armed Conflict in the Former Soviet Union*. New York: HRW.

(1994a) *The Mon: Persecuted in Burma, Forced Back from Thailand*. New York: HRW.

(1994b) *Violence against the Macuxi and Wapixana Indians in Raposa Serra Do Sol and Northern Roraima from 1988 to 1994*. New York: HRW.

(1995) *Return to Tajikistan: Continued Regional and Ethnic Tensions*. New York: HRW.

(1996a) *Uzbekistan: Persistent Human Rights Violations and Prospects for Improvement*. New York: HRW.

(1996b) *Return to Violence: Refugees, Civil Patrollers, and Impunity*. New York: HRW.

(1997) *Communal Violence in West Kalimantan*. New York: HRW.

(1998a) *Crackdown in the Farghona Valley: Arbitrary Arrests and Discrimination*. New York: HRW.

(1998b) *Sowing Terror: Atrocities against Civilians in Sierra Leone*. New York: HRW.

(1998c) *War without Quarter: Colombia and International Humanitarian Law*. New York: HRW.

(1999a) *Indonesia: Why Aceh Is Exploding*. New York: HRW.

(1999b) *Indonesia: The May 3, 1999 Killings in Aceh.* New York: HRW.

(2000) *Justice for East Timor.* New York: HRW.

(2001) *Indonesia: The Violence in Central Kalimantan (Borneo).* New York: HRW.

(2002a) *Swept Under: Torture, Forced Disappearances, and Extrajudicial Killings during Sweep Operations in Chechnya.* New York: HRW.

(2002b) *Indonesia: Accountability For Human Rights Violations in Aceh.* New York: HRW.

(2002c) *Four Years of Communal Violence in Central Sulawesi.* New York: HRW.

(2002d) *Guatemala: Political Violence Unchecked.* New York: HRW.

(2003a) *The Horn of Africa War: Mass Expulsions and the Nationality Issue.* New York: HRW.

(2003b) *Trapped between Two Wars: Violence against Civilians in Western Côte d'Ivoire.* New York: HRW.

(2004) *Turkmenistan: Human Rights Update.* New York: HRW.

(2005a) *'Bullets Were Falling Like Rain': The Andijan Massacre, May 13, 2005.* New York: HRW.

(2005b) *Ali Hassan al-Majid and the Basra Massacre of 1999.* New York: HRW.

(2005c) *The Horn of Africa War: Mass Expulsions and the Nationality Issue.* New York: HRW.

(2005d) *'Clear the Filth': Mass Evictions and Demolitions in Zimbabwe.* New York: HRW.

(2005e) *'They Came and Destroyed Our Village Again': The Plight of Internally Displaced Persons in Karen State.* New York: HRW.

(2007) *'My Heart Is Cut': Sexual Violence by Rebels and Pro-Government Forces in Côte d'Ivoire.* New York: HRW.

(2008a) *'So Much to Fear': War Crimes and the Devastation of Somalia.* New York: HRW.

(2008b) *Collective Punishment: War Crimes and Crimes against Humanity in the Ogaden area of Ethiopia's Somali Region.* New York: HRW.

(2008c) *Ballots to Bullets: Organized Political Violence and Kenya's Crisis of Governance.* New York: HRW.

(2008d) *Politics as War: The Human Rights Impact and Causes of Post-Election Violence in Rivers State, Nigeria.* New York: HRW.

(2008e) *Broken People: Caste Violence against India's 'Untouchables'.* New York: HRW.

(2009) *On Vulnerable Ground: Violence against Minority Communities in Nineveh Province's Disputed Territories.* New York: HRW.

(2010a) *'Where is the Justice?': Interethnic Violence in Southern Kyrgyzstan and Its Aftermath.* New York: HRW.

(2010b) *Paramilitaries' Heirs: The New Face of Violence in Colombia.* New York: HRW.

(2011a) *'You Don't Know Who to Blame': War Crimes in Somalia.* New York: HRW.

(2011b) *'Turning Pebbles': Evading Accountability for Post-Election Violence in Kenya.* New York: HRW.

(2011c) *'They Killed Them Like It Was Nothing': The Need for Justice for Côte d'Ivoire's Post-Election Crimes.* New York: HRW.

(2012a) *'What Will Happen if Hunger Comes?' Abuses against the Indigenous Peoples of Ethiopia's Lower Omo Valley.* New York: HRW.

(2012b) *'Untold Miseries': Wartime Abuses and Forced Displacement in Burma's Kachin State.* New York: HRW.

(2012c) *'The Government Could Have Stopped This': Sectarian Violence and Ensuing Abuses in Burma's Arakan State.* New York: HRW.

(2012d) *Mexico: Widespread Rights Abuses in 'War on Drugs': Impunity for Torture, 'Disappearances,' Killings Undermines Security.* New York: HRW.

Huttenbach, H. (2009) 'From the Editor: An Editor's Swan-Song'. *Journal of Genocide Research*, 11(4), 417–19.

IAGS (International Association of Genocide Scholars) (2006) *Resolution Condemning Iranian President Ahmadinejad's Statements Calling for the Destruction of Israel and Denying the Historical Reality of the Holocaust; and Calling for Prevention of Iranian Development of Nuclear Weapons.* www.genocidewatch.org/images/Iran-IAGS_Resolution.pdf (accessed 7 March 2012).

Independent International Commission on Kosovo (2000) *The Kosovo Report: Conflict, International Response, Lessons Learned.* Oxford University Press.

Internal Displacement Monitoring Centre (2008) *Internal Displacement: Global Overview of Trends and Developments in 2007.* Geneva: IDMC.

International Commission of Inquiry on Darfur (2005) *Report of the International Commission of Inquiry on Darfur.* www.un.org/News/dh/sudan/com_inq_darfur.pdf.

International Crisis Group (ICG) (2006) *The Next Iraqi War? Sectarianism and Civil Conflict.* Brussels: ICG.

(2008) *Kenya in Crisis.* Brussels: ICG.

International Rescue Committee (2007) *Mortality in the Democratic Republic of Congo: An Ongoing Crisis.* www.rescue.org/sites/default/files/migrated/resources/2007/2006-7_congomortalitysurvey.pdf.

Iraq Body Count (2012) www.iraqbodycount.org.

Jackson, R. (2006) 'Africa's Wars: Overview, Causes and the Challenges of Conflict Transformation', in Furley and May, eds., pp. 15–30.

Kahn, Y. (2007) *The Great Partition: The Making of India and Pakistan.* New Haven: Yale University Press.

Kaldor, M. (1999) *New and Old Wars.* Cambridge: Polity.

Kalyvas, S. N. (2001) '"New" and "Old" Civil Wars: A Valid Distinction?' *World Politics*, 54(1), 99–118.

(2004) 'The Urban Bias in Civil War Research'. *Security Studies*, 13(3), 160–90.

(2006) *The Logic of Civil War.* Cambridge University Press.

(2010) 'Internal Conflict and Political Violence: New Developments in Research', in E. Chenoweth and A. Lawrence, eds., *Rethinking Violence: State and Non-State Actors in Conflict.* Cambridge, MA: MIT Press, pp. xi–xiii.

Kalyvas, S. and L. Balcells (2010) 'International System and Technologies of Rebellion: How the End of the Cold War Shaped Internal Conflict'. *American Political Science Review*, 104(3), 415–29.

Kalyvas, S. and N. Sambanis (2007) 'Bosnia's Civil War: Origins and Violence Dynamics', in P. Collier and Sambanis, eds., *Understanding Civil War: Evidence and Analysis.* 2 vols., Washington, DC: World Bank, Vol. II, pp. 191–229.

Kasozi, A. B. K. (1994) *The Social Origins of Violence in Uganda, 1964–1985.* Montreal: McGill-Queen's University Press.

Katz, S. T. (1994) *The Holocaust in Historical Context.* New York: Oxford University Press, Vol. I.

Kenya Human Rights Commission (2011) *Lest We Forget: The Faces of Impunity in Kenya.* Nairobi: KHRC.

Khalaf, I. (1991) *Politics in Palestine: Arab Factionalism and Social Disintegration, 1939–1948.* Albany, NY: SUNY Press.

Khan, N. (2010) *Mohajir Militancy in Pakistan: Violence and Transformation in the Karachi Conflict.* London: Routledge.

Kiernan, B. (1996) *The Pol Pot Regime: Race, Power and Genocide in Cambodia under the Khmer Rouge, 1975–79.* New Haven: Yale University Press.

(2007) *Blood and Soil: A World History of Genocide and Extermination from Sparta to Darfur.* New Haven: Yale University Press.

Kissi, E. (2006) *Revolution and Genocide in Ethiopia and Cambodia.* Lanham, MD: Lexington Books.

Korman, G. (1972) 'The Holocaust in American Historical Writing'. *Societas: A Review of Social History*, 2, 251–70.

Krain, M. (1997) 'State-Sponsored Mass Murder: The Onset and Severity of Genocides and Politicides'. *Journal of Conflict Resolution*, 41(3), 331–60.

(2005) 'International Intervention and the Severity of Genocides and Politicides'. *International Studies Quarterly*, 49(3), 366–88.

Kratoska, P. H., ed. (2005) *Asian Labor in the Wartime Japanese Empire*. New York: M. E. Sharpe.

Kuhn, T. (1996 (1970)) *The Structure of Scientific Revolutions*. 3rd edn. University of Chicago Press.

Kuper, L. (1981) *Genocide*. Penguin: Harmondsworth.

Kuperman, A. J. (2001) *The Limits of Humanitarian Intervention: Genocide in Rwanda*. Washington, DC: Brookings.

(2008) 'The Moral Hazard of Humanitarian Intervention: Lessons from the Balkans'. *International Studies Quarterly*, 52, 49–75.

Kuperman, A. J. and T. W. Crawford, eds. (2006) *Gambling on Humanitarian Intervention: Moral Hazard, Rebellion and Civil War*. New York: Routledge.

Lake, D. A. and D. Rothchild (1998) 'Spreading Fear: The Genesis of Transnational Ethnic Conflict', in Lake and Rothchild, eds., *The International Spread of Ethnic Conflict*. Princeton University Press, pp. 3–32.

Lawson, G. (2010) 'Introduction: The "What", "When" and "Where" of the Global 1989', in Lawson, C. Armbruster and M. Cox, eds., *The Global 1989: Continuity and Change in World Politics*. Cambridge University Press, pp. 1–20.

Leezenberg, M. (1997) 'The Anfal Operations in Iraqi Kurdistan', in S. Totten and W. S. Parsons, eds., *Century of Genocide: Critical Essays and Eyewitness Accounts*. New York: Garland, pp. 375–95.

Lemarchand, R. (1996) *Burundi: Ethnic Conflict and Genocide*. Cambridge: Woodrow Wilson Center Press and Cambridge University Press.

(2002) 'Disconnecting the Threads: Rwanda and the Holocaust Reconsidered'. *Journal of Genocide Research*, 4(4), 499–518.

(2009) *The Dynamics of Violence in Central Africa*. Philadelphia: University of Pennsylvania Press.

Lemkin, R. (1944) *Axis Rule in Occupied Europe*. New York: Carnegie.

Levene, M. (1999) 'The Chittagong Hill Tracts: A Case Study in the Political Economy of "Creeping" Genocide'. *Third World Quarterly*, 20(2), 339–69.

(2005a) The Meaning of Genocide. Vol. I of *Genocide in the Age of the Nation State*. London: I. B. Tauris.

(2005b) The Rise of the West and the Coming of Genocide. Vol. II of *Genocide in the Age of the Nation State*. London: I. B. Tauris.

(2006) 'Britain's Holocaust Memorial Day: A Case of Post-Cold War Wish Fulfilment or Brazen Hypocrisy?' *Human Rights Review*, 7(3), 26–59.

(2007) Review of I. Pappé, *The Ethnic Cleansing of Palestine*. *Journal of Genocide Research*, 9(4), 675–81.

Lindsey, T. (2011) 'From Soepomo to Prabowo: Law, Violence and Corruption in the Preman State', in C. A. Coppel, ed., *Violent Conflicts in*

*Indonesia: Analysis, Representation, Resolution*. London: Taylor & Francis, pp. 19–36.

Longerich, P. (2010) *Holocaust: The Nazi Persecution and Murder of the Jews*. Oxford University Press.

Lovejoy, P. E. (2010) 'The Slave Trade as Enforced Migration in the Central Sudan and West Africa', in R. Bessel and C. B. Haake, eds., *Removing Peoples: Forced Removal in the Modern World*. Oxford University Press, pp. 149–66.

Luttikhuis, B. and A. D. Moses (2012) 'Mass Violence and the End of the Dutch Colonial Empire in Indonesia'. *Journal of Genocide Research*, 14(3–4), 257–76.

Lynch, G. (2011) *I Say to You: Ethnic Politics and the Kalenjin in Kenya*. University of Chicago Press.

MacDonald, D. (2009) *Identity Politics in the Age of Genocide*. London: Routledge.

Malkki, L. M. (1989) *Purity and Exile: Violence, Memory, and National Cosmology among Hutu Refugees in Tanzania*. University of Chicago Press.

Mamdani, M. (2002) *When Victims become Killers: Colonialism, Nativism, and the Genocide in Rwanda*. Princeton University Press.
  (2007) 'The Politics of Naming: Genocide, Civil War, Insurgency'. *London Review of Books*, 29(5), 5–8.

Mann, M. (1986, 1993) *The Sources of Social Power*. 2 vols. Cambridge University Press.
  (2005) *The Dark Side of Democracy*. Cambridge University Press.

Mannheim, K. (1936) *Ideology and Utopia*. London: Routledge.

Mansfield, E. D. and J. Snyder (1995), 'Democratization and the Danger of War'. *International Security*, 20(1), 5–38.
  (2002) 'Democratic Transitions, Institutional Strength, and War'. *International Organization*, 56(2), 297–337.

Markusen, E. and D. Kopf (1995) *The Holocaust and Strategic Bombing: Genocide and Total War in the Twentieth Century*. Boulder: Westview.

Martínez, L. (2000) *The Algerian Civil War, 1990–1998*. New York: Columbia University Press.

Marx, K. and F. Engels (1970 (1846)) *The German Ideology*. London: Lawrence & Wishart.

Mazower, M. (2009) *No Enchanted Palace: The End of Empire and the Ideological Origins of the United Nations*. Princeton University Press.
  (2010) *Hitler's Empire*. London: Allen Lane.

McMichael, P. (1990). 'Incorporating Comparison within a World-Historical Perspective: An Alternative Comparative Method'. *American Sociological Review*, 55(3), 385–97.

McSherry, J. P. (2010) '"Industrial Repression" and Operation Condor in Latin America', in Esparza et al., eds., pp. 107–23.

Melander, E. and M. Oberg (2007) 'The Threat of Violence and Forced Migration: Geographical Scope Trumps Intensity of Fighting'. *Civil Wars*, 9(2), 156–73.

Melson, R. (1996) *Revolution and Genocide: On the Origins of the Armenian Genocide and the Holocaust*. University of Chicago Press.

Melvern, L. (2000) *A People Betrayed: The Role of the West in Rwanda's Genocide*. London: Zed.

Midlarsky, M. (2005) *The Killing Trap*. Cambridge University Press.

Miles, W. F. S., ed. (2003) 'The Nazi Holocaust and the Rwandan Genocide', Round Table, *Journal of Genocide Research*, 5(1), 131–48.

Mills, C. W. (1959) *The Sociological Imagination*. Oxford University Press.

Mkandawire, T. (2002) 'The Terrible Toll of Post-Colonial "Rebel Movements" in Africa: Towards an Explanation of the Violence against the Peasantry'. *Journal of Modern African Studies*, 40(2), 181–215.

Mojzes, P. (2011) *Balkan Genocides: Holocaust and Ethnic Cleansing in the Twentieth Century*. Boulder: Rowman and Littlefield.

Moore, W. H. and S. M. Shellman (2004) 'Fear of Persecution: Forced Migration, 1952–1995'. *Journal of Conflict Resolution*, 48(5), 723–45.

Morris, B. (1989) *The Birth of the Palestinian Refugee Problem, 1947–1949*. Cambridge University Press.

(2004) *The Birth of the Palestinian Refugee Problem Revisited*. Cambridge University Press.

Moses, A. D. (2000) 'An Antipodean Genocide? The Origins of the Genocidal Moment in the Colonization of Australia'. *Journal of Genocide Research*, 2(1), 89–107.

(2002) 'Conceptual Blockages and Definitional Dilemmas in the Racial Century: Genocide of Indigenous Peoples and the Holocaust'. *Patterns of Prejudice*, 36(4), 7–36.

ed. (2004) *Genocide and Settler Society*. Oxford: Berghahn.

(2006) 'Toward a Theory of Critical Genocide Studies'. www.massviolence. org/Toward-a-Theory-of-Critical-Genocide-Studies?artpage=5–5 (accessed 30 January 2009).

ed. (2008) *Empire, Colony, Genocide: Conquest, Occupation and Subaltern Resistance in World History*. New York and Oxford: Berghahn.

(2010) 'Introduction', in Moses, ed., *Genocide*. London: Routledge, vol. I, pp. 1–10.

(2011) 'Paranoia and Partisanship: Genocide Studies, Holocaust Historiography and the "Apocalyptic Conjuncture"'. *The Historical Journal*, 54(2), 553–83.

Moses, A. D. and D. Stone, eds. (2007) *Colonialism and Genocide*. London: Routledge.

Mueller, J., M. Desch, S. Kalyvas and B. Valentino (2004) 'Final Solutions, Further Questions: A Symposium on Final Solutions by Benjamin Valentino'. *Security Studies*, 13(3), 204–18.

Murphy, C. N. (1994) *International Organization and Industrial Change: Global Governance since 1850*. Cambridge: Polity.

Naimark, N. M. (2003) *Fires of Hatred: Ethnic Cleansing in Twentieth-Century Europe*. Cambridge, MA: Harvard University Press.

(2010) *Stalin's Genocides*. Princeton University Press.

Newman, E. (2004) 'The "New Wars" Debate: A Historical Perspective is Needed'. *Security Dialogue*, 35(2), 173–89.

Noon, D. H. (2004) 'Operation Enduring Analogy: World War II, the War on Terror, and the Uses of Historical Memory'. *Rhetoric and Public Affairs*, 7(3), 339–64.

Norwegian Refugee Council/Global IDP. Project (2002) *Profile of Internal Displacement: Angola*. Geneva: Global IDP.

Novick, P. (1999) *The Holocaust in American Life*. New York: Houghton Mifflin.

Ohlson, T., ed. (2010) *From Intra-State War to Durable Peace: Conflict and Conflict Resolution in Africa after the Cold War*. Dordrecht: Republic of Letters Publishers.

Onwudiwe, E. and C. Berwind-Dart (2011) *Breaking the Cycle of Electoral Violence in Nigeria*. Washington, DC: United States Institute of Peace.

Palmer, A. (2000) *Colonial Genocide*. Adelaide: Crawford House.

Palyi, M. (1946) Review of Raphael Lemkin, *Axis Rule in Occupied Europe*. *American Journal of Sociology*, 51(5): 496–7.

Pappé, I. (2006) *The Ethnic Cleansing of Palestine*. New York: Oneworld.

Pepper, S. (1999) *Civil War in China: The Political Struggle, 1945–1949*. Lanham, MD: Rowman and Littlefield.

Petersen, W. (1958) 'A General Typology of Migration'. *American Sociological Review*, 23(3), 256–66.

Platzky, L. and C. Walker (1985) *The Surplus People: Forced Removals in South Africa*. Johannesburg: Ravan Press.

Popper, K. (2002 (1957)) *The Poverty of Historicism*. London: Routledge.

Powell, C. (2011) *Barbaric Civilization: A Critical Sociology of Genocide*. Toronto: McGill-Queen's University Press.

Power, S. (2002) *'A Problem from Hell': America and the Age of Genocide*. New York: Basic Books.

Prendergast, J. (2007) 'Debate on Darfur', *H-Genocide*. www.h-net.org/ ~genocide.

Preston, P. (2012) *The Spanish Holocaust: Inquisition and Extermination in Twentieth-Century Spain*. New York: Harper.

Prunier, G. (2009) *From Genocide to Continental War: The 'Congolese' Conflict and the Crisis of Contemporary Africa*. London: Hurst.

Rae, H. (2002), *State Identities and the Homogenisation of Peoples*. Cambridge University Press.

Ragin, C. C. (1982) 'Comparative Sociology and the Comparative Method', in Armer and Marsh, eds., pp. 102–20.

  (1989) *The Comparative Method: Moving beyond Qualitative and Quantitative Strategies*. Berkeley: University of California Press.

Record, J. (2005) 'Appeasement Reconsidered: Investigating the Mythology of the 1930s'. www.strategicstudiesinstitute.army.mil/pdffiles/pub622.

Richards, P. (1998) *Fighting for the Rain Forest: War, Youth and Resources in Sierra Leone*. Oxford: James Currey.

Rieff, D. (1996) *Slaughterhouse: Bosnia and the Failure of the West*. New York: Simon & Schuster.

Robb, G. (2009) *The Discovery of France*. London: Pan Macmillan.

Robins, N. A. and A. Jones, eds. (2010) *Genocides by the Oppressed: Subaltern Genocide in Theory and Practice*. Bloomington: Indiana University Press.

Roniger, L. (2010) 'US Hemispheric Hegemony and the Descent into Genocidal Practices in Latin America', in Esparza et al., eds. pp. 29–43.

Rotberg, R. I. (1999) *Creating Peace in Sri Lanka: Civil War and Reconciliation*. New York: Brookings.

Rousseau, D. (2005) *Democracy and War: Institutions, Norms, and the Evolution of International Conflict*. Stanford University Press.

Rubenstein, R. L. (2010) *Jihad and Genocide*. Lanham, MD: Rowman and Littlefield.

Rubinstein, W. (2004) *Genocide: A History*. London: Pearson.

Rummel, R. (1997) *Death By Government*. New Brunswick, NJ: Transaction Publishers.

Saideman, S. M. (1997) 'Explaining the International Relations of Secessionist Conflicts: Vulnerability versus Ethnic Ties'. *International Organization*, 51(4), 721–53.

Salvatori, M. (1979) *Karl Kautsky*. London: New Left Books.

Sambanis, N. (2001) 'Do Ethnic and Nonethnic Civil Wars Have the Same Causes? A Theoretical and Empirical Inquiry (Part 1)'. *Journal of Conflict Resolution*, 45(3), 259–82.

Sand, S. (2009) *The Invention of the Jewish People*. London: Verso.

Sands, P. (2005) *Lawless World: America and the Making and Breaking of Global Rules*. Harmondsworth: Penguin.

Sartre, J.-P. (1968) 'On Genocide'. *New Left Review*, 1(48), 13–25.

Schabas, W. A. (2000) *Genocide in International Law*. Cambridge University Press.

(2006) *The UN International Criminal Tribunals: The Former Yugoslavia, Rwanda and Sierra Leone*. Cambridge University Press.

Scherrer, C. P. (1999) 'Towards a Theory of Modern Genocide. Comparative Genocide Research: Definitions, Criteria, Typologies, Cases, Key Elements, Patterns and Voids'. *Journal of Genocide Research*, 1(1), 13–23.

Sells, M. A. (1996) *The Bridge Betrayed: Religion and Genocide in Bosnia*. Berkeley: University of California Press.

Sémelin, J. (2007) *Purify and Destroy*. London: Hurst.

Shaw, M. (1996) *Civil Society and Media in Global Crises: Representing Distant Violence*. London: Pinter.

(1998) 'The Historical Sociology of the Future'. *Review of International Political Economy*, 5(2), 322–7.

(2000) *Theory of the Global State: Globality as Unfinished Revolution*. Cambridge University Press.

(2001) 'Democracy and Peace in the Global Revolution', in T. Barkawi and M. Laffey, eds., *Democracy, Liberalism and War: Rethinking the Democratic Peace Debate*. Boulder: Lynne Rienner, pp. 173–92.

(2003) *War and Genocide: Organized Killing in Modern Society*. Cambridge: Polity.

(2005) *The New Western Way of War: Risk-Transfer Warfare and Its Crisis in Iraq*. Cambridge: Polity.

(2007) *What Is Genocide?* Cambridge: Polity.

(2010) 'Palestine in an International Historical Perspective on Genocide'. *Holy Land Studies*, 9(1), 1–24.

(2011) 'Darfur: Counter-Insurgency, Forced Displacement and Genocide'. *British Journal of Sociology*, 62(1), 56–61.

Simms, B. (2001) *Unfinest Hour: Britain and the Destruction of Bosnia*. London: Allen Lane.

Sivanandan, A. (2009) 'An Island Tragedy: Buddhist Ethnic Cleansing in Sri Lanka'. *New Left Review*, 2(60), 79–100.

Snyder, J. (2000) *From Voting to Violence: Democratization and Nationalist Conflict*. New York: Norton.

Snyder, T. (2010) *Bloodlands: Europe between Hitler and Stalin*. London: Bodley Head.

Stannard, D. E. (1992) *American Holocaust: The Conquest of the New World*. Oxford University Press.

(2001) 'Uniqueness as Denial: The Politics of Genocide Scholarship', in A. S. Rosenbaum, ed., *Is the Holocaust Unique?* Boulder: Westview, pp. 245–90.

Steele, A. (2011) '*Electing Displacement: Political Cleansing in Apartadó, Colombia*', Households in Conflict Network (HiCN) Working Paper 96. www.hicn.org/papers/wp96.pdf.

Stepanova, E. (2009) 'Trends in Armed Conflicts: One-Sided Violence against Civilians', *SIPRI Yearbook 2009*, Oxford University Press, pp. 39–68.

Stone, D., ed. (2008) *The Historiography of Genocide*. Basingstoke: Palgrave Macmillan.

Straus, S. (2005) 'Darfur and the Genocide Debate'. *Foreign Affairs*, 84(1), 123–33.

(2006) *The Order of Genocide: Race, Power, and War in Rwanda*. Ithaca, NY: Cornell University Press.

(2007) 'Second-Generation Comparative Research on Genocide'. *World Politics*, 59, 476–501.

(2011) '"It's Sheer Horror Here": Patterns of Violence during the First Four Months of Côte d'Ivoire's Post-Electoral Crisis'. *African Affairs*, 110(440): 481–9.

(2012) 'Wars Do End! Changing Patterns of Political Violence in Sub-Saharan Africa'. *African Affairs*, 111(443), 179–201.

Talbot, I. (2008) 'The 1947 Partition of India', in Stone, ed., pp. 420–37.

Tanter, R., G. A. Van Klinken and D. Ball, eds. (2006) *Masters of Terror: Indonesia's Military and Violence in East Timor*. Lanham, MD: Rowman and Littlefield.

Taylor, C. C. (2002) 'The Cultural Face of Terror in the Rwandan Genocide of 1994', in A. L. Hinton, ed., *Annihilating Difference*. Berkeley: University of California Press, pp. 137–78.

Teschke, B. (2003) *The Myth of 1648: Class, Geopolitics, and the Making of Modern International Relations*. London: Verso.

Thaler, K. (2012) 'Foreshadowing Future Slaughter: From the Indonesian Killings of 1965–1966 to the 1974–1999 Genocide in East Timor'. *Genocide Studies and Prevention*, 7(2–3), 204–22.

Thawnghmung, A. M. (2012) *The 'Other' Karen in Myanmar: Ethnic Minorities and the Struggle Without Arms*. Lanham, MD: Rowman and Littlefield.

Toal, G., and C. C. Dahlman (2011) *Bosnia Remade: Ethnic Cleansing and Its Reversal*. Oxford University Press.

Toscano, A. (2010) 'The Spectre of Analogy'. *New Left Review*, 2/66, 152–60.

Travis, H. (2010) *Genocide in the Middle East: The Ottoman Empire, Iraq and Sudan*. Durham, NC: Carolina Academic Press.

Tull, D. (2009) *Peacekeeping in the Democratic Republic of Congo: Waging Peace and Fighting War*. London: Routledge.

UN Office of the High Commissioner for Human Rights (2010) *Report of the Mapping Exercise Documenting the Most Serious Violations of*

*Human Rights and International Humanitarian Law Committed within the Territory of the Democratic Republic of the Congo between March 1993 and June 2003*. Available at www.ohchr.org.

UN (United Nations) (1948) *Convention on the Prevention and Punishment of the Crime of Genocide*.

(2011) *Report of the Secretary-General's Panel of Experts on Accountability in Sri Lanka*. Available at www.un.org.

Uppsala Conflict Data Program (UCDP) (2009) '*UCDP Definitions' and 'UCDP Conflict Encyclopaedia*'. www.ucdp.uu.se/.

Valentino, B. (2004) *Final Solutions: Mass Killing and Genocide in the Twentieth Century*. Ithaca, NY, and London: Cornell University Press.

Valentino, B., P. Huth and D. Balch-Lindsay (2004) 'Draining the Sea: Mass Killing and Guerrilla Warfare'. *International Organization*, 58(2), 375–407.

Verwimp, P. (2003) 'Testing the Double-Genocide Thesis for Central and Southern Rwanda'. *Journal of Conflict Resolution*, 47(4), 423–42.

(2011) *The 1990–1992 Massacres in Rwanda: A Case of Spatial and Social Engineering?* Households in Conflict Network (HiCN) Working Paper 94. www.hicn.org

Vétillard, R. (2008) *Sétif. Mai 1945. Massacres en Algérie*. Paris: Editions de Paris.

Waltz, K. (1979) *Theory of International Politics*. Reading, MA: Addison-Wesley.

Weber, E. (1977) *Peasants into Frenchmen: The Modernization of Rural France 1870–1914*. London: Chatto & Windus.

Weber, M. (2011 (1949)) *The Methodology of the Social Sciences*. New Brunswick, NJ: Transaction Publishers.

Wheeler, N. J. (2000) *Saving Strangers: Humanitarian Intervention in International Society*. Oxford University Press.

Weiner, M. (1996) 'Bad Neighbors, Bad Neighborhoods: An Inquiry into the Causes of Refugee Flows'. *International Security*, 21(2), 5–42.

Weinstein, J. M. (2006) *Inside Rebellion: The Politics of Insurgent Violence*. Cambridge University Press.

Weiss-Wendt, A. (2010) 'Introduction: Toward an Integrated Perspective on the Nazi Policies of Mass Murder', in Weiss-Wendt, ed., *Eradicating Differences: The Treatment of Minorities in Nazi-Dominated Europe*. Newcastle-upon-Tyne: Cambridge Scholars Publishing, pp. 1–22.

Weitz, E. D. (2005) *A Century of Genocide: Utopias of Race and Nation*. Princeton University Press.

(2008) 'From the Vienna to the Paris System: Entangled Histories of Human Rights, Forced Deportations and Civilizing Missions'. *American Historical Review*, 113(2), 319–40.

Wemheuer, F. (2010) 'Dealing with Responsibility for the Great Leap Famine in the People's Republic of China'. *China Quarterly*, 201, 176–94.

Werth, N. (2008) 'Crimes of the Stalin Regime: Outline for an Inventory and Classification', in Stone, ed., pp. 400–19.

Westad, O. A. (2003). *Decisive Encounters: The Chinese Civil War, 1946–1950*. Stanford University Press.

(2005) *The Global Civil War: Third World Interventions and the Making of Our Times*. Cambridge University Press.

(2012) *Restless Empire: China and the World since 1750*. New York: Basic Books.

Whitaker, B. E. (2005) 'Citizens and Foreigners: Democratization and the Politics of Exclusion in Africa'. *African Studies Review*, 48(1), 109–26.

Wilkinson, S. I. (2006) *Votes and Violence: Electoral Competition and Ethnic Riots in India*. Cambridge University Press.

Williams, P. (2011) *War and Conflict in Africa*. Cambridge: Polity.

Wilson, C. (2011) *Ethno-Religious Violence in Indonesia: From Soil to God*. London: Taylor & Francis.

Wolfe, P. (2001) 'Land, Labour and Difference: Elementary Structures of Race'. *American Historical Review*, 106, 865–1,095.

(2008) 'Structure and Event: Settler Colonialism, Time and the Question of Genocide', in Moses, ed., *Empire, Colony, Genocide*, pp. 102–32.

Yick, J. K. S. (1995) *Making Urban Revolution in China: The CCP-GMD Struggle for Beiping-Tianjin*. New York: M. E. Sharpe.

Yoshida, T. (2006) *The Making of 'The Rape of Nanking': History and Memory in Japan, China and the United States*. Oxford University Press.

Zarrow, P. G. (2005) *China in War and Revolution, 1895–1949*. London: Routledge.

Zimmerer, J. (2007) 'The Birth of the Ostland out of the Spirit of Colonialism', in Moses and Stone, eds., pp. 101–23.

(2009) *Von Windhuk nach Auschwitz*. Münster: Lit Verlag.

# Index